Kathleen Jamie

Essays and Poems on Her Work

Edited by Rachel Falconer

D1610693

EDINBURGH
University Press

Edinburgh University Press is one of the leading university presses in the UK. We publish academic books and journals in our selected subject areas across the humanities and social sciences, combining cutting-edge scholarship with high editorial and production values to produce academic works of lasting importance. For more information visit our website: www.edinburghuniversitypress.com

First published in hardback 2015

Edinburgh University Press Ltd
The Tun – Holyrood Road
12(2f) Jackson's Entry
Edinburgh EH8 8PJ
www.euppublishing.com

Typeset in 10/12pt Goudy Old Style by
Servis Filmsetting Ltd, Stockport, Cheshire,
and printed and bound in Great Britain by
CPI Group (UK) Ltd, Croydon CR0 4YY

A CIP record for this book is available from the British Library

ISBN 978 0 7486 9600 0 (hardback)
ISBN 978 1 4744 3145 3 (paperback)
ISBN 978 0 7486 9601 7 (webready PDF)
ISBN 978 1 4744 1419 7 (epub)

Published with the support of the Edinburgh University Scholarly Publishing Initiatives Fund.

Contents

Acknowledgements

First thanks go to Kathleen Jamie, for journeying across Europe by train to deliver a memorable poetry reading in the Grange Theatre of the University of Lausanne in the spring of 2013, and for graciously answering my questions over the following year. With thanks also to Jackie Jones, the exemplary editor of Edinburgh University Press, to Edinburgh's anonymous external readers, and to the EUP production team, especially Ellie Bush, Rebecca Mackenzie and Dhara Patel.

Thanks are due to the Scottish Poetry Library and its excellent staff: Lilias Fraser, Robyn Marsack, and especially the peerless librarian Lizzie MacGregor. I am also grateful to Dean François Rosset and the Faculté des Lettres of the University of Lausanne for hosting Kathleen Jamie, and to John McAuliffe, for organising the panel discussion of Jamie's work at the 2013 British and Irish Contemporary Poetry Conference at Manchester University.

Special thanks are due to Anas Sareen for his heroic copy-editing, and to Amy Player for casting a peregrine's eye over the whole MS. And warm thanks to the students in my Kathleen Jamie seminars at Lausanne, whose enthusiasm helped speed this project on its way tremendously.

The poem 'Little man, homunculus' quoted in Lucy Collins's essay is reproduced by kind permission of Kathleen Jamie, from *This Weird Estate* (Edinburgh: Scotland and Medicine, 2007).

'Even If' by Michael O'Neill also appears in his volume *Gangs of Shadow* (Arc, 2014).

The cover image, 'Dog Rose', reproduced by kind permission of artist Brigid Collins and photographer Angus Bremner, originally appeared in Kathleen Jamie and Brigid Collins, *Frissure* (Edinburgh: Polygon, 2013), p. 6, and is now held in the collection of the University of Stirling.

Abbreviations and Citations

Works by and about Kathleen Jamie are detailed in the Bibliography at the back of the volume. The Bibliography also contains a section of General Ecocriticism, which includes works cited several times in different chapters.

A 'Works Cited' section at the end of each chapter details all other primary and secondary texts cited in that particular chapter.

The following abbreviations of Jamie's major works will be used throughout the volume, where the number following the capital letter(s) refers to the page number of the volume in question.

FYH	*A Flame in Your Heart* (1986)
WWL	*The Way We Live* (1987)
AR	*The Autonomous Region* (1993)
QS	*The Queen of Sheba* (1994)
J	*Jizzen* (1999)
MMS	*Mr and Mrs Scotland Are Dead* (2002)
AM	*Among Muslims* (2002)
TH	*The Tree House* (2004)
F	*Findings* (2005)
WE	*This Weird Estate* (2007)
O	*The Overhaul* (2012)
S	*Sightlines* (2012)
Fr	*Frissure* (2013)

Since many of the poems and essays included in the book respond to the extraordinary soundscape of Jamie's poems, an audio recording of Kathleen Jamie reading her poems is available to readers of this volume at: www.euppublishing.com/page/kathleenjamie/audio

The poems selected for the audio recording are all discussed in the essays:

'Black Spiders'
'The Way We Live'
'Arraheids'
'Skeins o geese'
'Bolus'
'Meadowsweet'
'Alder'
'The Fountain of Lions'
'Water Lilies'
'Little man, homunculus'
'A Raised Beach'
'The Stags'
'Tae the Fates'
'Healings 2'

Introduction

Rachel Falconer

> *and there, with tremendous patience,*
> *I'd teach myself to listen*   (Kathleen Jamie, 'The Whales')

The 'green and ventricular cave', where this speaker imagines teaching herself to listen, might also stand for the space where poetry is being read these days – somewhere quiet and removed, one would hope – somewhere the word can still shudder up against silence in the reader's mind. Kathleen Jamie's work has been around in the public domain since 1982. She has been the recipient of numerous national awards, and in the past decade, has frequently been in the public eye or ear – in the national newspapers, or on BBC Radio. We are so used to having her around (by 'we' I mean the cave-frequenters, the readers of poetry and other weird matter, those many and various who are studying to be Leviathan listeners), we may have failed to notice how her poetry has grown in stature. Some people have noticed: the poet John Burnside has called her 'one of our handful of really important . . . actively important lyric poets.'[1] But who is 'our'? Kathleen Jamie doesn't just belong to Scotland; Keats might have said, she will be among the European poets.[2] But even that isn't enough, since she is at home among folk in Pakistan, Tibet, China, Nunavut and elsewhere. Her writing is 'really important' even though it does not trumpet its presence; in fact, this is one reason why it is so important.

Reading Jamie is a lesson in learning how to wait patiently for the marvellous to swim into view. It's a lesson that goes against the grain of much twenty-first-century Western culture, where to be faster, louder and shinier than the competition is a sign of success. Jamie's writing explores weighty issues – questions of nationhood, subjectivity, the relation between art and medicine, the health of the planet, what it means to be human – with all our freakish inner landscapes – and the primacy of the human connection to other species. But it does so with disarming quietness, with 'tremendous patience'. Comparisons with George Herbert, or John Clare, or Elizabeth Bishop, spring to mind. All these writers have penned astonishing, life-shifting poems, but you wouldn't notice it at first glance; their radicalism is the kind that seeps into you unawares.

Finally, though, Jamie's writing is like no-one else's. The contributors to this volume aim collectively to delve deeper into her poetry and prose writing than has been attempted before, and to consider the full range of her published writing from 1982 to the present day. It will be for future generations to assess the whole arc of her writing career, but our vantage point, here at mid-point in her career, reveals the paths by which her writing reached its maturity.

Born in Johnstone, Renfrewshire in 1962, Kathleen Jamie grew up in Currie, a suburb of Edinburgh, where she attended a comprehensive high school. The eldest of three siblings, she started writing poetry around the age of fifteen, although her family was not bookish (her father was an accountant and her mother worked in a solicitor's office). She studied philosophy at Edinburgh University, there becoming interested in Islam, and while at university, showed a sheaf of poems to the publisher Tom Fenton (brother of the poet James Fenton), who published them in a pamphlet under the title of *Black Spiders*. It was 1982, and Jamie was just twenty. After graduating from Edinburgh in 1984, she worked at odd jobs and was appointed as Writer in Residence to several organisations including the Workington Docks Project and the University of Dundee, before being elected as a lecturer in creative writing at the University of St Andrews in 1999, where she wrote and taught alongside other 'new generation' poets, Robert Crawford, John Burnside and Don Paterson.

From *Black Spiders*, which won a Scottish Arts Council Award in 1982, to *Sightlines*, which won the John Burroughs Medal in 2014, nearly all of Jamie's published works have won or been shortlisted for national awards: the Eric Gregory, Forward, Geoffrey Faber, T. S. Eliot and Costa Prizes and others (details are listed in the Bibliography). Her poems have been chosen to adorn national monuments in Scotland, and in the British Isles and North America her 'nature writing' (by which is usually meant *The Tree House*, to a lesser extent *The Overhaul*, and two books of essays, *Findings* and *Sightlines*) has won her an admiring and wide-ranging readership. In 2010, she took up the newly established Chair in Creative Writing at Stirling University, where she now works part-time. In addition to writing poetry and prose non-fiction, Jamie contributes regularly to *The Guardian*, *The London Review of Books*, and *Orion Magazine* in the USA, as well as to BBC radio programmes. She currently lives with her family in Fife, outside Edinburgh.

In 'At Point of Ness', Jamie describes a view from the shore at night, 'where night's / split open, the entire archipelago set as sink-weight / to the sky.' (QS 62) This sense of entities set in tension, of weights opposing and counter-balancing each other, recurs frequently in her writing. It might serve as an image of the complexity with which Jamie approaches questions of cultural, national and gender identity. From the first, her poetry has concerned itself with Scots language, land and culture. Jamie writes on her website, 'I have what Robert Louis Stevenson called "a strong Scots accent of the mind".'[3] But her poetry could hardly be described as straightforwardly nationalist, unless to be Scots is to be skeptical of concepts like 'Scottishness'. *Black Spiders* attracted criticism for 'inject[ing] little or nothing of her native places.'[4] Her 'intelligent and sensitive' gaze, according to that early reviewer, fastened on worlds whose only commonality was 'a removedness from Scotland'.[5] In a strong riposte, Andrew Greig pointed out the volume's references to Orkney and indigene Beaker burials, while insisting that Scots poetry need not be only a 'poetry of locale'.[6]

While *A Flame in Your Heart* (1986), co-authored with Greig, imagines the lives of a British couple during the Second World War, Jamie's third volume, *The Way We Live* (1987), sets in tension two apparently contrasting poetics: a careful, vivid rendering of everyday textures, sounds and images; and a romantic evocation of alluring, far-distant worlds. In 'Poem for a Departing Mountaineer', she writes, 'Regarding the skyline longingly / (curved as a body, my own, I desire you)'. Yet the speaker turns her gaze indoors: 'I must be distant, / draw the curtains for bed' (MMS 48), a phrase which succinctly juxtaposes the tug of 'home' against the desire to be 'away', since it is the speaker at home who is paradoxically 'distant'. In the collection as a whole, the poems in the first and third sections are loosely concerned with 'home' while they flank a middle sequence of poems about Jamie's journey along the Karakoram Highway between China and Pakistan.

A still more extreme 'removedness from Scotland' is evident in *The Golden Peak* (1992), a prose narrative about Jamie's experiences in Pakistan, and *The Autonomous Region* (1993), a collaborative volume of poems by Jamie and photographs by Sean Mayne Smith, based on their travels in China up to the border of Tibet, the 'autonomous region' of the title. While Mayne Smith's striking black and white photographs document actual places and people, Jamie's poems constitute a modern double-stranded ballad, whose principal protagonists are based on two historical characters: Fa-hsien, a fourth-century Chinese Buddhist monk, and Wen Cheng, a seventh-century Chinese princess betrothed to the king of Tibet. But perhaps the strangest, most haunting passages in this intensely imagined narrative poem – quite different to anything she has written before or since – are those in which the features of a Scottish landscape and the sound of a Scots language are found at home in this austere desert realm. *Among Muslims* (2002), a reissue of *The Golden Peak*, provides another instance of cultural palimpsest, since the new prefatory chapter begins with an account of Jamie encountering a group of Pakistani pilgrims on the streets of Edinburgh. Published in the aftermath of 9/11, Jamie's narrative of rural life in Pakistan takes on a new political urgency.

'Women beware gravity' becomes a major theme in Jamie's next poetry collection, *The Queen of Sheba* (1994). The resplendently liberating figure of the title poem appears on the streets of Currie and Edinburgh, in response to the traditional Scots put-down, '*whae do you think y'ur?*' (QS 11). As a whole, though, the collection sets the lightness of geographical escape against the weight of domesticity in an ongoing, unresolved tension. If the fate of 'Wee Wifey' is to be avoided, still, the poem concludes, 'It's sad to note / that without / WEE WIFEY / I shall live long and lonely as a tossing cork.' (QS 30) In 'Rooms', the rocking rhythm of a ship at sea captures the complex yearning of a traveller who longs to be home so that she can throw open the doors of her imagination (QS 58). The conflicting tensions of female identities – mother, daughter, poet, explorer – are subtly negotiated in *Jizzen* (1999). The final poem of this volume, 'Meadowsweet', harks back not only to Jamie's own 'The Queen of Sheba', but also to Seamus Heaney's 'Punishment' and Sylvia Plath's 'Lady Lazarus'. Jamie imagines a female Gaelic poet, ritually buried face down, digging herself out of the ground 'when the time came'. But unlike Lazarus or the sacrificed bog girl of Heaney's poem, this rejuvenated, auroral poet is beyond exact, tribal revenge; her desire is 'to surface and greet' those who buried her, 'mouth young, and full again / of dirt, and spit, and poetry.' (J 49)

This pivotal figure appears to usher in a new direction in Jamie's writing, the 'writing towards nature' for which she is thus far most widely celebrated. In fact, there are many lines of continuity between this 'phase' and her earlier work. In *The Tree House* (2004), the ambiguous, dead-yet-living house of the title poem speaks of 'our difficult, / chthonic anchorage / in the apple-sweetened earth' (*TH* 41), and is closely akin to 'The Sea-House' of *The Queen of Sheba* (57). The 'stone boat,/ a miracle ship' (*QS* 43) returns as an ethereal blue boat, 'with, slung from its mast, a lantern / like our old idea of the soul' (*TH* 19). It is not that Jamie became a 'nature writer' overnight, but her conversations with the natural world shifted to centre stage in her work just as 'new nature writing' or 'environmental literature' came to be recognised as a major literary movement in the first decade of the twenty-first century.[7]

The Tree House is arguably Jamie's most lyrical work, demonstrating her mastery of ballad quatrains, Dantean tercets, unrhymed couplets, experimental sonnets and many new forms of her own making. The volume abounds with birdlife, both in movement and song, and in some ways it is her 'song of the earth', her response to Jonathan Bate's impassioned study of Romantic ecopoetics in *The Song of the Earth* (2000). Her engagement with German (rather than English) Romanticism is also in evidence in the influence of Rilke on poems such as 'Daisies', as well as in the translations of Hölderlin in *The Tree House* and *The Overhaul*. But Jamie's understanding of the relation between language and the natural world is more ambivalent than Bate's Heideggerian model of 'ecopoetics' would suggest (Bate defines 'ecopoetics' as the study of poetry that makes the earth our dwelling-place).[8] The 'Wishing Tree', that chokes on the 'small change / of human hope, / daily beaten into me' (*T* 4), signals a more conflicted relation with the earth, and stresses the costs, as well as the hope, of human dwelling. All the same, in its newfound lyricism, *The Tree House* seems to have absorbed both Rilke's fascination with aural effects, and Bate's conviction that 'metre itself – a quiet but persistent music, a recurring cycle, a heartbeat – is an answer to nature's own rhythms, an echoing of the song of the earth itself' (76).

Jamie's two books of essays, *Findings* (2005) and *Sightlines* (2012), extend this 'writing towards nature' in new directions, while also creating a complex echo chamber between her prose and poetry, since many of the essays correspond in situation or theme to poems in *The Tree House* and *The Overhaul* (2012). In *Findings* and *The Tree House*, she discovers analogues and points of connection between the domestic affairs of humans and other animals. She enters into a daily ritual of watching peregrines come and go near her home: 'between the laundry and the fetching kids from school, that's how birds enter my life.' (*F* 39) Attending to these incidental, daily encounters, she sets her prose against a tradition of nature writing about solitary, extreme experience of the wild. Here she is referring to J. A. Baker, whose intense and dazzling narration of a lonely, ten-month pilgrimage following two pairs of peregrines culminates in a scene of heart-wrenching separation from his Beatrice, the peregrine who has absorbed all his waking consciousness.[9] But Jamie's daily 'findings' amidst the routines of her ordinary life also lead her to a muted but no less powerful sense of revelation: 'The peregrine flickers at the edge of one's senses, at the edge of the sky, at the edge of existence itself.' (F 47) The edge which gives us a sense of mortal existence, and which sets poetry resonating, becomes increasingly important in the later poetry, especially *The Overhaul* and *Frissure*.

In her essay 'Surgeons' Hall' (F 129–45), Jamie narrates a visit to the Surgeons' Hall Museum in Edinburgh. The essay finds its harmonic echo in *This Weird Estate* (2007), a collection with a series of poems commissioned by Scotland and Medicine for the touring exhibition 'Anatomy Acts'. Considered together, this writing demonstrates her interest in medicine as a field of study which ballasts her artistic exploration of the human relation to nature. Each poem in *This Weird Estate* is paired with a full-page photograph of a specimen from the 'Anatomy Acts' collection. These poems challenge the notion of a natural world existing beyond and in opposition to the human, for they discover weirdly exotic creatures with staring eyes, and fantastical landscapes – birch trees, rivers, coracles, gateways, oceans, glens, 'a kingdom ye micht gang tae / in Elfyn-ballads an dreams' (WE, Plate III) – all within the body's interior: the cross-section of human brain, a human foetus, an amputated tumour, and the severed stomach of a young boy.

Sightlines is dedicated to 'the island-goers', and travels geographically further afield than *Findings*, in part because, as Jamie has remarked, her children were older and she was less constrained by domestic ties.[10] But the two genres of 'travel writing' and 'indigene' or 'local' writing are increasingly fused in Jamie's later work, because her external landscapes have begun to echo and mirror interior ones, within and across different genres of writing. In her essay 'Pathologies' (S 21–42), Jamie describes looking into a microscope at a section of tumour, in Ninewells Hospital, Dundee. In the amplified image she discovers 'another world . . . an estuary with a north bank and a south . . . wing-shaped river islands or sandbanks, as if it was low tide. It was astonishing, a map of the familiar; it was our local river, as seen by a hawk.' (S 30) Jamie is usually careful to name the species of her birds, but another generic hawk appears in *The Overhaul*, where the twinned image of the gliding bird and its shadow comes to mirror the speaker's own 'so-called soul, / part unhooked hawk / part shadow on parole' (O 15). There is, if anything, an even closer relation between essays and poems in *Sightlines* and *The Overhaul*, with many subjects – gannets, the moon, whales, light and darkness – overlapping in the two works. But the two genres are also handled more distinctly, with the one pushing the other farther in its given form.

Introducing *The Overhaul* amongst other contenders for the 2012 T. S. Eliot Prize, Ian McMillan commented that writing essays seems to have 'freed up Jamie's poetry to become even more poetic'.[11] That, of course, depends on what you mean by 'poetic', but *The Overhaul* certainly explores many different poetic forms, from the ballad quatrains, tercet and couplet forms featured in *The Tree House* to long narratives such as 'The Gather' and ragged, loosely-woven sonnets (possibly another sign of Rilke's influence). While all poetry plays against white space and silence, the poems of *The Overhaul* do so consciously and daringly, as if this flight towards the edge has become the central challenge. Here, and even more so in *Frissure* (2013), the words are in dialogue with silence, taking shape in response to and anticipation of that 'edge of existence' alluded to in *Findings*.

It is too early to reach a critical consensus about the direction and overall significance of Kathleen Jamie's writing, and in any case, great writing rarely leads to a consensus. The aim of the present volume is twofold: to give a critical account of the full range of her writing from 1982 to the present day, and also to stimulate discussion and debate about her work from a variety of different critical and creative perspectives. The first aim sets itself polemically against a tendency in the public reception of contemporary writers to find a single box for their work. Jamie's writing has evolved through many distinct phases, though there are also strong lines of continuity and an inner coherence to her corpus. To think of her mainly as a nature writer, or as a Scots woman writer, or as any other fixed thing, is to miss out on Jamie's openness to the new, her defiance of predictability.

The second aim continues in the direction of the first. Gathered together here are a series of responses to Jamie's work by poets and scholars, young, middling and mature; taken together, they attend to many different facets of her artistry.

Seven poets, an aptly fairy-tale number, have contributed original poems. Amongst the essayists, Faith Lawrence argues that the practice of 'listening with attention'[12] constitutes the ground of Jamie's poetics. Influenced by Rilke's notions of auditory empathy, it involves an ethical stance toward the other that is complicit with the other's presence. Alan Riach's essay surveys Jamie's early work, from *Black Spiders* through to *The Queen of Sheba*, and traces a trajectory moving from personal and lyrical, but oblique, perception through dialogue and excursion, to a confident series of negotiations with Scottish nationhood. Robert Crawford discusses the evolution of Jamie's use of Scots, from a studied avoidance in her earliest poems, through a turning point in *Autonomous Region*, to a total immersion, at important moments, in her latest published collections. While most readers think of *The Tree House* (2004) as the earliest of Jamie's volumes written 'toward the natural world',[13] Amanda Bell demonstrates how the 'seeds of her ecological sensibility' are already present in *The Queen of Sheba*, published a decade earlier.

David Wheatley considers how Jamie 'maps the land' in her more recent poetry, from *Jizzen* (1999) to the present day; 'mapping', in Wheatley's sense, refers to the poet finding her bearings in nation, history, geography, and literary tradition. Timothy L. Baker argues that *Jizzen* exemplifies the notion of identity as difference rather than belonging (to a nation, race or gender), and he illustrates ways in which selfhood emerges through contact with the other in this collection. Juliet Simpson explores the weights and counterweights at play in *Jizzen*'s figuring of birth: birthing as both homely and un-homely experience, one which recharges the poet's connections with Scots language and landscape, but which also summons up histories of severance and linguistic diaspora.

Peter Mackay's essay brings us to Jamie's 'writing toward nature' and again to the notion of poetry as a listening in or attentiveness. In Jamie's emphasis on 'unchanciness', and her portrayal of a dynamic dialectic between resistance to, and immersion in, the natural world, Mackay finds a kinship with the philosophy of Emmanuel Levinas. Lynn Davidson explores the significance of repeated 'folding' and 'unfolding' words in *The Tree House* in a reading that emphasises the uncertainty of human relations to evolving natural environments. Michael O'Neill's essay also focuses on *The Tree House*, this time for an exploration of Jamie's inventive use of traditional poetic forms such as the sonnet, the couplet and quatrain, rhyme and near-rhyme; at times, O'Neill suggests, form 'does the work of divination . . . it enables migration between one dimension and another'.

In her reading of *This Weird Estate*, a volume published three years after *The Tree House*, Lucy Collins turns our attention to nature as the 'other within' the human body. Collins's reading shows how Jamie's anatomical poems meditate on the relation between anatomist, poet, and the human subject of study from different angles – private, public, empathetic or detached. Eleanor Bell's essay situates Jamie's prose collections, *Findings* and *Sightlines*, within the context of an earlier generation of Scottish Renaissance writing about nature; Bell finds a particularly close affinity between Jamie's prose and Nan Shepherd's *The Living Mountain*, in that both writers find 'the domestic within the wild, and vice versa'. Louisa Gairn's essay on *Sightlines* and *The Overhaul* returns us to the question of how and where we belong, or dwell, in relation to nature. Drawing on the work of anthropologist Tim Ingold, Gairn sees Jamie creating spaces of negotiated settlement, in both her recent poetry and prose collections.

In her introductory essay to *Frissure*, Jamie notes of the process of composition with artist Brigid Collins, '[a]lways we began with conversation' (F iii). Eleanor Spencer's essay explores this conversational aspect of Jamie's art, discussing the range of her collaborative works from *A Flame in Your Heart* (1986) to *Frissure* (2013). Spencer discovers in these diverse texts a consistent preoccupation with 'line' – of verse, brush stroke, landscape, scored body, temporal mark. In my essay on *The Overhaul* and *Frissure*, I suggest that Jamie's two 'midlife' collections perform, while listening out for, a distinctively musical kind of presence, in which every sound resounds against an outer edge – whether a web of rhyme, or a sonorous chamber, or a listening ear, or a sense of finitude. Maria Johnston's essay weaves together many of the thematic concerns explored elsewhere in this volume, showing us further how such concerns form part of a web of conversation between poets. She explores ways in which Jamie and Michael Longley are both 'out on the edge of things', creating forms that are 'makeshift shelters' for something passing through. The present volume is another makeshift shelter, where the reader may hear the crisscross of different conversations – between the essays, between the poetry and prose, and not least, between the reader's own thoughts and Kathleen Jamie's writing.

NOTES

1. Scott interview, 'In the nature of things'.
2. John Keats, letter to George and Georgiana Keats, 14 October 1818.
3. http://www.kathleenjamie.com/about (last accessed 6 May 2014).

4. Rush, 'Elephants in Anstruther'.

5. Ibid.

6. Greig, 'A White Elephant in Anstruther', p. 5. Greig goes on to define being Scottish as 'qualities of skepticism, of sarcasm, of curiosity, of a persistent identification with the underdog, of a distrust of striking attitudes, of a refusal to be easily impressed' (p. 7).

7. See for example Cowley, 'The New Nature Writing'.

8. Bate, *The Song of the Earth*, p. 75.

9. According to Mark Cocker, Baker may in fact have spent ten years following his wild peregrines, and then compressed the experience into a fictional ten-month period in his narrative. See Cocker, 'Introduction', in Baker, *The Peregrine*, pp. 6–7. I am grateful to Amy Player for this reference.

10. Crown interview, 'Kathleen Jamie: a life in writing' (2012).

11. McMillan continues, 'because the essays can contain a kind of description and a kind of narrative . . . then somehow the poems have been allowed to become themselves'. https://www.youtube.com/watch?v=g8GZmLt3Ook (last accessed 6 May 2014).

12. Scott interview, 'In the nature of things'.

13. Jamie, 'Author statement', British Council website.

Inlet

for Kathleen Jamie

I have seen your face
Among the pebbles
In a Highland pool.

Seeping into grass
The sea at spring tide
Leaves bladderwrack there.

You will have noticed
A planetary rose-hip
Hanging from the sky,

A slippery plank
Bridging the inlet
And the last of the sea,

A mussel shell
Filling up with rain
As you reach the pool.

Michael Longley

1. A Poetics of Listening

Faith Lawrence

> *Isn't that a kind of prayer? The care and maintenance of the web of our noticing,*
> *the paying heed? (Findings 109)*

This 'web of our noticing' is a significant image in Kathleen Jamie's work, and the precursor of another web: the one woven by the 'sulphur-and-black-striped' spider in her 2012 collection *The Overhaul*.

> – had you never considered
> how the world sustains?
> The ants by day
> clearing, clearing,
> the spiders mending endlessly – (O 20)

The mundane ('mending') and the eternal ('endlessly') come together in the last line of this poem, and then the pronouns change. The spider has been speaking in the first person, 'when I appear to you / by dark', but now it uses the third – 'the spiders mending'; the shift means it makes no special claims for itself outside of its genus. In reading that line too quickly, one could easily mistake it for the voice of the poet. This is resonant, useful confusion, for as Jamie once said, 'we [humans] do language like spiders do webs'.[1] Her persona, one could argue, is somewhat like that modest spider, almost happy to efface its own ego in the act of creation.

For Jamie, the making and maintenance of this 'web of our noticing' is more than a talent, or a mere component of the writing process; it is *the* solution to an ethical question – how can I justify writing?

> It is inexplicable to me why I should be a poet. Why me, and not the girl next door? Why not my classmates, whose lives were so similar to my own? Why are poets still born at all? There must be some reason, that poets still occur ...Writing was necessary to me, and I published young, but for years I felt almost ashamed to be making a spectacle of myself. Ashamed that I had a talent or speciality which others didn't. A very Scottish cringe![2]

The idea that a poet's attention is one of distinctive things he or she can offer, gives Jamie not just the constitutive elements of her writing but a place to stand, where service rather than self-expression ('making a spectacle') is the point:

> When we were young, we were told that poetry is about voice, about finding a voice and speaking with this voice, but the older I get I think it's not about voice, it's about listening and the art of listening, listening with attention. I don't just mean with the ear; bringing the quality of attention to the world. The writers I like best are those who attend.[3]

This emphasis on the poet's ear as witness recalls the work of Rainer Maria Rilke, for whom the act of paying attention also had ethical and ontological value:

> Yes – the springtimes needed you. Often a star
> was waiting for you to notice it. A wave rolled toward you
> out of the distant past, or as you walked
> under an open window, a violin
> yielded itself to your hearing. All this was mission.[4]

It's not surprising, given this parallel between these two poets, to find (as we shall see) that Jamie cites Rilke as one of her influences. Comparing their work helps to interpret that curious notion, the idea of the poet listening '[not] just. . .with the ear', and to understand how listening as a trope enables their poetry.

First, though, it's worth noting that Jamie has been called a 'supreme listener' in a literal sense.[5] Although the verb 'to listen' doesn't appear in her poems very often, there is a notable, unassuming exception in *The Overhaul*,

> I'd discover a cave
> green and ventricular
>
> and there, with tremendous patience,
> I'd teach myself to listen:
>
> what the whale-fish hear
> answering through the vastnesses
>
> I'd hear too. (O 46)

Ironically, the rarity of such explicit references indicates the pervasiveness of Jamie's listening, rather than its absence. It's not an exceptional practice for her, and what it yields is more important; we can take her listening for granted:

> Between the laundry and fetching kids from school, that's how birds enter my life. I listen. During a lull in the traffic: oyster catchers; in the school play-ground, sparrows – (F 39)

This habit of 'listening in the gaps' is already evident in one of her earliest prose works, *Among Muslims*:

> I lay for a few minutes enjoying peace. Children's voices reached me, and the occasional bleat of a goat. I noticed the river's rush which pervades every village, so constant and ubiquitous that you become unaware of it until it reappears at times of silence like your own heartbeat. Another sound: of an axe thudding into wood. Softly the door opened, and closed again before I could see who was there. (AM 194)

In *Findings* Jamie continues to show delight in the experience of sound, especially when she shares it with the like-minded:

> I grew to appreciate the company of people who listen to the world. They don't feel the need to talk all the while. They were alert to bird cries, waves sucking on rocks, a rope frittering on a mast. (F 54)

That capacity – to be a listener, not just a speaker – reveals a particular orientation; it's about valuing an awareness of the physical world outside ourselves, but which nevertheless incorporates our listening.

If the evidence of Jamie's listening practice is in the prose, the fruits are in the poems. Respectful and scrupulous in her descriptions, she transcribes the varied sounds of creatures, the nuances of bird calls: 'the wild birds' / faint strangulated cries' (O 24), the swifts' 'terse screams' (19), the rooks' 'Kaah . . . kaah . . . kaah . . . kaah . . .' (44) (taking care, in the last example, to represent not only bird-calls, but the silence between the rooks' cries). No such 'art of listening' could be acquired without an accompanying fascination with the soundscape. Less obvious is the tenacity such an art requires:

> – And gulls too,
> uttering the same
> torn-throated cries
> as when you first imagined
> hours hunched
> against the wind-
> abraded wall might yield some
> species of understanding. (O 41)

For Jamie, listening means being prepared to fail, to endure the times when it feels as if nothing useful is being retrieved. The backdrop of the 'torn-throated' gulls is awful continuous consolation for what cannot be heard. Jamie shows a facility for the patience listening requires, and for auditory empathy – hearing herself as other creatures might hear her:

and you shriek, you shriek
so prettily, I'm reminded
of the birds – (O 20)

This is inventive listening, but it is still listening in a literal sense. To understand what it means for Jamie to listen '[not] just . . . with the ear', we must ask what it means to *be* a listener, not simply to imagine other 'listenings'.

Few writers have been as engaged with the notion of what it means to *be* a listener as Jean-Luc Nancy. In *Listening* he argues that hearing is the liminal sense par excellence: 'To be listening is always to be on the edge of meaning, or in an edgy meaning of extremity.'[6] If this sense leads us, metaphorically, to the edge of meaning, what is heard will perforce not be intelligible at first. It will entail bringing what has not yet found expression into the language of the poem. Whereas vision is the ultimate 'distance' sense (where the subject and the object perceive each other, yet remain separate), our ears necessarily mix us up with the world, blurring our boundaries:

> to listen is to enter that spatiality by which, at the same time, I am penetrated, for it opens up in me as well as around me, and from me as well as toward me: it opens me inside me as well as outside, and it is through being such a double, quadruple, or sextuple opening that a 'self' can take place. To be listening is to be at the same time outside and inside, to be open from without and from within, hence from one to the other and from one in the other.[7]

If one draws on these two ideas of Nancy's, a listening poetics should foreground and trouble the boundaries of the self rather than shore them up. Hence the ear has often been associated with strange meetings, or mystical encounters. The fourteenth-century author of *The Cloud of Unknowing* is one of many mystics from differing faiths who have emphasised listening as a route to union with God.

> There he [Christ] will show you the wonderful kindness of God, and he wants nothing so much as that you should listen to him . . . Before you know where you are you are disintegrated beyond belief! And the reason? Simply that you freely consented to listen to that thought, and responded to it, accepted it, and gave it its head.[8]

For Jamie, writing poetry offers union of a different kind – it's 'a sort of connective tissue, when my self meets the world and rises out of that, that liminal place'.[9] It makes sense that she should first and foremost think of herself as a listener. Like the wishing tree in *The Tree House*, to be a 'listening poet' means to stand on the threshold – the 'fold in the green hill', 'the tilt from one parish / into another' – in order to hear 'each wish / each secret assignation' (*TH* 3).

The adoption of this liminal 'listening position' tells us something about the ambition of Jamie's poems (one must talk about the ambition of a Jamie poem itself, rather than her ambitions for it). These are poems that are not content to turn inward and simply mine the experiences of the poet for material. Jamie once advised competition entrants to 'write the poem that wants to be written', explaining that she is always grateful 'to be taken far beyond myself'.[10] The ideal of the transporting experience is a far cry from what Sean O'Brien calls the 'indulgently anecdotal' poem, a species he found relatively common in the mid-noughties.[11] This verdict appeared in an essay within which he explored the 'intensification of interest' in the work of Rainer Maria Rilke. His suggestion was that Rilke was offering a less limiting mode of expression:

> some of the most interesting contemporary poets are powerfully drawn to the work of a modern poet who was prepared to stake everything on the imagination's resources.[12]

At the time O'Brien was writing, close to the publication of *The Tree House*, Jamie hadn't published any versions of Rilke's poems (like Don Paterson), direct responses to his work (like Jo Shapcott) or poems 'after' Rilke (like Seamus Heaney or Paul Farley). She had, however, already testified to the nature of his appeal:

> I remember being introduced to the work of Rilke, especially the Duino Elegies; and Elizabeth Bishop. I loved Rilke for his heights and range, Bishop for her care and cool exactitude.[13]

Her comments around the significance of listening '[not] just . . . with the ear' certainly came out of the same climate as this general 'intensification of interest' in Rilke, a poet profoundly engaged with the idea of the poet as a careful listener:

> At one period, when I began to interest myself in Arabic poems, which seem to owe their existence to the simultaneous and equal contributions from all five senses, it struck me for the first time, that the modern European poet makes use of these contributors singly and in varying degree, only one of them – sight overladen with the seen world – seeming to dominate him constantly; how slight, by contrast, is the contribution he receives from inattentive hearing.[14]

Rilke's own emphasis on a listening practice resulted in some of his most astonishing achievements. He thought it was responsible for the fifty-five *Sonnets to Orpheus* (described as 'an inner dictation, completely spontaneous') and for enabling the 'heights' of a poem like the 'First Duino Elegy', which started with a voice 'heard' whilst out walking,

> Listen, my heart, as only
> saints have listened: until the gigantic call lifted them
> off the ground; yet they kept on, impossibly,
> kneeling and didn't notice at all:
> so complete was their listening.[15]

Whether or not he really 'heard' this voice is beside the point; it's certainly true that for Rilke listening became a useful trope, giving him a metaphorical place to stand and receive – just as it does for Jamie. And they both manifest a 'listening poetics', in the sense that their poems seem to 'listen'. Or, as Jamie herself has said:

> When I'm asked what is the difference between poetry and prose, I reply the status of the line. Lines that were both controlled and breathed, that listened to language, that revealed and slowed . . . or raced and paced – these were hard to find.[16]

For a poem to work, each word in a line must 'hear' all the others, since it can only be properly experienced within the resonance of all the other words circling it. Jamie is arguing here for an attentiveness between words, distinctive to poetry. Beyond this act of micro-listening, there is also a broader 'listening' rhetoric in the language, apparent in the way the poems acknowledge the reader. In Rilke's *Sonnets to Orpheus* we find lines like, 'But you now, dear girl, whom I loved like a flower whose name / I didn't know'[17]. O'Brien argues that this manner of address is key to Rilke's contemporary appeal:

> sometimes involving 'you', often using 'we' to active effect rather than as mere rhetorical reinforcement – [the address] does work to implicate the reader as a companion of a sort, a privileged listener rather than an accidental passer-by . . .[18]

In Jamie's poems, we must exchange the word 'privileged' for 'complicit'. Her way of talking to the reader implies equality rather than flattery.

In 'The Tree House', the proximity experienced by the 'chamber' with the branch of the tree is compared to the relationship between the poet and reader(s) – 'a complicity / like our own' (*TH* 41). 'Complicit', from the Old French for 'associate', ultimately deriving from the Latin verb 'complicare' ('to fold together'), is a choice of word which corroborates the cool yet inclusive tone that pervades so many of Jamie's poems. In 'Materials' it's assumed the reader shares another kind of 'complicity', an ironic sense of humour:

> half a dozen waders
> mediate between sea and shore, that space confirmed
> – don't laugh – by your own work. (*O* 50)

Conceived as a conversation, a poem like this allows the poet to sit at the boundary – not just between two ways of speaking, but two ways of hearing.

It also makes for other listening opportunities; questions, for example, are threaded through Rilke's and Jamie's writing, a gesture which Don Paterson has described as 'our most honest prepositional stance towards the universe'.[19] Listening spaces inevitably follow question marks (a question mark could be described as a listening notation), and when a question enters a Jamie poem, the poems are at their listening best:

> What was it
> I'd have asked, to exist
> so bright and fateless
>
> while time coursed
> through our every atom
> over its bed of stones – ? (*TH* 33)

And:

> The world's
> mind is such interstices;
> cells charging with light of day –
> is that what they were telling us? (*TH* 30)

The most important question in *The Tree House* comes in 'Alder':

> won't you teach me
>
> a way to live
> on this damp ambiguous earth? (*TH* 7)

In *The Tree House* questions often come at the end of a poem, and are often rhetorical. In *The Overhaul*, however, responses arrive frequently:

> . . . Moon,
> why have you turned to me
> your dark side, why am I
> examining these stones?
> *Our friendship lapsed.* (*O* 18)

These 'listening' poems are able to detect fissures in attention, but they also offer reparation:

> [. . .] imagine
> we could mend
>
> whatever we heard fracture:
> splintering of wood, a bird's
>
> cry over still water, a sound
> only reaching us now. (*O* 11)

This idea of listening as a healing practice resonates towards the end of Jamie's most recent prose collection, *Sightlines*. Here she presents an elegy for the eardrums of whales:

> I find them [the eardrums] beautiful and sad and complete; all that can be said about sea-waves and sound waves, song and utterance, is rolled together in these forms.
>
> The Stromness one is grey and old, and as you look at it lying on its shelf you have to wonder. What did it hear, in life? Across what distances? Whales apparently hear through their jawbones; they have no external ears as we do – so the very jawbones now raised around the country at large would, in life, have picked up sound waves in the ocean. What did they hear, these jaws, these eardrums? They heard us coming, that's what. (S 233)

Again Jamie is imagining another listening orientation – one capable of offering absolution, if only symbolically:

> I suggest that if they cared to listen, if we could indeed whisper into those eardrums, they'd hear something, at least in this country, like atonement. (S 235)

Where Rilke and Jamie part company, though, is in their conception of where the poet's listening receptivity should begin and end. Rilke came to define himself as an *empfanger* (a receiver), but it became an overwhelming responsibility:

> I am like the little anemone I once saw in the garden in Rome: it had opened so wide during the day that it could no longer close at night. It was terrible to see it in the dark lawn, wide open . . . I too am as hopelessly turned outward thus also distracted by everything, refusing nothing.[20]

One of the *Sonnets to Orpheus* draws on the same image of exposure, amplified here in Don Paterson's version of the poem, 'Anemone'.

> By noon, the sky's polyphony
> will flood her white lap till she drowns
>
> The tiny muscle in her star
> is tensed to open to the All,
> yet the daylight's blast so deafens her
> she barely heeds the sunset's call.[21]

Jamie's 'Daisies' could almost be in conversation with Rilke's sonnet; characteristically, she chooses to give a voice to the flowers themselves:

> We are flowers of the common
> sward, that much we understand.

[. . .] Evening
means sleep, and surely it's better
to renew ourselves than die
of all that openness?
But die we will, innocent
or no, (TH 32)

There are limits to everything, the poem argues, to what we can hear, and to what
we will experience on this earth. Jamie's listening poetics (unlike Rilke's) is tempered by pragmatism, and a balancing attention paid to her own physicality:

Be quiet, I tell myself. Listen to the silence. I take my eye off the raven for a
moment, and when I look back it's gone.

How long we sit there I don't know. I know only that I'd never heard
anything like it, a silence that could dismiss a sound, as wind would dismiss a
feather. Five minutes, ten, minutes in a lifetime.

Some people say you can never experience true silence, because you come
to hear the high whine of your own nerves. That is to say, you hear the very
nervous system which allows you to hear at all. Nerves because we are animals,
not ice, not rock. Driven by cold and hunger. It's cold, our animal bodies say;
best get moving. Keep warm, keep hunting. So, after maybe ten minutes, by
some unspoken assent, a movement, a cough, our experience of deep silence
is over, and life begins to whip us on our way. We all begin slowly to stand
and move downhill, back toward the waiting boats. It's a while before anyone
speaks. (S 5)

This realism feels less like limitation in Jamie's writing and more like revelation.
The presence of boundaries confers meaning on poems and on our own lives. Daisies
draw in their petals, missing the night sky, but it is in the nature of all living things
to experience closure of one kind or another. It is all too typical of Rilke that the
image of the receiving flower, even when it becomes closed in his famous epitaph,
retains a kind of boundlessness, an eternal multiplicity:

Rose, oh pure contradiction, delight of being no-one's sleep under so many
lids.[22]

Ultimately it is the relationship between listening and our experience of time that
makes listening not 'just . . . with the ear' into such an apposite trope for Rilke and
Jamie. Don Paterson writes that within the Sonnets to Orpheus Rilke achieved

the perfect balance between death and life, eternity and the living present, by
singing across the gap and inhabiting both at once . . . For a human to sing is to
do something unique and with no analogue in other species. It is to unite the
discrete quanta of passing time through music and lyric. These things offer a
stay against time's passing.[23]

We shouldn't forget that the power of Orphic song is met in the sonnets by an equal listening. In the first poem of the sequence, the creatures fall 'quiet in neither stealth nor fear,/ but in their listening', and finally, the 'temple rises in their hearing'.[24] Such absorbed attention is as much a part of this 'stay against time passing' as the song itself.

In contrast, Jamie uses a listening poetics to find a way to live with, rather than protest our impermanence. Monuments are made of stone because it outlasts us, whereas sound is always in the act of disappearing. But like the spider's web at the start of this essay, sound is always being re-made; it is 'supple, undammable', like Jamie's birdsong in 'The Dipper' (*TH* 49).

The almost-answer which follows Jamie's central question ('won't you teach me / a way to live / on this damp ambiguous earth?') begins in sound ('The rain showers / release you from a broken tune'). This attention paid to listening, to the moment of the poem, is a kind of liberation, a *modus vivendi*.

To be a listener, but '[not] just . . . with the ear': this is what Jamie's poems say we may do in the face of 'the provisional'. For, as she tells us in the last line of *Sightlines*, 'a wing's beat and it's gone'.

WORKS CITED (SEE ALSO BIBLIOGRAPHY)

O'Brien, Sean, 'Rilke and the Contemporary Reader', *Poetry Review* 77, 2005, pp. 77–87.
Nancy, Jean-Luc, *Listening*, tr. Charlotte Mandell (New York: Fordham University Press, 2007).
Paterson, Don, *Orpheus* (London: Faber and Faber, 2007).
Rilke, Rainer Maria, *Ahead of all Parting: The Selected Poetry and Prose of Rainer Maria Rilke*, ed. And tr Stephen Mitchell (New York: Random House, 1995).
Snow, Edward, and Michael Winkler (eds and trs), *Rilke and Andreas Salome: A Love Story in Letters* (New York: Norton, 2006).
Walters, Clifton (ed.), *The Cloud of Unknowing* (London: Penguin, 1978).

NOTES

1. Goring, 'Kathleen Jamie: The SRB Interview'.
2. Jamie, 'Author statement', British Council website.
3. Scott interview, 'In the nature of things'.
4. Rilke, 'First Duino Elegy', *Ahead of All Parting*, p. 331.
5. Mabey, review of *Findings*, quoted on the author page of Sort of Books website: http://www.sortof.co.uk/authors/kathleen-jamie (last accessed 18 May 2014).
6. Nancy, *Listening*, p. 7.
7. Ibid., p. 14.
8. Walters, *The Cloud of Unknowing*, pp. 58–69.
9. Scott interview, 'In the nature of things'.
10. Jamie, 'Kathleen Jamie: Judge's Report'.
11. O'Brien, 'Rilke and the Contemporary Reader', p. 1.
12. Ibid., p. 1.
13. Jamie, 'Author statement', British Council website.
14. Rilke, 'Primal Sound', *Ahead of All Parting*, p. 301.

15. Rilke, 'First Duino Elegy', *Ahead of All Parting*, p. 333.
16. Jamie, 'Kathleen Jamie: Judge's Report'.
17. Rilke, 'Sonnets to Orpheus XXV', *Ahead of All Parting*, p. 459.
18. O'Brien, 'Rilke and the Contemporary Reader', p. 79.
19. Paterson, *Orpheus*, p. 67.
20. Snow and Winkler, *Rilke and Andreas Salome*, p. 248.
21. Paterson, *Orpheus*, p. 35.
22. Rilke, *Ahead of All Parting*, p. 195.
23. Paterson, *Orpheus*, p. 69.
24. Ibid., p. 3.

2. Mr and Mrs Scotland Are Taking a Vacation in the Autonomous Region

Alan Riach

At the end of an essay published in 2008, Kathleen Jamie said that 'wildness' was:

> not a place to stride over but a force requiring constant negotiation. A lifelong negotiation at that: to give birth is to be in a wild place, so is to struggle with pneumonia. If you can look down a gryke, you can look down a microscope, and marvel at the wildness of the processes of our own bodies, the wildness of disease. There is Ben Nevis, there is smallpox. One wild worth protecting, one worth eradicating. And in the end, we won't have to go out to find the wild, because the wild will come for us.[1]

A 'gryke' is a fissure in flat limestone, in which can be seen hundreds of plants thriving in the shelter of a miniature wilderness, and the delight in such a vision is described by Robert Macfarlane in his book *The Wild Places* (2007), which Jamie's essay reviews. Her point is that, attractive as Macfarlane's work is, there is a liability in a comfortable narrator's honeyed prose recounting an expedition from which he and the reader both know they will safely return. The wild places evoke not only open, expansive, uninhabited land, but locations in time, where land-ownership might be a matter of violence, where the language of place names offers a history far from serene, where the 'preservation' of 'Nature' might come at the cost of neglecting or obscuring threatened or tortured realities, from which or through which people might – or sometimes, must – go fearfully. When the wild places are sporting-grounds for families or guests of royalty, or under-the-radar practise-space for war planes, wildness is not an exotic resort but a condition of social life that might, or should, be changed.

The contexts so far have been personal or geographical localities – the body (in childbirth or disease), the territory (wherever the excursion takes us), but there is another wild place in Jamie's poetry: the nation. For Jamie, Scotland is contextualised with co-ordinate points that arise from the foundations of her understanding of socially gendered, power-structured identities, in which nationality is only one component and redefinable part. The nation is a wild place of contesting forces.

Affirmation of statehood is not likely to change that. No simplification of the political power structures can alter the priorities of demarcation, legalities, limits and what is beyond them. And from her earliest books, Jamie has been working to develop poetic forms of articulation that acknowledge clear structure while moving through its securities. What might be described as the character of the work of her contemporaries – Liz Lochhead, Jackie Kay, Meg Bateman, Carol Ann Duffy, for example – might be quite firmly delineated. Jamie's work is more erratic than theirs, less certain, less emphatic, more tentative. The space it occupies is transformational. Their poems are frequently reports on, or playful engagements with, experience; Jamie's are more often about its potential, prospects or possibilities arising from it. This essay is an attempt to explore and justify this proposition.

Mr and Mrs Scotland Are Dead: Poems 1980–1994 (2002) is a selection of her poems from her first collection, Black Spiders (1982) through to The Queen of Sheba (1994). The poems chart Jamie's exploration of understanding what ideas of position, power, place and personality might mean, as they change in conditions of desire, enquiry and decisive judgement. Following Mr and Mrs Scotland, Jamie's later work develops further and her prose essays in Findings (2005) and Sightlines (2012) testify to specific engagements with nature, wilderness, the wild, and what these words mean. The potential for the later developments is inherent in the early work.

Pre-eminently, from the title itself, the promise of mortal demise delivered upon conventional, reactionary, intimidated articulations of 'Scottishness' is complemented by fully charged assertions of value in social, gendered and regenerated self-determination. Yet this binary opposition oversimplifies the way the poems work, which is to deliver nuanced, subtle explorations of experience, ideas and physical locations being discovered, tentatively, as well as inhabited, fully, with great strengths of attachment, but going further, being considered in terms of what future potential such experience portends, what it might bring. The ideas and locations take her far from Scotland, but, as the title insists, her native country is not erased by this. This dynamic in Jamie's writing extends to her prose, where a sensitivity to particularities and the exercise of the power of critical judgement combine in situations both of hard extremity and transition. Her work brings together some of the most delicate perceptions and argumentative, oppositional propositions, in modern Scottish writing. This is a key method in her writing practice.

The trajectory of the book may be simply described as beginning in lyrical, personal but oblique perception, opening into a dialogue in a tragic love affair represented by personae from the Second World War, resuming and deepening a sense of personal authority via an excursion along 'The Karakoram Highway' and a further excursion to 'The Autonomous Region'. The final selection from The Queen of Sheba reoccupies and redefines the poet's position and authority in Scotland, with a more confidently assertive and defined presence which nevertheless insists upon the unavoidability of the uncontrollable world. Jamie's poems open and invite us to encounter this world beyond securities of category and definition. Their slight, hesitant movement at times belies the certainty of what she is delivering.

This is evident in her first collection, Black Spiders (1982). The title refers to the hair around the nipples of an unnamed man caught sight of by an unnamed woman.

In the title poem's opening lines, she leaves him to go 'up to the convent' and he looks towards her, then goes swimming 'to the caves' (MMS 15). In the closing lines, she glimpses him 'below', 'brushing salt' from his chest hair, and her desire to tickle and kiss him there is lightly, delicately noted. The sensitivity of physical attraction, the delicacy of the emotional relation, the evocation of hunger and need, impatience and movement, are all registered in the opening five and closing three lines; between them are nine lines depicting the convent abandoned ('The nuns have retreated' but for the 'eldest' nun pealing the bell 'in glee', as if demented) and the collection boxes empty. The praying was over once the nuns saw 'the Turks' / swords reflecting the sun'. The poem begins and ends with unfulfilled personal sexual desire, physical proximity and distance, the elements, a man and a woman; but its central lines depict the aftermath of a collective violent raid. The 'he' of the opening and closing lines is mysterious, undefined. The careful manipulation of past and present tense evokes retrospection and projection, recording desire that only a future might fulfil. But the whole intricate weave of imagery and action, tenderness and violence leaves a sense of the fragility of that future, an uncertainty about what it might bring, just as the need and want that is felt remains definite, but insecure.

This is a poetry representing diffidence, faltering, hesitation and desire, yet its assurance in delivering these qualities is constant. The locations are explicitly unfamiliar: one poem is entitled 'Women in Jerusalem' (MMS 16–17); in 'The Harbour' we read, 'the harbour could be anywhere' (MMS 20); in 'The Leaving of an Island' (MMS 21) the word 'an' rejects cartographic specificity. In 'November' the named month gives calendrical place, but vagueness and universals inhabit the lines: 'On the shore / where he insists we walk, he holds me like a man / at a deck-rail in a gale' (MMS 22). When we do get a location, it is occupied by an anonymous company: in 'Cramond Island', the group are 'Most who', 'them' and 'They' and once back in 'the study', 'they stare to sea, and heal, / marking pages with salt and sand / shaken from windblown hair' (MMS 25). This vagueness invites the reader's accompaniment, a recognition that as we read these poems, we too are of these people. Yet at the same time, the figures Jamie refers to are not only others, depicted and seen as if in a film, but also personae, speaking and acting aspects of herself. Every one of these early poems is an exploration of these possibilities, which her later work carries to greater and more various realisation.

Her collaborative book-length poem-sequence *A Flame in Your Heart* (1986), written with Andrew Greig, takes the personae to a defined historical location where a Second World War fighter plane pilot and his wife, and finally widow, voice a series of oblique dialogic poems representing their relationship, their isolated experiences and reflections, their desires, hopes and failings. In *Mr and Mrs Scotland* only Jamie's half of the earlier book is reproduced, so that reading her poems in this sequence, outside of the dialogic totality, delivers a character-based story centred on a persona who inhabits an inherently dramatic, or indeed theatrical, form (MMS 29–41). The nuances and undefined qualities of her earlier poems are more fixed and co-ordinated here, so there is a sense of development, but not of definition. She is still seeing where these modes might take her.

In *The Way We Live* (1987), the self-determination and security of her voice is unmistakable. Yet it arrives in a remarkable confluence of local, specific reference with emphatically international and universal imagery. For example, the title of 'Havers' is a Scots word for spoken nonsense, flights of fancy, talking rubbish, and the poem begins: 'She once went to Girvan on horseback / it's said.' (MMS 71) Girvan is an Ayrshire seaside holiday resort, popular in the 1960s, and the reference might depend on knowledge extraneous to the poem, but 'once' suggests 'once upon a time' and 'it's said' gives a cautionary note. The romantic idea of riding by the sea is built up further, then deflated:

> Wind from the hillsides
> through her hair and its mane, sheep
> on the roadside. Havers. Her hair
> never felt breezes, caught to her neck
> like grey fleece to wire. (MMS 71)

'She' appears from the memories of childhood, her hands like saint's bones and her cheek like flaky grey parchment. Far from a figure idealised in romantic abandon, she seems more like a spinster aunt. Yet what tone prevails in this poem? Scorn for the urge to romanticise a more mundane reality? Affection for the fact of memory, helplessly giving more to the unrealised life only glimpsed and hardly comprehended by the observer? There is a melancholy quality to the clash of local idiom, the Scots word and place, a sense of diminishment, and a stronger sense of the contemporary moment bringing this past person into the poem's presence.

The culmination of this process of bringing together these seemingly disparate things is in the title poem, 'The Way We Live' itself, beginning with the command to 'Pass the tambourine, let me bash out praises' and the elision from that opening (a quotable unit) into the second and third lines: 'to the Lord God of movement, to Absolute / non-friction, flight,' then on into the fourth line: 'and the scary side: / death by avalanche, birth by failed contraception' (MMS 76). The use of capital 'A' in 'Absolute' and the apparently arbitrary imagery of avalanche and contraception (both vague, non-specific references) all keep the lines active and almost abstract. The only clear visual image in these four lines (apart from avalanche, which is generic) is 'tambourine' – a word that immediately evokes a hand, two hands, a body in movement, rhythm, music and dance. It is not a conventionally familiar Scottish musical instrument, and the references that immediately follow, to chicken tandoori and reggae, run straight into tenements, tee shirts on pulleys and dreaming waitresses, which are both Scotland and other places just as well. Airports, motorways and the symbolic and real 'mountains' lead to geography: Rannoch moor, 'endless gloaming in the North' but also 'Asiatic swelter' and 'the skeletal grip / of government'. The ninth line of the poem ends, 'waking to uncertainty', but the last two lines return to the opening command and invert the syntax brilliantly: 'To the way it fits, the way it is, the way it seems / to be: let me bash out praises – pass the tambourine.' No exclamation mark is required, for the self-assurance delivers the sense of preference without exaggeration, and the placing of 'the way it seems' at the end of the penultimate line makes sure that touch of uncertainty is still present.

Whatever it is, this seeming, whatever is there *apparently*, is something we must deal with as surely as whatever is *actually* there, 'the way it is'. Both what 'is' and what 'seems' require the engagement and the promise to be engaged, being made in the poem.

The excursus that informs the poems selected from the 1993 collection, *The Autonomous Region* (MMS 77–108) takes us to Lake Qinghai and the Tibetan plateau in China, one of the far places, or the 'wild places' to use Robert Macfarlane's term. By now, however, Jamie's character and the methodology of her poetic enquiry are clear, and clearly her own. In the distance of her travels, there are conventional exoticisms ('a high pass over the mountains', 'the Sun–Moon mirror', 'jasmine / air', 'dear Uygar boys', yaks), but there is also the infiltration of Scots words, a language that registers that nationality in the context of the other 'autonomous region': Fa-hsien has bathed in the 'joyous lake' and made himself fresh and clean:

> and now his hand and cards have changed
> reveal

> a hanker for his ain folk,
>   his auld hert follows suit. (MMS 95)

So when this sequence comes to its final poem, Jamie is using Scots throughout. The journey into the wild place of a distant and different geography has retuned the voice and returned the language to her. She hears,

> Wave droonin wave
> on a pebbly shore,
> the *ahe* o machair, o slammach,

> o impatience; ahent the saft saltire
> i trashed, an sheep;
> wha's drift on the brae

> is a lang cloud's shadda. (MMS 106)

Upon wakening, there is the realisation: 'A'm far fae hame, / I hae crossed China.' The poem abjures apostrophes, varies the spelling of one-letter words ('i' and 'A' and 'I'), works through the uncertainties of diction, yet delivers the conviction in, and commitment to, self-realisation.

This is most elaborately and compellingly affirmed in *The Queen of Sheba* (1994). The title poem is well known, but it is important to read it as opening the way for what follows in the book, collecting individuals, experiences, registers and idioms of language, characters changed through time (both in personality and in social history), hopes for possibilities and curses on constraints. The Queen of Sheba arrives to visit revenge upon the dead hand and oppressive spirit of 'Scotland'. The word recurs in the caricature couple who give their name to the title of the whole collection, *Mr and Mrs Scotland*. Identities of nation and gender are confirmed, confined and constricted by convention, and demolished by the appetites – both sensual and intellectual – of the exemplary Queen and all the 'thousand laughing girls' who draw not 'their' but 'our' hot breath to shout out their affirmation of self-extension (MMS 113). The element of fantasy or dream in the title poem is tempered by the use of vernacular, working-class urban Scots phrases, and this technical procedure is evident in 'School Reunion' (MMS 121–5), 'Bairns of Suzie: a hex' (126–7), 'Wee Baby' (128) and 'Wee Wifey' (129). In these poems, domestic, small-town, small-minded clichés of Scottishness are sharply satirised and ambiguously reimagined. The 'wee baby' might be a sentimental horror, slavering on the future, but she is also 'cradled in the sieve of all potential'. The 'wee wifey' might be 'out to do me ill' but she is 'a demon' caught by the persona in the poem, and 'we love each other dearly'. There is an affinity and indeed affection in this horrible connection. If these diminutive terms make subordinate identities that are no more than parts of the woman writing the poems, they remain attached. Dividing 'land from sea, sea from sky' may be tidy, but things are always on the move, and won't stay apart: 'The kingdom of Wee Baby is within. / She curls her fists and holds tight.' Like the nocturnal creatures in Robert Lowell's paranoid poem, 'Skunk Hour', Baby and Wifey 'will not scare'.[2]

These conventional representations of 'Scottishness' regenerate identities and find form in Jamie's plurality of idioms, voices and tonalities. This is clear in 'Arraheids' (MMS 137), where prehistoric arrowheads are identified as 'the hard tongues o grannies' that have been lying in the land for generations, 'in wicked cherms'; and in 'Skeins o Geese':

Whit dae birds write on the dusk?
A word niver spoken or read.
The skeins turn hame,
on the wind's dumb moan, a soun,
maybe human, bereft. (159)

Writing, inscription, becomes an elision, as 'word' is negated as something that is neither voiced to be heard nor made visible on paper to be seen. Birds 'write' nothing on the dusk, and then the sound in nature of the wind's 'moan' is 'dumb', meaning, perhaps, not soundless but inarticulate, and in that respect, suggesting ('maybe') something human, a song of loss, grief or sorrow, as in the Scots phrase, to 'mak' moan' or 'makin' a main' (familiar from the traditional ballad, 'The Twa Corbies'). These words are all connected in the poem syntactically, through rhetorical question and answer and visual image depicted in a sky whose twilight clarity is evoked by the reference to the wind, which is, like the geese, moving through its empty space. Yet each word or phrase seems weightless, the different linguistic registers of Scots and English terms and verbal idioms artfully placed yet almost imperceptibly distinct. 'Whit', 'dae', 'niver', 'hame' and 'soun' are Scots, and all other words are standard English. The subtlety here is unobtrusive but deft.

Jamie's poetics of juxtaposition of voices has been carefully analysed by Nancy Gish in her essay, 'Complexities of Subjectivity'.[3] Gish discusses the work of Liz

Lochhead and Jackie Kay as well as Jamie, and perceptively notes that in the 'distinct lexicons, spellings, sounds, and pronunciations' of their poems, the readers' participation is engaged and the language forms become interactive, not to be assumed. Lochhead puts it succinctly: 'I would say that the big split in Scotland is between the self and the other self.'[4] Up until *The Queen of Sheba*, Gish argues, Jamie's poems are 'conventionally "expressive"' – though as we have seen, there are clear indications of the process of 'othering' that was to become so decisively characteristic. Although Jamie was using Scots words and inflections before *The Queen of Sheba*, this volume does mark an important deepening of conviction and assurance. Jamie has said that when she moved to Sheffield in England in 1989, and registered the distinct languages of Scots and English, she was more capable of dealing with and making use of 'the Scots polyphony'.[5] This discovery and the inhabitation it led to helped bring about her sense of what the 'wild places' really are, the locations of extremity and liminality. In this way, 'Scottishness' in the new Scotland must mean something very different from what had been accepted heretofore. The Autonomous Region is no longer an exoticised location on the Tibetan plateau, but comes into its own across the history of generations, from MacDiarmid, through the generation of great poets, all men, writing after the Second World War, to the post-1970s generation of women rewriting the identity of the nation. If MacDiarmid set an example of multi-faceted national identity, and the 'seven poets' generation created their work from the geographical places each one distinctively favoured, then the gendered world of the generation since has made the national identity even more complex and welcoming, home to different diversities, accommodating – not always easily – the wild places of nature and domesticity, chaos and order, states and movements, internationality and self-determined nationality.

Eavan Boland, in her essay *A Kind of Scar*, describes her own determination to write herself into a national tradition, as a woman.[6] To do so was to break the identity of masculine authority and to redefine the discourse of nationalism. She wanted to write defiantly and definitively as an Irish poet, she says, in other words, emphatically to be part of the national tradition in its complex totality; and at the same time, she wanted to write decidedly as a woman, in work that arises from her own self-conscious experience and might deal with any matter on equal terms with her male contemporaries. This assertion begins with recognition of the predominance of male poets eulogising the nation as a principle of womanly virtue – Kathleen Ni Houlihan, Mother Ireland – but instead of opposing and rejecting nationalism as something hopelessly contaminated by the masculine imagination, and thus to be rejected, Boland's strategy was to reclaim both the nation and the provenance of poetry as her own domain. This strategy deconstructs the polarised associations of male provenance as state–nation–authority–law–literature–art–poetry and claims for female engagement the state, nation, authority, law, literature, art and poetry. Women equally with men, therefore, this strategy insists, are to be understood as citizens and artists. This degendering of secular politics was an act of enablement. The fictions of gendered prioritisation could therefore be understood as historically engineered. They may have been purposeful and useful; they may have been psychotic or pathological; but they could not be maintained unselfconsciously any longer.

Now, in Scotland, that had already been taking place, first in the work of Hugh MacDiarmid, then in the generation of male poets who came out of the Second World War, who began publishing mainly in the 1950s and 1960s. Two decades on, though, the scene had changed. The women who were published increasingly in the following decades used the achievements of their predecessors gainfully, game-somely, in the development of their own distinctive work. Meg Bateman learned from, respected, honoured and made creative use of the work of Sorley MacLean. The same could be said of Liz Lochhead and Edwin Morgan, or any younger poet writing in English and Norman MacCaig, just as each one of that generation of men – MacLean, MacCaig, Morgan, Iain Crichton Smith, George Mackay Brown, Robert Garioch, Sydney Goodsir Smith – learned from and acknowledged the achievement of Hugh MacDiarmid. None of them were to be emulated, and MacDiarmid especially repudiated the notion of 'disciples', but they each showed that things could be done – different things, in different ways, and in different loca-tions. In this respect, they were exemplary.

Characteristic of the generational change that took place in the 1970s and 1980s is Liz Lochhead's 'Mirror's Song', which begins with the command to the reader and the poet's persona and the mirror of the poem's title: 'Smash me looking-glass glass . . . ' and ends with the line, 'a woman giving birth to herself'.[7] It is as if in such an act of self-generation, and regeneration, the exemplary struggle enacted in the poem takes its place, along with the work of all the poets named, in the process of a nation giving birth to itself. From MacDiarmid through the geographical locations favoured by the next generation of men, to Lochhead and the complex identities embodied by the generation of women after them, and Jamie in that generation, the multi-faceted, plural nationality is redefining and qualifying itself, and extending into new forms and preferences. It is a continuing epic work. As Wole Soyinka describes the nature of the form: 'The epic celebrates the victory of the human spirit over forces inimical to self-extension. It concretises in the form of action the arduous birth of the individual or communal entity, creates a new being through utilising and stressing the language of self-glorification to which human nature is healthily prone.'[8]

Soyinka argues in his essay 'The Fourth Stage' that in the cosmogony, the understanding of what humanity is in the cosmos, in which he grew up as a Yoruba in Nigeria, there are three worlds: the worlds of the ancestors, the living and the unborn. It is possible to see how, in the world of western capitalism, commercial priorities are dynamic because they are pre-eminently about the living, resources are exploited and the future can look after itself; and it is possible to see how con-servative, moribund societies (like those places where, generation after generation, Mr and Mrs Scotland once lived) can be dragged down by doing things the way they've always been done in the imagined world of the ancestors; but the world of the unborn needs more attention. More than in the work of Lochhead, Kay, Duffy, Bateman, this sense of what we might provide for, or keep in mind for the well-being of, future generations, is characteristic of Jamie. The sustained strength of character of Lochhead, the clever turns and challenges of Duffy, the self-assurance and poise of Kay, and balance of self-centredness and vulnerability of Bateman, are very different from the hesitancies, gingery decisions, multivalent perspectives, tentative annotations of experience that typify Jamie's poems. This is because each poem is less a declaration than a proposition, less an assertion than an attempt, less the oil painting, more the sketch, indicating rather than fully embodying. Yet these are inadequate metaphors because they do not convey the achievement, which is singular and as great – though perhaps less easily described – than those of her contemporaries.

Soyinka goes on to say that there is a fourth stage, the realm of transition, when things change, and human beings enter onto this fourth stage, or into this fourth space, to risk transition, to bring about change. This is the space of tragedy, but it is also the space where change does happen, transition can take place. In the whole cosmos of creative and destructive being, Soyinka says, according to the wisdom he acquired in his own upbringing in Nigeria, offences against humanity and even against nature 'may be part of the exaction by deeper nature from humanity of acts which alone can bring about a constant rejuvenation of the human spirit.'[9]

Tentative yet certain, willing to risk the destructive potential of this stage, where wildness is, Kathleen Jamie's best work reminds us that the values of Enlightenment and reason are not the only ones. The decisiveness with which Jamie has taken this risk has been clearly characterised since the beginning of the new millennium by a direct engagement with the politics of Scotland and national identity. As with Eavan Boland's decision to write as a woman while redefining national identity by writing within it, rather than rejecting or denying it, Jamie's explicit engagements are strong. For example, the poem published in 2001, on the design chosen for the new parliament building designed by Catalan architect Enric Miralles, entitled 'For a new Scottish Parliament', consists in its entirety of two lines. The first delivers the image of the upward-looking hull of an overturned boat, but then the second line describes this as a 'watershed', meaning both a transitional historical moment full of future potential, and a visualisation of a wooden shelter made of a construction normally associated with being at sea.[10]

Further, on 22 August 2013, it was reported online by the BBC that Jamie had won the open vote to write a commissioned poem for the refurbished Battle of Bannockburn site, looked after by the National Trust. This has been inscribed on the rotunda monument there. The poem gestures towards 'our land' in its mixed weather, owned not by people but part of the whole earth, with its particularities of 'westlin' winds and fernie braes, / Northern lights and siller tides'.[11] Jamie commented on the BBC online page:

From the start I wanted this piece of work to make a nod to the Scottish literary tradition and the Scottish landscape, to evoke the deep love of a country that makes one community out of many people. As Bannockburn is so important in Scottish history, it seemed proper to acknowledge our cultural traditions, especially poetry and song about landscape. Of course I'm pleased 'my' poem was chosen, but I don't think of this work as 'mine' any longer. It's built from traditional materials, so to speak, and it's spun into the future, and like the land it describes, it belongs to everyone that appreciates it.[12]

Jamie made clear her position on Scotland's independence in a 2014 article: 'We want independence because we seek good governance, and no longer think the Westminster government offers that, or social justice or decency. We find the prospect of being a small, independent nation on the fringe of Europe exciting, and look forward to making our own decisions, even if that means having to fix our own problems. We'll take the risk.'[13]

However explicit this alignment with nationality and the politics of national identity, Jamie's qualifications are a safeguard against the ossification of identity which nationalism sometimes inclines towards. Her poems continue to emphasise the liminal space that even something as seemingly secure as nationality is always in the process of moving *through*. Scotland may be 'our land' but we are 'mere transients', acknowledging Robert Burns and Hamish Henderson (in her references to the songs, 'Now westlin winds' and 'Freedom, Come All Ye') but also the conundrum of love in the poem's last line: 'You win me, who take me most to heart.' This is reminiscent of the opening lines of Hugh MacDiarmid's poem 'Scotland': 'It requires great love of it, deeply to read / The configuration of a land . . .'.[14] And just as MacDiarmid evokes a constant process of change and unending renewal, a redisposition of things in a world that takes the risks of regeneration, so Jamie in her later work keeps us in mind of what that liminality must mean, in her poem 'Crossing the Loch' from *Jizzen* (1999).

This poem begins with a quiet, conversational question, asking the reader if she or he might remember 'how we rowed toward the cottage' across a bay, after a night drinking in a pub (J 1). The poet says that she cannot remember who rowed, but only how the jokes and voices went quiet and the sound of the oars in the water 'reached long into the night'. The crossing is scary, the breeze is cold, the hills 'hunched' around the loch and the water itself seems to conceal nuclear submarines, nightmares lurking below, real and metaphorical. Yet the water is phosphorescent and beautiful, shining on fingers and oars, and the passengers are like pilgrim saints making a crossing to another place, a destination from which they will enter their futures. They are 'twittering' (small birds in a nest washed out from shore, with no idea of what the future might bring), 'astonished' (in awe, confronted by the immensity of the unknowable universe around them), and 'foolhardy' (they could have capsized and been drowned). But, the poet tells us – mixing tenses so that past, present and what can be seen retrospectively from a future position: 'we live – and even have children / to women and men we had yet to meet / that night we set out'. Travelling through the night, the poet and her companions were 'calling our own / the sky and salt-water, wounded hills' and recollecting

> the glimmering anklets
> we wore in the shallows
> as we shipped oars and jumped,
> to draw the boat safe, high at the cottage shore. (J 2)

As the poem ends, the boat may be safe, the travellers ashore, but the wild is still there, and the autonomous region is always in need of new creation. Mr and Mrs

Scotland may find new meaning and purpose there. Kathleen Jamie's poems show us how that can be made.

WORKS CITED (SEE ALSO BIBLIOGRAPHY)

BBC News, 'Poem inscribed on Bannockburn battle monument' (2013), www.bbc.co.uk/news/uk-scotland-tayside-central-23795000 (last accessed 18 May 2014).

Boland, Eavan, *A Kind of Scar: The Woman Poet in the National Tradition* (Dublin: Attic Press, 1989).

Gish, Nancy, 'Complexities of Subjectivity: Scottish Poets and Multiplicity', in Romana Huk (ed.), *Assembling Alternatives: Reading Postmodern Poetries Transnationally* (Middletown, CT: Wesleyan University Press, 2003), pp. 259–74.

Lochhead, Liz, 'Mirror's Song', in *Dreaming Frankenstein & Collected Poems* (Edinburgh: Polygon, 1984), pp. 67–8.

Lowell, Robert, 'Skunk Hour', in *Life Studies* (London: Faber and Faber, 1972), pp. 103–4.

MacDiarmid, Hugh, 'Scotland', in Alan Riach and Michael Grieve (eds), *Selected Poetry* (Manchester: Carcanet, 2004), pp. 197–8.

Soyinka, Wole, *Myth, Literature and the African World* (Cambridge: Cambridge University Press, 1978).

NOTES

1. Jamie, 'A Lone Enraptured Male'.
2. Lowell, 'Skunk Hour', p. 104.
3. Gish, 'Complexities of Subjectivity: Scottish Poets and Multiplicity'.
4. Quoted in Gish, 'Complexities of Subjectivity', p. 266.
5. Quoted in Gish, 'Complexities of Subjectivity, p. 268.
6. Boland, *A Kind of Scar*.
7. Lochhead, 'Mirror's Song'.
8. Soyinka, *Myth, Literature and the African World*, p. 2.
9. Soyinka, 'Appendix: The fourth stage', in *Myth, Literature*, pp. 140–60.
10. Jamie, 'For a new Scottish Parliament'.
11. BBC News, 'Poem inscribed on Bannockburn battle monument'.
12. Ibid.
13. Ibid.
14. MacDiarmid, 'Scotland'.

Off the Page

for Kathleen Jamie
(The Queen of Sheba *and* Sightlines)

I used to live there   scuffing
the reek and rattle of dead leaves
cycling inside the keep-out fences
digging things up   throwing stones
in the quarry   building and burying
tins of treasure. The world
would never be so close again
as close as the dirt under your nails.

And I remember another's tale
of tree-houses   arra-heids and
skinned knees in the Republic of Fife.
Or she's brushing earth from fired clay
thinking of graves in the bronze age
or standing under a whalebone gateway
– in the jaws of the beast right enough –
waiting for the long tunes.

And she's tracing them   grounded
on some beach at the edge of things –
the scars   skelfs   roots and leaves
the close connections of nerve and bone
that seek to bind us to the real
and its wanchancy shapings:
off the page   out of bounds
as close as skin.

Roderick Watson

3. Kathleen's Scots

Robert Crawford

Kathleen Jamie's first collection of poetry, *Black Spiders*, contains the words 'abaheys', 'kaffiyas', and 'shequel', but not a word of Scots.[1] Five years later, in 1987, her second collection has just a tiny infusion of Scots words: there's a poem called 'Havers' ('Nonsense'); someone says '"It jist disnae matter!"'; we hear of 'the Kirk' (*WWL* 45, 46, 47). For a person whose own speech deploys many Scots words and phrases, this poet's avoidance of the Scots tongue in her early collected poetry is striking. Kathleen sounds Scottish as soon as she opens her mouth; yet on the page in her early work it can appear that she wants to sound otherwise, or at least to eschew the most obvious linguistic markers that would identify her as Scottish. Who among her early readers would have predicted that this poet would publish a collection called *Jizzen*?

I first saw Kathleen in the distance when I was a student of English and a fledgling poet at Glasgow University around 1981, and she was a student of philosophy and a more assured poet at Edinburgh University. Ever since that period I have read her work with confirmatory excitement, but we were not in touch until about 1988; later I was delighted to play a part in her becoming a colleague at St Andrews University in 1999, and I enjoyed teaching alongside her for over a decade. As a colleague and as a poet of Kathleen's generation who has written in Scots, from *Sterts & Stobies* (1985) and *Sharawaggi* (1990) to *Simonides* (2011) and beyond, I write this piece as what anthropologists might term a partisan 'participant observer'. Like many readers, I feel an instinctive as well as an intellectual closeness to Kathleen's work, and recognise in it not least an attraction to the Scots tongue that is both heartfelt and brainily astute.

There may be a politics to Kathleen Jamie's avoidance of Scots in her first book, or at any rate a wish to avoid certain predictabilities of politics. For many Scottish writers of her generation, the use of Scots was hard to separate from political trajectories. Hugh MacDiarmid's synthetic Scots seemed to have given the language an almost obligatory Scottish Nationalist inflection, and seemed to some younger writers suspect in terms of the politics of gender. Though Kathleen's sympathies might incline towards the political left and towards Scottish independence, early on at least MacDiarmid was a stumbling block. With regard to Scotland's greatest twentieth-century Scots-language poet, she recalled in 1992,

> When I was being told in this loud but subliminal way 'You must read MacDiarmid and take those ideas on and espouse his ideas,' I was told there was this poem that I had to read; it was called *A Drunk Man Looks at the Thistle*. Drunk? Men? Thistle? What? This is what we'd been striving to get away from for umpteen years. This is the smoky darkness of those pubs that you weren't allowed into because you were a woman. Yes? No. No, not for me.[2]

Though Tom Leonard's urban Scots was very different from MacDiarmid's, again it was bound up with an insistent politics, one of class rather than nation. Inevitably, Jamie's generation of Scottish poets was aware of such inheritances and sought variously to engage with or avoid them. For several of her contemporaries this impulse has continued. So, even where the poet writes principally in English, Scots remains a significant presence in the work of W. N. Herbert, Jackie Kay, David Kinloch, Don Paterson, and the present writer.[3] Other poets, including John Burnside, Carol Ann Duffy and Robin Robertson, have made at least sparing use of it; while for some, such as Rab Wilson, it is their principal medium of expression.

Jamie's early work sought to avoid or wrong-foot assumptions about the way language might be loaded in Scotland. She did not engage, for instance, in tedious arguments about whether Scots should be regarded as a language in its own right or as a northern dialect of English; and she liked, on occasion, to provoke. Her use of the word 'Clearances' as the title of the opening poem in *The Way We Live* is dazzling in a Scottish context: it signals forcefully that we do not have to go on living in the way we used to. Instead of lamenting the Highland Clearances, Jamie's poem, rich in oriental images such as 'Mandarins' and 'scimitar', relishes the idea of simply clearing off, 'of leaving: for Szechwan, or Persia' (*WWL* 11). In such an emotional and intellectual climate, the Scots tongue and all the sometimes wearisome language-politics associated with it might be regarded as baggage to be jettisoned, rather than as an inheritance to be preserved.

What happens in a few poems in *The Autonomous Region* (a 1993 book whose preface calls no attention to the way its title might wink towards Scotland while also indicating Tibet) is that the impulse to head out, to clear off, comes into contact with a Scots voice that was always Kathleen's but which was hardly part of her literary utterance until that date. It's as if the experience of travelling in Asia was needed to give her the freedom to write in a Scots that felt her own, rather than a speech laden with other people's politics and prejudices. When the reader encounters 'a hanker [longing] for his ain folk' in this book, the phrasing is saved from undue predictability by being applied to Fa-hsien in an Asian location, not to some auld Scots worthy (*WWL* 51). We are far from Scotland, 'At the shore of a loch called Qinghai' (*WWL* 49). This application of the word 'loch' to very un-Scottish terrain may owe something to the publication in the previous decade of that greatest work of Scots prose, William Laughton Lorimer's *The New Testament in Scots*, which has Jesus 'gaein alangside the Loch o Galilee'.[4] Yet Jamie's use of 'loch' is even more culturally estranged from that word's Scots moorings; she has had to travel very far to locate her Scots voice. Linguistically, location and dislocation are fused.

Her 'discovery' of Scots is part of an awareness apparent in some of her earliest poems, including 'Women in Jerusalem': a consciousness of a 'dance' (as *The Autonomous Region* puts it) 'through many people's many tongues' (*AR* 57). For me, *The Autonomous Region*'s most striking line is the last line of 'Xiahe', one of Jamie's first published poems in Scots: 'I hae crossed China.' (*AR* 78) Simply to add the letter 'v' to the word 'hae' would render that line into plain English; but the power of this Chinese-titled poem comes not least from its being in a Scots that resonates all the more strongly for being infused with some sense of 'Tibetan sang'. In the context of the book, this fusion and exploration feel sufficiently hard-won to be justified; they are no mere Chinoiserie. Playing off the title word's last two syllables against Gaelic and Scots lexis in the words 'machair' (a grassy, sandy plain) and 'slammach' (a slab), the poem (occasionally hard to follow: what does 'ahent the saft saltire / i trashed, an sheep' mean?) gains from its usually clear imagery and often (to a good number of Lowland Scottish people) familiar Scots utterances; but these are spoken in what is for most Western readers an unfamiliar context – one which, as the poet makes clear, enforces a conclusive sense of being 'far fae hame' (*AR* 78). It is this long-distance clearance, this clearing out, which gives Jamie an increasingly sure access to a home vernacular, one whose grain can make it sound more intimate than standard English, but whose use in this remote Asian context rescues it from the charge of sentimentality or any too easily predictable political manipulation.

This is how Scots makes its way from the very periphery to the centre of Jamie's poetry, and with it comes an access of poetic power. Shrewdly, Helen Vendler argues that often poets deliberately have to 'break' their earlier style in order to mature.[5] In Jamie's work such a breaking, such a breakthrough, into a more assured voice occurs most clearly after the publication of the work later collected in *Mr and Mrs Scotland are Dead: Poems 1980–1994*. Yet the 1993 foregrounding of Scots in her verse marks an important move in this direction, and is surely at one with her ability to access a style of poetic speech at once more finely balanced and more subtly distinctive than that of some of her earlier verse.

This is very evident in the verve of 'The Queen of Sheba'. That poem owes something to the feminine and feminist accents heard in Liz Lochhead's poetry and drama, but also draws on Jamie's own discoveries in *The Autonomous Region* about how Scots can be fused with markedly non-Scottish material to provide an access of power. If 'Vi-next-door', whose high-heeled slippers 'keek' from under her dressing gown 'like little hooves', sounds as if she might be a character from one of Lochhead's monologues, then other phrases (including 'vixen's bark of poverty' and 'fruity hemispheres') mark out a poetic idiom very substantially Jamie's own (*QS* 9–10). The fusion of the Sheba-world and the Scots-world of housing schemes generates comedy. Yet, for all the relishing of Scots idioms, ultimately the sexist, Scots-accented put-down – '*whae do you think y'ur?*' – which gives the poem its bite is subverted; the 'otherness' of the Queen of Sheba is deployed (a little like the unfamiliarity of Xiahe) to redirect the poem's ubiquitous and conventional Scots in a new, liberating direction that is both intellectually ambitious (hence the mention of the National Library) and noisily empowering. The poem gains energy from skipping nimbly between English and Scots, and its final yell is hard not to hear as Scots-inflected.

Building on the work of Willa Muir (whose 1965 *Living with Ballads* is a book Jamie admires) and of the late-twentieth-century Scottish scholar Catherine Kerrigan, who presented the ballads as an importantly female tradition, a number of recent poets have drawn on the Scots ballads to produce a Scots idiom far less in thrall to MacDiarmid or Tom Leonard than to older ballad traditions. In the earlier twentieth century such traditions were drawn on by Marion Angus, Violet Jacob, and Helen Cruickshank. Liz Lochhead, too, has been fascinated by ballad figures including Tam Lin, but no one in recent Scottish poetry has engaged so productively with the ballad tradition and its early-twentieth-century mediation as has Kathleen Jamie. The point is not that she writes ballads, but the way in which her poetry engages in Scots with notions of a female-accented verse tradition. *Jizzen* and *The Tree House* develop this. Earlier, 'Arraheids' in *The Way We Live* presents 'a show o grannies' tongues' in the form of flint arrowheads; such 'wicked cherms' (charms) are passed down 'fur generations', carrying a vein of hard practicality while quickening the imagination (*QS* 40). Though Jamie's poem does not say so, this makes them similar to Scots ballads.

In 'Arraheids' the analogy with 'tongues' is important. The Scots tongue and the tongue-shaped arrowhead are fused, not as a mother tongue but as a grandmother tongue – something older, perhaps wiser, and certainly enduringly stubborn. Yet the impulse, too, to be wary of the associations of such a Scots tongue (associations including kinds of subjection) is part of what makes the poem strong. In 'Wee Wifey', a Scots phrase gives the poem its title, but the rest of the poem is in English. This English struggles against the 'wee wifey' stereotype, but is also bonded intensely to that Scots-tongued expression – 'because we love each other dearly' (*QS* 30). Clearly, as she later puts it in 'Heredity 2' in the remarkable *Frissure* (2013), Jamie admires 'rich Scots speech', often associating it with older generations: 'My grandmother called her breast her "breist", her bosom her "kist"' (*Fr* 25).

As her work develops, Jamie, like Gwyneth Lewis in Wales, looks steadily at the issue of mother tongue and other tongue, integrating into her work elements of conflictedness, as well as a love of accessing more than one kind of speech. Scots becomes an essential element of her linguistic palate. At times she likes to mix phrases which sound as if they might have come from the world of the ballads – 'Ablow the pine-tree' or 'Bairns of the witch' – with clearly different elements (*QS* 25, 26). This mixture powers several poems in *The Queen of Sheba*, many of which are neither in English nor (like 'Arraheids') wholly in Scots, but constitute enlivened splicings of both. In 'Bairns of Susie: a hex', for instance, the lines 'the rustling whin, / the black / Giaconda smile of the broom pods' gains traction on the ear by passing readily from the Scots 'whin' (gorse)' to the foreign but familiar 'Giaconda' (*QS* 25).

While Jamie's poetry is honest in confronting some unwanted, sometimes sexist baggage that comes with certain Scots phrases, her mature work also delights in a tongue that can be used not just for hectoring but for vernacular lyricism, giving a distinctive twist, for example, to her imitation of Tsvetayeva with its 'cushie-doos' (doves) and 'quaich' (a drinking vessel) (QS 36). Here we have neither Tibetan Scots nor Sheban Scots, but Russian Scots; the drive to meld Scots with some 'other' remains consistent, each part of the mixture enhancing its complement to produce an admirable hybridity, a Scots open to the world rather than huddled away from it. The way Scots locutions are used in 'Sky-burial' and 'A Dream of the Dalai Lama on Skye' reinforces just such usage. Moreover, one of Jamie's finest predominantly Scots lyrics, 'Skeins o Geese', confirms a sense that Jamie's Scots is all the better for being migratory, at home with displacement as well as with place. That poem's 'archaic script', like the ancient artefacts of 'Arraheids', invokes the deep past while aware of moving onwards (QS 64). As in 'Arraheids', so in 'Skeins o Geese' the use of Scots may be linked to a sense of ancientness, but it carries, too, a deep respect and sometimes difficult love.

Jizzen, that 1999 volume whose back cover explains that its title is 'old Scots for childbed', may also at times associate Scots with the 'old'; but Jizzen is predominantly a book of birth and rebirth, not only in the sense that several of its poems deal with pregnancy, birth, and looking after a baby, but also in that it marks a further poetic rebirth, a thoroughgoing 'breaking of style' which moves beyond The Queen of Sheba. Part of this stylistic advance lies in a refined sense of cadence and greater clarity of line, but part of it also comes from a sense of having made peace with the Scots tongue so that there is a more fluid integration of Scots words, phrases, and whole poems into the collection. On occasion the poems' English is very lightly caressed by a grace of Scots: the word 'Loch' in the first poem's title and the mention of 'blaeberries' in its fourth-last line give a distinguishing tincture; the collection's second poem, 'The Graduates', is, like the first, one of crossover. It signals an emigration to a new world of 'bright, monoglot bairns' (J 3); yet whereas on one level that last phrase envisages children's access to only a single linguistic inheritance, Jamie's very use of the Scots word 'bairns' declares a deep continuing allegiance to Scots which is bound up with parental love – a mother's love for a mither tongue.

Issues of moving on and carrying forward are important to these poems; the use and status of Scots are part of their preoccupations, often in discreet ways: the deployment of the Scots term 'press' (meaning cupboard) in 'Forget It' signals that though, perhaps, 'Some history's better forgot', an intimate adherence to the 'old' language continues to inflect this poet's present-day speech (J 5). The 'Ultrasound' sequence begins with a deep listening to the tradition of Scots song as represented by Robert Burns's lyric, 'Whistle & I'll Come to You, My Lad' whose first verse and chorus run:

O whistle & I'll come to ye, my lad,
O whistle & I'll come to ye, my lad;
Tho' father & mither & a' should gae mad,
 Whistle & I'll come to ye, my lad.[6]

As elsewhere (not least in 'Healings 2' in Frissure), Burns is a touchstone for Jamie. She reorients this Scots love song in the direction of a 'wee shilpit [puny] ghost', but not one that belongs to a nostalgic past (J 11). Instead, 'summonsed from tomorrow' through the technology of the ultrasound scan's 'keek-aboot' (look around), the 'ghost' is already taking on flesh and bone for the future (J 11).

Part of the history of the Scots tongue is its use in intimate situations – love songs, lullabies, familial speech – rather than in formal situations such as school classrooms, where its vernacular was often scorned in favour of English. Though the 'Ultrasound' sequence is predominantly Anglophone, its tincture of Scots invokes vernacular intimacy. It gives rise to an intimate lullaby, a 'Bairnsang' wholly in a Scots that is not just tender but also playful, as when, with a nonsensical, loving wink, it weaves into itself place names – 'an greetna, girna, Gretna Green' (J 15). 'Greetna' could mean in Scots, 'Don't cry'; 'girna' could mean 'don't complain'; and Gretna Green is a place in southern Scotland associated with elopements and weddings. Like the more frolicsome poem 'Lucky Bag' with its 'golach' (beetle) and its 'shalwar-kameez', this poem may call for the use of a Scots (plus a further) dictionary, and invites a very attentive listening as the reader scans its ultrasound; but its reward is lyrical, ludic, tenaciously tender (J 42). Its loving at-homeness with Scots acknowledges, also, as modern poets who use Scots must, that the language carries for many readers a sense not just of intimacy but also, in shifting proportions, an acoustic of strangeness and even estrangement. Yet that, too, is appropriate to the phenomena of ultrasound, of childbirth, and of prospective as well as new parenthood.

The Scots vestiges in 'The Tay Moses' and 'A Miracle' continue this note. A mixture of intimacy and otherness, characteristic of *Jizzen* and of a good deal of Jamie's work, is maintained deftly in the use of the distinctively Scottish word 'crofts' (smallholdings) in 'Flower-sellers, Budapest', bringing the continental women of the poem with 'their mild southern crofts' empathetically close to a Scottish poet always alert to 'several languages', and often aware of how languages can be bound up with kinds of 'invasion' (J 27). Following on from 'Arraheids', an association between the hard history of women's lives and the use of the Scots tongue continues in 'Hackit'. This English-language poem has as its title and centre of gravity a Scots adjective used of skin that is chapped and worn (J 33). Though that word gives the poem its resonant centre, and is applied to a Scotswoman, the poem's Canadian setting shows Jamie once again using Scots in a context of displacement rather than simply emplacement. As in 'Rhododendrons', she shows how emplacement and displacement may coexist. This disturbing 'Hackit', too, is a poem about moving into a new world, but one far less attractive than that of the paradisal 'Lochan', which offers a longed-for place for 'When all this is over' (J 36).

In *The Tree House* (2004), very few of the English-language poems contain any Scots locutions: a favourite word ('lochan's'), a plant name ('Stane-raw'), one or two simple terms such as 'muckle' (big) and a couple of names linked to 'sandbanks: the *Reckit* [wrecked] *Lady*, the *Shair as Daith* [Sure as Death]' – that's about all (*TH* 34, 35, 44, 41). While this volume was being written Kathleen was my St Andrews colleague, teaching there alongside her editor at Picador, Don Paterson. As someone who loves to deploy Scottish place names in verse, I remember being shocked when she explained that she had deliberately combed these out of *The Tree House*: she wanted to let the poems speak for the earth without the interference of imposed nomenclature. So, for instance, though the poem 'The Puddle' (which draws on her observation of a flooded field on the road beside the North Haugh in St Andrews) was published as a card from the Poetry House at the university's School of English and bore the subtitle 'St Andrews', no such specific place could be identified from the poem as it appears in *The Tree House*.

If most of the English-language poems in that collection are almost as free of Scots as they are of place names, the book does not mark a renunciation of Scots. Instead, there are four poems in that tongue: two are versions of lyric fragments by Hölderlin – probably relying on David Constantine's English translations and in part on the bilingual edition by Michael Hamburger and Jeremy Adler.[7] All show a confident, fluent sense of Scots. Jamie turns the 'Pfaden' (paths) of Hölderlin's 'Heimath' (Home) into 'back-braes', and his 'Linden' (lime-trees) into 'gean-trees' (cherry trees). Her version, 'Hame', though not literal, is beautiful and confident. Its abrupt ending has a clipped quickness – 'An a's weel' – that may even improve on the original 'So gehet es wohl.'[8] Jamie's Scots versions of this German poet establish an intimate link with landscape that is Scottish in idiom but does not involve the naming of any particular place. Her 'Yird' (Earth) is as wide as Hölderlin's 'Erd'.

The impulse to translate European poetry into Scots has a very long ancestry, reinforced in the later twentieth century by poets including Robert Garioch and Edwin Morgan and by Peter France and Duncan Glen's 1989 anthology *European Poetry in Scotland*, which contains translations from German and other languages into Scots. In Jamie's two original Scots lyrics from *The Tree House* there is, too, a sense of wishing to bond her own work to older Scots poetic traditions: the use of 'ma jo' (my dear) in 'Selchs' ('Grey Seals') (*TH* 26) conjures up Burns's love song 'John Anderson my jo', while the phrase 'caller-water' (fresh water) in the last line of 'Selchs' echoes the title of a Scots poem by Burns's favourite Scottish poet, the eighteenth-century Robert Fergusson – to whom Jamie addressed her Scots poem of March 2000, 'At Robert Fergusson's Grave'.[9] A sense that she has been reading a good deal of Scots poetry is reinforced later by her recent poetic inscription for the rotunda at the Bannockburn battle site, though her Scots is used also to summon up quite different poets including Hölderlin and Yeats: it's surely the latter's 'The Cold Heaven' that undergirds the 'cauld hivvin' of Jamie's 'Speirin' ('Asking') in *The Tree House*, where the speaker longs to go with a 'hinny' (honey) and 'loss wirsels' (lose ourselves) in bluebell woods (*TH* 14).[10] The Scots poems in this book are at once distinct from yet attuned to the rest of a volume which craves to be at one with nature, while remaining aware of being set apart.

Jamie's custom of gracing her English poems with a very light dusting of Scots continues in *The Overhaul* (2012). However, when she returns to Hölderlin in that collection, his 'An die Parzen' ('To the Fates') is recast in a thoroughly Scots voice. Whereas Jamie's fellow poet and St Andrews colleague John Burnside is thoroughly versed in the thought of Martin Heidegger, whose essays such as 'What Are Poets For?' and '"Poetically Man Dwells"' attend particularly to Hölderlin, it may be that her own continuing attraction to Hölderlin comes more from Jonathan Bate's *The Song of the Earth*. That book's last chapter is also entitled 'What Are Poets For?' In summarising some of Heidegger's thought, it emphasises the way Hölderlin 'says to us, "poetically man dwells on this earth"'.[11] Emphasising that 'For Heidegger, poetry can, quite literally, save the earth', Bate explores Hölderlin's sacred sense of what it means to 'dwell'.[12] Though Jamie is a poet sometimes wary of ideas of the sacred, her vision of poetry (at least as articulated through her versions of Hölderlin) does see it as 'halie' (holy) (O38). Through its *poiesis*, poetry, like nature, can offer an experience of sacred immersion 'Ins heilignuchterne Wasser' – 'i' the douce, the hailie watter' (O 48).[13] As before, her admired Hölderlin speaks in an intimate lyrical vernacular. It is an indication of how central to her sense of language this mode of utterance is that for her readers Jamie's poetry must involve not just a sprinkling but at important moments a total immersion in this cherished, tenaciously-grained way of speaking – Kathleen's Scots.

WORKS CITED (SEE ALSO BIBLIOGRAPHY)

Corbett, John, J. Derrick McClure, and Jane Stuart-Smith (eds), *The Edinburgh Companion to Scots* (Edinburgh: Edinburgh University Press, 2003).

Crawford, Robert, *Bannockburns: Scottish Independence and Literary Imagination, 1314–2014* (Edinburgh: Edinburgh University Press, 2014).

Crawford, Robert, 'Hugh MacDiarmid: A Disgrace to the Community', *PN Review* 19.3, Jan–Feb 1993.

Crawford, Robert et al.(ed.), *Heaven-Taught Fergusson: Robert Burns's Favourite Scottish Poet* (East Linton: Tuckwell Press, 2003).

Crawford, Robert, and Christopher MacLachlan (eds), *The Best Laid Schemes: Selected Poetry and Prose of Robert Burns* (Edinburgh and Princeton: Polygon and Princeton University Press, 2009).

Heidegger, Martin, *Poetry, Language, Thought*, tr. Albert Hofstadter (New York: Harper Perennial, 2001).

Hölderlin, Friedrich, *Selected Poems and Fragments*, ed. Jeremy Adler, tr Michael Hamburger (London: Penguin, 1998).

Lorimer, William Laughton (tr.), *The New Testament in Scots* (Edinburgh: Southside, 1983).

Vendler, Helen, *The Breaking of Style* (Cambridge, MA: Harvard University Press, 1995).

Watson, Roderick, 'Living with the Double Tongue: Modern Poetry in Scots' in Ian Brown (ed.), *The Edinburgh History of Scottish Literature, Vol. 3, Modern Transformations: New Identities (from 1918)* (Edinburgh: Edinburgh University Press, 2007), pp. 163–75.

NOTES

1. On the nature and history of the Scots tongue, see Corbett et al., *The Edinburgh Companion to Scots*.
2. Jamie in Crawford et al., 'Hugh MacDiarmid: A Disgrace to the Community', p. 21.
3. For an overview, see Watson, 'Living with the Double Tongue', pp. 163–75.
4. Lorimer, *The New Testament in Scots*, p. 61.
5. Vendler, *The Breaking of Style*.
6. Crawford and MacLachlan, *The Best Laid Schemes*, p. 151.
7. Hölderlin, *Selected Poems* and *Selected Poems and Fragments*.
8. Hölderlin, *Selected Poems and Fragments*, pp. 266–7; Jamie, *The Tree House*, p. 28.

9. Jamie, 'At Robert Fergusson's Grave', in Crawford, *Heaven-Taught Fergusson*, pp. 85–6. Also published in *London Review of Books* (2001).

10. On Jamie's Bannockburn inscription, see Crawford, *Bannockburns*, pp. 236–7.

11. Bate, *Song of the Earth*, p. 257.

12. Bate, *Song of the Earth*, pp. 258, 260; Heidegger, *Poetry, Language, Thought*, pp. 87–159, 211–27.

13. Hölderlin, *Selected Poems and Fragments*, p. 170.

4. Transcending the Urban: *The Queen of Sheba*

Amanda Bell

Speaking in Enniskillen, Northern Ireland in August 2013, Kathleen Jamie remarked that her interest in writing about the natural world began a decade earlier, a reference to the 2004 publication of *The Tree House*.[1] However, the seeds of her ecological sensibility are evident in the 1994 collection *The Queen of Sheba*, which can be seen as the beginning of her mature work. Usually noted for its 'various forensic critiques of modern Scotland',[2] the collection can also be read as a paradigm for the development of an ecopoetics.

The Queen of Sheba appeared at an important moment in the raising of environmental awareness in Scotland. In 1990, the Scottish Green Party had separated from the UK Greens, and saw its membership surge from under 100 members to 1,250.[3] In 1995, the Environment Act (UK) made provision for the establishment of the Scottish Environment Protection Agency the following year. Perhaps most significantly in terms of impact on the public imagination, early in January 1993 the Liberian-registered oil tanker MV *Braer* ran aground off the Shetland Islands, spilling almost all of her cargo of 84,000 tonnes of light crude oil into the sea, with catastrophic implications for both wildlife and the fishing and tourism industries.[4] The spill was twice the volume of that lost from the Exxon Valdez in 1989. There was a strong volunteer response to the disaster, as local people braved the adverse weather conditions to rescue dead and dying seabirds and animals. Jamie's devastation at the event is recorded in her notebook from that year: 'Wreck of the Braer at Shetland / wretched, despair. / "Only when we have been truly heartbroken can we be whole" [. . .] After pain comes a security / wish for a new / seawashed / spirituality'.[5] Against this backdrop, *The Queen of Sheba*, in its struggle to determine what an ecological worldview might entail, captures both a personal turning point, and the zeitgeist. The collection is characterised by juxtapositions, which operate as heuristic devices in working towards an understanding of the gnarly relationship of the human to the non-human world, and of the role of the poet in portraying this dynamic. The struggle played out in these poems operates as what Josephine Donovan, in a collection of ecofeminist essays published in the same year, calls 'a vehicle for the revelation of being, rather than a mechanism for its domination'[6] or what

Jonathan Bate describes as the role of *ecopoesis*: to 'engage *imaginatively* with the non-human'.[7]

The Queen of Sheba implicitly problematises the idea of 'nature poetry' or 'ecopoetry' by questioning the concepts of nature and ecology, much as ecocriticism itself has done. As the collection progresses, Jamie sets up a series of dualisms between east and west, exotic Arabia and astringent Presbyterianism in the title poem, the old and the new, age and youth in 'Mr and Mrs Scotland are Dead', travel and return in 'Coupie' and 'Rooms', freedom and domesticity in 'Wee Baby' and 'Wee Wifey', modernity and prehistory in 'One of Us'. The overarching dualism in the collection is that of urban and rural, which she uses to represent different aspects of the constraints facing a young woman wrestling with the idea of how to be in the world.

Threaded through the collection are poems which chart the growth of a female sensibility, sometimes in the first person, sometimes in the second, from childhood through early parenthood and into independent self-awareness. The attainment of self-awareness coincides with an enriched understanding of the human relationship to the environment. In this paradigm, the urban is represented by the constructed human environment and the rules for normative behaviour; the rural by the natural, non-human, world outside. Jamie's idea of the 'rural' represents a sought-after alternative to the reality of lived urban experience, an exploration of the trope, common in popular culture, that 'there must be more to life than this'. The rural mutates according to circumstance, but always comes with the alluring idea that there must be something better, something beyond the judgemental, impoverishing restrictions of sexism, constructed environments, social constraints and the language which articulates them. The desire for the rural, or wilderness, is an appeal to the authority of nature, a search for the ecosublime, and the concomitant search for an originary language represents a desire to transcend political affiliation, to be identified on one's own terms.[8]

The constantly shifting aspect of the urban–rural dualism is central to *The Queen of Sheba*.[9] Juxtapositions of these in the Scottish context could be seen to represent the landed wealthy and the impoverished crofters or migrants of the Industrial Revolution. The urban could be seen as a dystopian condition, in contrast to the idyll of rural living, though in contemporary societies, albeit more in the USA than Britain and Ireland, cities are frequently seen as a civilising counterpart to degraded rustic life.[10] In *The Queen of Sheba*, rural is neither a traditional agrarian way of life, nor the wilderness conceived of by American transcendentalism, and certainly not the politically fraught spaces of land-cleared estates, but a prismatic concept best thought of as the 'anti-urban'.[11]

The impulse behind constructing these dichotomies demonstrates the poet's accelerating struggle to transcend inherited constraints, and charts the ever-strengthening lure of the non-human world as part of a maturation process. Looking at this process as it unfolds in the course of the collection, focusing on 'Mother-May-I', 'A Shoe', 'Child with Pillar Box and Bin Bags', 'Fountain', 'All Washed Up', 'Flashing Green Man', 'At Point of Ness' and 'Skeins o Geese', it is evident that the mutating urban–rural dualism is used in each one to represent different aspects of the struggle for voice and identity. These poems dealing with central aspects of female experience constitute a core coming-of-age narrative of environmental encounter.

'Mother-May-I' is exemplary in its establishment of multiple dualisms. Written in the voice of an urban child living near the edge of a housing scheme, and longing to escape it and flee to the woods and the wild, the poem proceeds like an inventory of obstacles to achieving this: the urban is used here to represent constraints of age, gender and normative behaviour. Mother-May-I is a children's game in which the players are entirely in the power of the 'mother' figure, sometimes also called 'Captain' or 'Mr Wolf', and have to ask permission for anything they want to do. It is in the power of the 'mother' to grant or deny the request, to specify how it should be done, or to impose an entirely different task on the asker. The convention of the game introduces the idea of disempowerment, a disempowerment in conflict with the huge ambition of the child. The child's requests in the poem start as small and reasonable, with a wish to go as far as the end of the lane, but rapidly become more daring and dangerous. The next request is to 'leave these lasses' games/ and play at Man-hunt' (QS 12). Man-hunt is a children's game of tag, but the capitalisation and hyphenation of the word, and the fact that this request comes straight after the description of the woods as a site of criminality and perversion, populated by anonymous child molesters, gives a sinister overtone to the game, evocative of the chase in William Golding's *Lord of the Flies*, and confirming that children's games function as an analogue for adult behaviour. The next question, seeking permission to 'tell small lies', proceeds along the continuum towards adulthood. The final request, 'Mother may we/ pull our soft backsides/ through the jagged may's/ white blossom' suggests a rite – literally of passage – which could represent either a social initiation, such as communion, confirmation, or marriage; or an experiential initiation, such as puberty, loss of virginity, or childbirth (QS 12). The narrator is hungry to experience the outside world, not the enclosed teenage world of discos and cinemas, but the wilderness of the burn and the woods, which she associates with freedom.

What is constraining the child from exploring the woods? First, the rules of the game – the need to request and be granted permission; second, the urban legends, tales of paedophiles and perverts which have just enough grounding in reality to be plausible – discarded pornography leading on to rumours of mouldering corpses and missing hitch-hikers. The use of myth to warn children, and particularly female children, away from exploration and possible transgression has its origins in medieval folk tales, but Jamie subverts the trope of the conventional antithesis between the safe town or village and the dangerous woods by ending the poem with the child's glee at attaining the superficially simple yet metaphorically significant pleasure of seeing the white dye from her gym shoes dissolve and run downstream.[12] By confronting the myths propagated about the world beyond the suburb, the child has attained a primal pleasure.

A third constraint on the child's explorations is that of clothing – the impractical skirts and dresses which hamper the activity of little girls by fanning out in the dirt, the white gym shoes which need to be kept clean. Fourth, there is the physical obstacle of the dump – the detritus of the city that forms a barrier between the built environment and what lies outside it. This could be the same 'civic amenity landfill site' which provides the setting for 'Mr and Mrs Scotland are Dead': a liminal space composed of the city's waste but overlaid with reminders of another way of being, as Mr Scotland's puncture repair kit, abandoned among the detritus, evokes memories of 'hedgerows / hanged with small black brambles' hearts' (QS 37). The choice of the dump as a defining liminal space between urban and rural in 'Mother-May-I' has resonances in the objects out of place that feature throughout the collection: the platform on the beach in 'A Shoe' (QS 13), the washed-up form in 'Another day in paradise' (QS 56): pieces of flotsam which spark a meditation on the impact of the human in the wider world. Dumps in *The Queen of Sheba* are morally neutral environments, holding areas where objects await triage, dispensed with not for intrinsic uselessness, but for having outlived their usefulness.[13] In the era of plastic, durability has ceased to be positive attribute, and the concept of disposability provides a strong starting point for a meditation on the human relationship to the environment.

So on the one side are rules, myths, conventions, barriers; on the other a powerful desire for escape and experience, both geographical and maturational. The transcendence of four types of urban constraint – conceived of in this poem as a loss of innocence – is a source of huge delight, and the double meaning of the last word in the phrase 'muck about at the woods and burn' lends a sacramental aspect to the child's achievement: the transcendence is itself a rite, a trial by fire.

The possibilities of escape to the anti-urban are fewer in 'Child with Pillar Box and Bin Bags'. The focus in this poem is on a young mother, and the paraphernalia of parenthood, both physical and emotional, proves a more powerful deterrent to connecting with the non-human world than the obstacles facing the small girl in the earlier poem. Lacking the egocentric ferocity of childhood, the young woman has more fear, and therefore less perceived choice. To photograph her baby she chooses the side of the street 'dark in the shade of the tenements' (QS 15). The tenements, the buildings, the bookies, though indicative of the crowded life of an urban proletariat, are not in themselves intimidating; they are neutral 'friendly buildings', and the implication is that they too have a type of life – 'the traffic ground, the buildings shook, the baby breathed': this is not a simplistic juxtaposition of the sun as a representation of nature and all things good versus buildings representing the urban and all things bad, but rather an awareness of choice – it is possible to choose the sun and its fascinating shadows. Fear for the baby's safety, 'fearful as Niagara', seems to eliminate the possibility of recognising that choice exists – 'if she'd chosen or thought it possible to choose'. The use of 'Niagara' as a simile for the kerb indicates a terror of natural phenomena – surely if a child's buggy is rolling off a kerb fear should be of traffic, the kerb itself, the hard road, but all of the terrors for the child are embodied in the image of a world-renowned geological feature. The most potent obstacle to the young woman who is the subject of this poem is fear – a societally engendered fear of the world outside of the constructed environment.

This sense of powerlessness to recognise choice, particularly once the subject is constrained by the demands of parenthood, is further developed in 'Fountain'. Young parents – and from the line 'who these days can thrust her wrists / into a giggling hillside spring', we can infer that these young parents are female – are caught in a man-made theme-park, a shopping mall full of escalators and hard surfaces, where everything is artificial: plastic bags, polystyrene cups, Perspex foliage, neon signs (QS 17). There is, nevertheless, something else, should people choose to see or feel it. The question 'who these days can thrust her wrists into a giggling hillside spring above some ancient city' seems rhetorical, raising once more the question of choice. The next question, 'who says we can't respond . . .', implies that the spring, as symbol of the natural world beyond the machine, is accessible to all, whether they know it or not. The reference to Virgil's *Eclogues* is a reminder of the enduring draw of the anti-urban for humankind, but in this poem the anti-urban is simmering below concrete surfaces, ready to erupt. The incongruity of the Arcadian well in the shopping centre relates back to 'A Shoe', which takes elements from both the manu- factured realm and the natural world and places them in the opposing environment: thus we find the thick sole of a platform shoe among pebbles on the beach, and on the bathroom shelf a collection of 'pretty/ Queeny shells' (QS 13). This superficially humorous mixing of register and context gives way to a sobering contemplation: how did the wearer of the shoe feel? Did she jump off the bridge, or rather choose to walk into the sea? The penultimate stanza poses a profound question, 'did she walk in, saying yes/ I recognise this/ as the water yanked heavy/ on thighs belly breasts?' This sense, or act, of recognition is pivotal to the collection – a connection to a point of origin, a return to the primordial. An unnerving blend of humour and gravitas, 'A Shoe' is a rallying call to engage on a deeper level with existence, with the reassurance that 'it's all right/ once you're out the other side'.

There is a dual aspect to the urban–rural dynamic in the collection. Those within the city feel, with mounting intensity, the draw of the anti-urban, whereas those portrayed as external to the constructed environment feel it as a threat, a symbol of destruction. In 'All Washed Up' the city is a metaphor for ruin and dereliction – emotional as much as physical. The foundering relationship, described in terms of shipwreck, is pronounced dead by invocation of the city. Clearly the city here is an emotional and imaginative space rather than a physical location: it is 'far from any shore', simultaneously landlocked and cast adrift (QS 35). Increasingly, as the collection progresses, there is an intimation of life just within reach of the con- structed environment, be it underground or overhead. In 'Fountain' it is intuited by the twitch of the dowser's rod in the baby's buggy; in 'Flashing Green Man' it is sig- nalled by the geese flying overhead. The voice in 'Flashing Green Man' is that of an urbanite, 'one of the city' (QS 38). The flashing green man, 'he too refuged in cities', is a constant reminder of what lies beyond, an avatar of the geese themselves. The image first conjured by the calling geese is that of 'ancient contraptions / abandoned on farms', a salute to rural depopulation and nineteenth- and twentieth-century migration to industrial centres. But the geese are also a reminder of how close the countryside is in the present moment, as they 'pull themselves North to the Sidlaws': this is not a huge sprawling metropolis, but a small city near to the mountains. There is a sense here, just over halfway through the collection, of breakthrough: the geese are a 'true sign', their wings 'more precious than angels'. Although the portents of the non-human world are stronger in this poem, they need to be – the cumulative effect of adulthood and city-living have deadened the senses: this state of adulthood, being 'one of the city', involves taking 'little time to consider', an emotional and sensory numbness. In contrast to this unreflective life, the moment of noticing the geese, gilded with sunlight reflected against windows, is characterised by stillness: the poet stands transfixed while people and traffic stream around her, everything else is movement: 'and people flowed around me / intent on home; from the round-about's hub / traffic wheeled off to the suburbs'. The trope of mindfulness, of taking time to consider, spools through the collection, from the sense of recognition in 'A Shoe' to the absence of time to consider in 'Flashing Green Man', to a moment of epiphany in 'At Point of Ness', which is discussed below.

From the restless child of 'Mother-May-I' through the young women in 'Child with Pillar Box and Bin Bags' and 'Fountain', the urban–rural relationship has become less dichotomous, the two facets of being are beginning to overlap: by 'Flashing Green Man' the voices of the geese bring the rural – past and present – into the city, anticipated by their avatar the flashing green man: they are accessible harbingers of an alternative way of being.[14] It is a paradigm for the increasing acceptance of the interconnection of all aspects of existence central to an ecopoetic worldview. It can be argued that the shift in focus to a true ecopoetic impulse occurs at the end of the collection, between 'At Point of Ness' and 'Skeins o Geese'. The former, in its epiphanic assertion that 'heart-scared, I have it/ understood:/   never   ever/ harm — this,/   you never could', uses a didactic form of statement of intent (*QS* 62). By the final poem, this conviction has been transformed into an attempt to make language itself, rather than words, articulate how it is to dwell in the world, mindful of the inherent contradictions of such an approach.

'Skeins o geese' picks up directly on the theme of 'Flashing Green Man'. The image of a stationary figure at the centre of milling activity in 'Flashing Green Man' is evocative of the time-lapse sequences in Godfrey Reggio's *Koyaanisqatski*, the cult film described as a visual tone poem, which depicts multiplicitous interactions between humans, nature and technology. The analogy between 'Flashing Green Man' and *Koyaanisqatski* is illuminating in terms of Jamie's representation of the geese in 'Skeins o Geese'. Godfrey Reggio explained his decision not to have dia-logue in the trilogy of films beginning with *Koyaanisqatski* by stating that 'it's not for lack of love of language, but because I feel our language is in a state of vast humilia-tion, I decided to make films without words'.[15] The same sense of the inadequacy of language to express the natural world is doubly indicated in 'Skeins o Geese'. The word written by the geese is both everlasting and unattainable: 'Skeins o geese write a word / across the sky. A word / struck lik a gong / afore I wis born' (*QS* 64). The Tibetan singing bowl or *rin gong*, continues at too high a frequency to be audible. Like the word, it 'whusstles / ower high for ma senses.' The meaning is there, but how can it be accessed? In describing both the inaccessibility of the geese's communica-tion, and the straining towards the non-human involved in trying to comprehend it, the poem enacts *ecopoesis* by imaginative engagement with the non-human, evoking George Mackay Brown's edict for poets to 'carve the runes / then be content with silence.'[16] The conundrum is partly answered by the shift into blended Scots.[17]

It is particularly noteworthy then that Jamie shifts into Scots to articulate this straining towards connection with the non-human world: to truly transcend the constraints hitherto represented by the urban–rural dichotomy, it may also be necessary to transcend the official language. This appropriation of language reflects the work pattern of Hugh MacDiarmid, who, as Louisa Gairn notes, felt that 'synthetic Scots was the only idiom [. . .] capable of representing the complex entanglements of man and environment in the modern world'.[18]

In the course of *The Queen of Sheba* Jamie has interrogated the possibilities of language, from the biblical to the inarticulate. The difficulty of finding a language reflects the difficulty of transcending the urban. Jamie has grappled with the idea of not using language at all before concluding that language is what, as humans, we do best. By moving away from English, she is taking a step towards freeing herself from the constraints heretofore represented by constructed environments. Her switch into Scots as a literary language represents a reclamation of linguistic biodiversity, a cogent demonstration of the power of literature to take tangible action in defense of a biosphere increasingly under threat.

WORKS CITED (SEE ALSO BIBLIOGRAPHY)

Bardini, Thierry, *Junkware* (Minneapolis: University of Minnesota Press, 2011).

Donovan, Josephine, 'Ecofeminist Literary Criticism: Reading the Orange', in Gaard and Murphy (eds), *Ecofeminist Literary Criticism* (Urbana, IL and Chicago: University of Illinois Press, 1998), pp. 74–96.

The Essence of Life, film, directed by Greg Carson. USA: MGM Home Entertainment, 2002.

Golding, William, *Lord of the Flies* (London: Faber and Faber, 1954).

Koyaanisqatski, film, directed by Godfrey Reggio. USA: Island Alive /New Cinema, 1983.

Kuin, Inger, 'Review: Green Party Membership', *Scottish Affairs* 55, Spring 2006, pp. 138–41; www.scottishaffairs.org/backiss/pdfs/sa55/Sa55_Kuin.pdf (last accessed 19 May 2014).

Mackay Brown, George, 'A Work for Poets', *Following a Lark* (London: John Murray Ltd, 1996); http://www.georgemackaybrown.co.uk/extracts%20from/WorkforPoets.htm (last accessed 19 May 2014).

Marine Accident Investigation Branch, Department of Transport, *Report of the Chief Inspector of Marine Accidents into the engine failure and subsequent grounding of the Motor Tanker Braer at Garths Ness, Shetland on 5 January 1993* (HMSO, 1993); www.maib.gov.uk/cms_resources. cfm?file=/braer-text.pdf (last accessed 23 September 2013).

McClure, J. Derrick, *Why Scots Matters* (Edinburgh: Saltire Society, 2009).

Neil, Andrew, 'History in a new scheme', *Magma* 16, Winter 2000; www.poetrymagazine.org.uk/magazine/notice.asp?id=291 (last accessed 27 January 2014).

Pullman, Philip, *Grimm Tales for Young and Old* (London: Penguin, 2012).

Ross, Andrew, 'The Social Claim on Urban Ecology' (interview with Michael Bennett), in *The Nature of Cities: Ecocriticism and Urban Environments* (Tucson, AZ: University of Arizona Press, 1999).

Scott, Alistair, Alana Gilbert and Ayele Gelan (Socio-Economic Research Group (SERG)), 'The Urban–Rural Divide: Myth or Reality' (Aberdeen: The Maccauley Institute, 2007).

NOTES

1. Kathleen Jamie in conversation with Tim Dee, 'Alone with Nature', *Happy Days Enniskillen International Beckett Festival*, 22–26 August 2013.
2. Neil, 'History in a new scheme', 2000.
3. Kuin, 'Review', p. 138.
4. Marine Accident Investigation Branch, *Report*. Ironically, the wreck of the MV *Braer* is now itself marketed as a tourist attraction for scuba divers, promoted on the official site for Shetland tourism (visit.shetland.org, last accessed 25 May 2014).
5. Jamie, Literary Papers, National Library of Scotland Accession 11599/8, pp. 41–2.
6. Donovan, 'Ecofeminist Literary Criticism', p. 88.
7. Bate, *Song of the Earth*, p. 199.
8. Rozelle defines the 'ecosublime' as 'the awe and terror that occurs when literary figures experience the infinite complexity and contingency of place' (*Ecosublime*, p. 1).
9. On the complex interrelationship between the concepts 'urban' and 'rural' in Scotland today, see Scott et al., 'The Urban–Rural Divide'.
10. Ross, 'The Social Claim on Urban Ecology', p. 24.
11. Gairn's discussion of 'Scottish literary technophobia' is illuminating on the division between the portrayal of the urban and the rural in post-WWII Scotland. See Gairn, *Ecology and Modern Scottish Literature*, pp. 110–55.
12. The use of the cautionary tale was formalised in seventeenth-century France by Charles Perrault's fairy tales, notably *Le Petit Chaperon Rouge*, and recurs throughout European fairy tales from the Grimm Brothers' German tales to those documented by Italo Calvino in twentieth-century Italy. Pullman points out how such tales are resuscitated during periods of heightened anxiety about paedophilia and 'stranger danger' (p. 142), now ubiquitous thanks to prurient media outlets. Kossick has noted Jamie's 'indebtedness to the baroque textual strategies of Angela Carter' in this poem, in 'Roaring Girls, Bogie Wives', p. 201.
13. Bardini defines junk as something which 'used to be useful, to serve a purpose, or . . . was meant to eventually serve a purpose. Its time is always in between, a bubble in the efficient, productive time we unfortunately enough got hooked on in the so-called developed world. Junk lives in a time stasis. Junk is a luxury for the well fed; it incarnates the sentimental scrap we choose to love tenderly in these parts of the world. It materializes the memories of consumption that we grew up idolizing.' (*Junkware*, p. 9).
14. In 'Flashing Green Man', the geese encapsulate nostalgia for the past, the sense of being in the moment, and a harbinger of a utopian future, thereby fulfilling the three orientations of pastoral – elegy, idyll and utopia – discussed by Garrard in *Ecocriticism*, pp. 37–8.
15. In *Essence of Life*, directed by Greg Carson, 2002.
16. George Mackay Brown, 'A Work for Poets'.
17. J. Derrick McClure argues that one reason for using Scots is that standard English is being reduced to utilitarian uses, becoming the language of technology, commerce, tourism and mass entertainment (*Why Scots Matters*, pp. 66–7).
18. Gairn, *Ecology*, p. 82.

Hibernaculum

'Hibernaculum' is his [Gilbert White's] word for the winter quarters a swallow
repairs to, but where was this hibernaculum?

Kathleen Jamie, Sightlines

I am here with the swallows that failed to migrate,
resting up, oiling my wings. *Here*, in case
you'd like to know, wherever you've intrepidly
flown off south to, hasn't an actual address –
there isn't much sun, or much anything
and the cold makes my head-magnet ache,
or is it a clock the creator implanted
to make our departures so effortlessly punctual?
I've been keeping bad time, and losing my way.

With impairment, I'm not ourself: I is
another – famous phrase of one hirondelle
who risked a solo flight to Africa
and only made it back when truly crippled,
scorched and songless. All that came
so naturally is now you've no idea
how much of an effort, but still
this cavern is like a pale blue crystal
magnifying the little light that remains.

Truth is, as you can see, my imagination
is suffering from a dearth of the facts yours
is always nourished by as you fly
into the clean north wind or alight
on a TV aerial, the edge of a townland.
On bad days, it's more like a hospital here
– with the staff and caterers out on strike –

than any kind of splendid winter residence,
but despite the dark, the long nights and this

particular winter's refusal to end;
despite the depleted store of tawny grubs
and the drab vexations I should have shed,
but just to give you one example:
some spotty fledgling in the *Avian Times*
calls my song 'awkward' and 'uninspired' – well
you should listen to *his* twittery scritchings;
despite the dark days and the splitting nights
I intend to hold out till your return.

Jamie McKendrick

5. 'Proceeding Without a Map': Kathleen Jamie and the Lie of the Land

David Wheatley

'Art proceeds without a map', Kathleen Jamie has written of the act of finishing a book: 'It seems to me that if you know precisely what you've done, or are going to do, then it's a project. Projects are not art.'[1] For all her sceptical embargo, the cartographical metaphor remains a compelling way of approaching Jamie's poetry. Also with cartography in mind, Elizabeth Bishop wrote: 'More delicate than the historians' are the map-makers' colors', suggesting ways in which the business of cartography, tied though it is to the business of nation-building, achieves a non-political surplus of aesthetic delight.[2] Access to such aesthetic pleasures is not achieved without a struggle. In 'Forget It', the second poem in her 1999 collection *Jizzen*, Jamie evokes the 'project' of school history lessons and the thick wall of intransigence presented by those who would rather forget. While the official record of Scottish history might be open to challenge, many of those with best reason to contest it have departed the scene, whether opting for emigration or violently cleared off the land. Thus, even the revisionist history studied by the young poet (*'We done the slums today!'*) is treated by her mother with suspicion, who retorts *'Some history's better forgot.'* (J 5) Those who stay become, in the words of 'The Graduates', 'emigrants of no farewell' (J 3), unmoored and at sea in their own country. Having submitted to her mother's injunction, the speaker takes stock of her world in a small but significant act of map-making: the garden 'shrunk for winter', the exotic spaghetti hoops her mother cooks for dinner, and savings from a part-time job at Debenhams that pay for the luxury of 'our first / foreign / holiday' (J 7). In 'Song of Sunday', later in the same collection, questions of history and cartography reappear in modified form. It is Sunday, that dreichest of days in God-fearing Scotland, and the young speaker is bored and with 'nothing to do' (J 31). After an unappetising dinner and *Songs of Praise* and African leopards on the television, the speaker takes out her stamp album. Last of the nations' miniature calling cards to be examined are those of 'Great Britain' (the poem's quotation marks), whose patch in her stamp album she tends carefully, folding and aligning its edges with the stamps' 'orderly squares' (J 32). The poem ends with three one-word sentences: 'Press. "Bedtime!" *There.*' Where exactly, 'there', one might ask? The disaffection from the official narrative of nation is hard to miss, and the act of placing the stamps so carefully in their album becomes, in its way, an act of displacing too, insisting on certainties capable once of eliciting childish assent, but now looking – in the present-day poem's act of framing – faded and threadbare.

Another form of miniature to be found in abundance in Scottish sitting rooms of yore is the decorative tea-tray, of the kind brandished by the poet in 'Interregnum'. This tray is emblazoned with an advert for McEwen's lager, but as she looks about for a place to put it the poet imagines herself laden down with a jigsaw, a haggis and a 'model-to-scale / of the SS *Balmoral*' (J 41). With its admixture of royalist kitsch, the melancholy domestic interior disorients the poet: she cannot re-enter the 'clear space' behind her 'because it won't now exist', still doesn't know where to place her load, and 'Besides, / what's the point of the tray?' The abjection of the Scottish interior genre-piece is complete. The sequencing of Jamie's collections is never less than canny, and the aforementioned 'Song of Sunday' is followed by a suite of poems about the emigrant experience, inspired by a visit to an Ontario museum. Historical displacement continues to play itself out in a museum attendant 'taken aback' at hearing the poet's Scottish accent, the poet by this stage 'bored' with her holiday and 'headed for home' (J 35). 'Should we have stayed at home, / wherever that may be?' Elizabeth Bishop asks in 'Questions of Travel',[3] but no sooner does Jamie establish her dichotomy, albeit a complex one, of home and elsewhere, than she abandons it in 'Lochan' for a notional destination instead: 'When all this is over I mean / to travel north, by the high // drove roads and cart tracks', at the end of which tracks a 'white boat' awaits her (J 36). Jamie's opening strongly echoes that of Eiléan Ní Chuilleanáin's 'Swineherd', and the Irish intertext lends weight to the Gaelic echo behind Jamie's 'white boat' – the *bád bán* being traditionally the emigrant ship.[4] Wherever home may be remains uncertain, but the itch of displacement remains a constant.

Like Ireland's, the Scottish literary landscape is much contested, but harbours dark zones not just at its periphery but also at its nominal centre. The same is as true of the historical as the strictly literary landscape: in a *New Statesman* essay on her being commissioned to write a poem for the 700th anniversary of the Battle of Bannockburn, Jamie begins by pointing out that no one knows exactly where this much-mythologised battle was fought.[5] This vagueness offers opportunities of its own, however, and informs the conditions of Jamie's response to the lie of the land in contemporary Scotland. Here my incomer's experience as a recently arrived immigrant proved eye-opening. Visible from my window as I type these words is the knobbly-topped peak of Bennachie, the Mither Tap, much hymned by local Renaissance Latin poet Arthur Johnston (1587–1641), but which manages to combine historical fame and obscurity (or mystery) in equal measures. At its summit is an Iron Age fort, once occupied by the elusive Picts. Descendants of the Caledonii, the Picts established a kingdom in the Scottish north-east that lasted from Iron Age times until the eleventh century. As the name suggests, they were the 'painted' people, and favoured the blue facial stylings anachronistically sported a thousand years later by Mel Gibson and associates in *Braveheart*. Amidst a welter of unknowns, one indubitable Pictish fact is their addiction to stone-carving, as reflected in the large number of ornate stones that dot the countryside in these parts.

The Brandsbutt stone in Inverurie, a particularly fine example with crescent and serpent markings, has been advanced as evidence that the Picts were Celts, but of the P rather than Q persuasion, the Q strain turning up later and violently supplanting them. 'IRATADDOARENS', reads its Ogham inscription (as mentioned in a W. N. Herbert poem), thought to be a version of a local saint's name, Etharnanus.[6] At a time when questions of national identity are much in the air in Scotland, I find it salutary to juxtapose our narratives of the post-Romantic nation-state with these more palimpsestuous worlds lurking beneath our current polity. 'We were a tribe, a family, a people', Edwin Muir begins his poem 'Scotland, 1941', but no sooner does he unfurl his historical tapestry than it begins to unravel. 'Out of that desolation we were born', he says of the Calvinist world of Knox and Melville, but in no time at all we are masochistically celebrating Scott and Burns as 'sham bards of a sham nation' before an inglorious collapse amid 'wasted bravery idle as a song' and tales of woe whose best hope is that they may in time 'melt to pity the annalist's iron tongue.'[7]

By and large, Jamie eschews such sweeping historical gestures. Poetry as archaeology finds its most celebrated contemporary laureate in Seamus Heaney, and in Jamie's 'Hoard' the earth becomes a Heaneyesque *chthonos*, releasing a bog body packed with sphagnum and still clutching a sword. The differences between the two poets are unmistakable, however, as Jamie deflects the poem's mythic ambitions by focusing on the dead man's final moments over the symbolic meanings he might have been expected to acquire in the poems of *North*. 'Reliquary' too screens out the voices of myth and history, passing over the exposed remains of ancient settlements in favour of bluebell seeds cast on the ground 'like tiny hearts in caskets / tossed onto a battle ground' (*TH* 37). The appropriation of the natural landscape to our historical concerns is subtly rehabilitated in Jamie's closing image of the battle ground on which the seeds are cast, but the contrast with Heaney remains. At issue in *North* is which of its warring male tribes will occupy the feminised earth, rather than the principle either of male authority or the rights of occupation it confers. In 'Reliquary', the human comparison is incorporated in the poem but the primary focus remains the natural world. The poem makes a virtue of its smallness in the face of history, declining to offer long disquisitions on the former 'plague pits' that now house fibre-optic cables, but embodying an exemplary toughness and durability in the face of historical nightmare. Unlike Derek Mahon's Fire King, Jamie is far from 'through with history', but history in her poems tends to be understood as subject to veiling, overwriting and silencing, a condition her poems imaginatively explore rather than presuming to overturn.[8] Where Scottish history for Edwin Muir was a 'painted field', for Jamie it is as likely to be a storm-blown beach, endlessly written, unwritten, and rewritten by the changing elements.

By the standards of the Cairngorms further up the road, my own study window peak of Bennachie is the merest tiddler at 1,733 feet, neither a Munro, a Corbett nor even a Graham (peaks over 3,000, 2,500 and 2,000 feet respectively). Stranded between the estuarine landscapes that animate so many of Jamie's poems and the North Atlantic fringe that inspires her prose, this corner of Aberdeenshire features only a few Scottish literary gazetteers, Arthur Johnston notwithstanding. As such, it occupies one of those in-between spaces we find in Jamie's 'The Wishing Tree', 'neither in the wilderness / nor fairyland' (*TH* 3). Yet with its five-pronged peak and most dramatically the angular Mither Tap, it dominates the plain for dozens of miles in all directions. It is the alleged site of the Battle of Mons Graupius in AD 89, an event both epic and obscure, at which up to sixty thousand Caledonians and Romans allegedly did battle, and in which the better-prepared Romans routed their foes according to the only account we possess of the stramash, Tacitus's *Agricola*. There is some uncertainty as to the site of the battlefield (and no cache of tongue-like, testifying 'arraheids' in the ground to help), with any number of other locations pressing rival claims. The leader of the Caledonians, Calgacus, is credited with the immortal line, '*Ubi solitudinem faciunt pacem appellant*' on the Romans' scorched-earth tactics ('Where they make a wilderness they call it peace')[9], the only problem being that Calgacus may never have spoken these words and in fact may not have existed at all. He awaits his *Braveheart* moment, but I would hope Mel Gibson is open to offers; in the meantime Jean-Yves Ferri and Didier Conrad have given us *Asterix and the Picts* (with versions in both Scots and Gaelic translation), a tall tale of Burns-quoting ancient Scots who communicate by 'pictogram'. Another obscure Scottish poet associated with these parts, I learned, is the tragically short-lived Robert Fergusson (1750–1774), whose liberation of his style from the Augustan decorum of his earliest efforts into the urban demotic of his long poem 'Auld Reekie' is one of the great eureka moments for vernacular verse in the pre-Romantic age. He is also the subject of Jamie's uncollected elegy 'At Robert Fergusson's Grave', in which the cult of official commemoration is contrasted with the more subversive afterlife that Fergusson has led, and through which he exercises his continuing influence ('Let dust be your memorial, no stane // then mibbe Scotia's grun-doon specks // and mites could fin in your name // a champion; a constant irritant, alive').[10] As a young man Fergusson spent time on an uncle's farm in Oldmeldrum, on the far side of Inverurie, returning in 1769 for an unhappy six months before walking home to Edinburgh – a period that left no trace on his work, unfortunately. Thinking I had found a more voluble Donside Fergusson, I alighted with interest on a copy in my village library of *Don: A Poem*, published in 1805 by the Kemnay schoolmaster Charles Dawson. Something in the poem failed to ring true, I felt, and further investigations revealed Dawson to have plagiarised the poem from a 1655 text. Though exposed in his lifetime, he shamelessly continued to reprint the poem, a minor Ossian of the Garioch.[11]

Getting to know the lie of the land in Aberdeenshire, I began to see Jamie's cultural geography and 'questions of travel' in a different light. Pictish stones and Latin poets would seem far removed from McEwen's tea-trays and the miserabilism of the Sabbath, but the lie of the land that emerges from Jamie's work – and in particular the trilogy formed by *Jizzen*, *The Tree House* and *The Overhaul* – is born of a complex knot of influences and strands of Scottish literary history. For Irish poets who came after him, the problem was how to stop sounding like Yeats; for Scottish poets coming after their own great modernist master, the problem was that almost no one had the slightest desire or inclination to sound like MacDiarmid. Introducing his *Faber Book of Twentieth-Century Scottish Poetry*, Douglas Dunn elegantly summarises the problem of an obligatory Scots-speaking nationalist modernism for poets who did not feel inclined to display any of these qualities in a conspicuous or performative manner. Revisiting MacDiarmid's sparring-match with Edwin Muir over the use of Scots versus English, he finds its legacy all too discernible in contemporary debate too. As he notes in relation to Tom Leonard: 'Accent is an audible yardstick for gauging social origins throughout the British Isles; but in Scotland it can seem as if the social controllers have turned up the volume'.[12] Of contemporary Scottish poets, perhaps only W. N. Herbert and Robert Crawford have continued in the MacDiarmid line, and while Scots has always been a presence in Jamie's work (and is the vehicle for some of the finest lyrics in Jizzen, The Tree House and The Overhaul) Matt McGuire's comment that Jamie 'wears her Scots lightly' seems designed to keep her at a safe distance from these controversies.[13]

Nevertheless, Jamie's choice of 'A Raised Beach' as the title for one of the short lyrics in The Overhaul places it self-consciously in the shadow of one of MacDiarmid's best-known poems, 'On a Raised Beach', his salute to the stones of the Shetland islet of West Linga, first published in Stony Limits in 1934. For MacDiarmid, the stones embody a permanence and authority that mocks all human endeavour. With its similarities to the 'inhumanism' of Robinson Jeffers, the poem's desire to find sermons in stones is a prime product, but also a querulous rejection, of the Romantic tradition and its desire to place man and nature on speaking terms, even if not always as equals. Twenty-six short lines in length, Jamie's poem works on a more modest compass. Beginning by accepting MacDiarmid's donnée of nature's indifference, the poem questions its own motives in trying to make this mute force speak ('Moon, / why have you turned to me / your dark side, why am I / examining these stones?'), before reaching a very different conclusion from MacDiarmid's (O 18). Replying to the poet's harangue, the sea informs Jamie that the poet is a 'grown-up now' and that she has 'sung to you / quite long enough'; the reader may also detect echoes here of Wallace Stevens' 'The Idea of Order at Key West'). Non-communication is given a human face, but non-communication it remains, even if Jamie's couthy conclusion more closely resembles a family squabble than a battle of the elements.

In responding to Jamie's recent work, critics have aligned her with ecopoetry,[14] though at a panel at the 2013 Contemporary Poetry Conference in Manchester (all of whose papers focused on Jamie's work since Jizzen) Peter Mackay rejected the label, and the Heideggerian baggage of the 'poetry of dwelling' ('This is not poetry as the song of the earth, or of a revelation of dwelling').[15] Writing in 2009, Matt McGuire applied the light-green paradigm of Jonathan Bate's The Song of the Earth, presenting Jamie as a neo-Romantic whose connection with the earth will heal our separation from nature while steering clear of ideological stridency, or, as he terms it, 'green fascism'.[16] This is a strangely depoliticised response to Jamie's work, in which she offers us 'reconnection and reclamation' but is carefully steered away from anything as vulgar as eco-activism ('the dreadlocked tree-hugger'), not that Jamie's engagements with ecopolitics are easily reducible to this or any other label. To subject MacDiarmid's apocalyptic vision to some gentle satire is one thing, but to revert to a timeless pastoralism something else again; nor does such a stance sit easily with Jamie's hard-hitting review of Robert Macfarlane's The Wild Places, and the Romantic fantasies of an innocent terra nullius she finds therein. As she writes:

We see [Macfarlane] swimming, climbing, looking, feeling, hearing, responding, being sensitive, and because almost no one else speaks, this begins to feel like an appropriation, as if the land has been taken from us and offered back, in a different language and tone and attitude. Because it's land we're talking about, this leads to an unfortunate sense that we're in the company, however engaging, of another 'owner', or if not an owner, certainly a single mediator.[17]

When Jamie's contemporary Alice Oswald edited her anthology *The Thunder Mutters* in 2005, she staged a small protest against the acquisitive side of the Romantic imagination by leaving the Romantic poets out altogether. To title a collection *The Tree House* signals an interest in the natural spaces one passes through without inhabiting, exactly, and in 'The Bower' Jamie explores an exemplary non-colonised natural space. The bower is neither 'born', 'gifted', 'crafted' nor 'bequeathed' (*TH* 17). Its modesty is stressed in the line-break 'this forest dwelling's little / but a warp or tease', the modifier not entirely cancelling the temporary image of its essential littleness. Jamie likes the effect so much she repeats it a few lines later: 'Though it's nothing / but an attitude of mind'. The true inhabitant of the bower, it emerges, is the song it inspires in those who visit it, and which when projected 'from such frail enclaves' journeys to the edge of the forest and 'returns in waves'. Jamie's Scots translations of Hölderlin are among the high points of her recent work, and given the centrality of the Swabian poet to Heidegger's thinking, one might see 'The Bower' as a poem of Heideggerian *Holzwege*, forest trails in search of an epiphanic clearing. Jamie is careful to locate her bower within an 'entailed estate', reminding us of the complex question of land-ownership in Scotland, but achieving freedom from such concerns with a primal insistence on the question of song ('sure only of its need to annunciate').

'The Bower' establishes a back-and-forth between these primal questions and more local or political accidents of time and place, without either side gaining an outright victory. In 'The Tree House' Jamie uses the word 'complicity' to describe the human dwelling contained in a tree, with freedoms and human obligations neatly juxtaposed. Peculiarly, stepping inside the tree house provokes an escape to wider horizons, only for these escapist fantasies to culminate in another tree house, described with some ambivalence as 'a dwelling of sorts', but one freighted with loss: 'a gall / we've asked the tree to carry / of its own dead, and every spring / to drape in leaf and blossom, like a pall' (*TH* 43). Only occasionally does Jamie succumb to a more didactic imperative, as when she wonders whether the alder tree might 'teach me // a way to live / on this damp ambiguous earth?' (*TH* 7) Perhaps, in the words of the following poem, 'Water Day', this is to make 'heavy weather' of the relationship between poet and her environment (*TH* 8), but when Jamie appeals like this to the song of the earth (or the alder tree), it is often the voice of older contemporaries that answers, as in the previously-noted echoes of Heaney, but also in the witty reprise of Ian Hamilton Finlay minimalist poems we find in 'On the Design Chosen for the New Scottish Parliament Building by Architect Enric Miralles'. The ungainly title suggests the creaking worthiness of public art, which Jamie then short-circuits with the five words of the poem itself (*J* 48).

More so than in *Jizzen* or *The Tree House*, Jamie's forms begin to look beyond their borders in *The Overhaul*. In 'Fragments', the sighting of a deer (also the theme of 'The Stags' a few pages further on) sets up a familiar encounter of the human and the non-human, with the difference that this encounter becomes for the poet primarily a question of form. Using the interpellative second person, Jamie asks 'how can you tell / what form I take?' (O 10) With its vague punctuation, the answer 'What form I take / I scarcely know myself' might be a repetition of the question blurring into a punningly evasive answer: the poet scarcely knows what form she takes, or more generally, scarcely knows herself at all. Birds are ubiquitous in Jamie's recent work, and in 'Hawk and Shadow' a hawk gliding over a hill becomes the basis for a dialogue of self and soul, as the poet seeks to establish the contours of identity amid the transience of nature. The poem is written in short, predominantly dimeter and trimeter lines, and with one exception uses monosyllables throughout for its rhyme-words. The impression of a poem turned in on itself is heightened by the self-inwoven simile Jamie employs of the hawk seeming to carrying its 'own dark shape' in its talons 'like a kill', combining part and whole metonymically, but also life and death (O 15). The hawk's shadow takes the place of its prey, suggesting the thin line between the imagination achieving the form it seeks and a vain capture of one's own shadow. As Maria Johnston has written of this poem, 'The lines' compulsive rhythmic stress-pulse amplifies the mounting panic, while their dark nursery-rhyme endings vibrate with disjunctive energy as boundaries dissolve to terrifying effect.'[18] With its reference to the 'so-called soul', the poem is uneasy with abstractions, and finds the effort of a divided self finally too much to bear. The hawk drifts upwards, forsaking its shadow self on the ground, 'till hill and sky were empty, / and I was afraid' (O 15).

Yeats will return at the end of *The Overhaul*, but 'Hawk and Shadow' too is rich with Yeatsian intertexts. 'The Second Coming' opens with an image of a falcon breaking away from its falconer, going beyond its usual circumscribed flights into a zone of freedom that is also a harbinger of chaos, prompting the poem to its famous pronouncement that 'Things fall apart; the centre cannot hold'.[19] Another Yeats poem in which a creature is doubled by a shadow is the short lyric 'Memory', in which the memory of beautiful women is compared to a mountain hare. The charm and beauty of the remembered women is somehow 'in vain' because 'the mountain grass / Cannot but keep the form / Where the mountain hare has lain.'[20] The qualifying 'but' appears paradoxical on first reading. The hare's impression on the grass is surely short-lived, but for Yeats its transience is an integral part of the effect the poem savours ('form' is also a word for a hare's nest). So strong is the effect produced by this aesthetic delight that it trumps the facts of ageing and decay, and also, it would seem, the women's original beauty. Such is the richness of the self-delighting Yeatsian style, but Jamie's 'Hawk and Shadow' prefers to leave its element disassembled and the poet in a state of fear and confusion.

When Yeats exclaims 'Another emblem there!' in 'Coole Park and Ballylee',[21] he is responding to the Midas-like transformative side of his style. Nothing is merely itself; all is heightened and changed utterly by the application of his bardic gaze. Jamie's 'Highland Sketch' continues to undershoot the Yeatsian style, commenting as it goes along on its poetic map-making, but refusing to apply the necessary finishing touches for the bardic payoff (nor can one easily imagine a Yeats poem whose speaker is too lazy or nonplussed to make love.) 'Another landscape, / another swept glen' (O 17), Jamie begins, and when the poem answers its injunction to 'rouse ourselves' it does so by way of a Burns quotation before a downbeat closing 'sklent of sunlight to the heart'. Between Jamie's distrust of the artistic ego and the will-to-power required for her poems to 'rouse' themselves lies a zone of tension resolved at last in the closing poem of *The Overhaul*. With its vision of unravelling and incompletion, 'Materials' is a superficially audacious poem on which to end. *The Materials* was the title of George Oppen's second poetry collection, after his lengthy mid-career hiatus, and Jamie's poem honours the Objectivist approach in returning all to process and bricolage. We began with Jamie's dislike for the word 'project', and 'Materials' begins with a vision of 'the entire project / reduced to threads of moss' (O 50). The poem imagines following 'just one strand' of this unravelled project, in a winter landscape denuded of most of its birds and pounded by waves, but at the end of her beach-combing appears to have nothing to show for herself: 'And look at us! Out all day and damn all to show for it.' The poem then finds its vision at last not in transcendence but the recognition of immanent truth. Where Yeats had his 'mound of refuse or the sweepings of a street' in 'The Circus Animals' Desertion',[22] Jamie has 'Bird-bones, rope-scraps, a cursory sketch', or 'bruck' as she dismissively labels it, but which is nevertheless 'all we need to get us started, all we'll leave behind us when we're gone' (O 50). In lingering on the 'sweepings of a street' Yeats is marking one stage of the gestation of the poet's 'masterful images' ('These masterful images, because complete, / Grew in pure mind, but out of what began?') – but one stage only. They are shaped by, and pressed on the reader as examples of artistic mastery, a condition that ennobles the medium in which it works. Jamie refuses the Irish poet's grandiloquence, and in the absence of bardic self-aggrandisement would rather the landscape of 'Materials' spoke for itself. An 'unsung cleft of rock' is another sheltering space going a-begging ('a place you could take to, / dig yourself in') whether or not the poet chooses to occupy it, and even amidst natural disarray the shoreline is a 'space confirmed / – don't laugh – by your own work' (O 50).

Yet a central absence remains: this landscape is 'all we need to get us started' and 'all we'll leave behind us', but the poem declines to present its author in the moment of the appropriative artistic act itself. It declines, in other words, and yet again, to become a self-conscious 'project', preferring to go about its business under cover of the self-cancelling, painstaking attention to its landscapes that is Jamie's signature. It is on such terms that Jamie's negotiations with the natural world allow it to answer back and people the space the poem has left empty with its probing, provisional epiphanies – the bird's voice in 'Even the Raven' suddenly (and without answer) 'ask[ing] you what you're waiting for' (O 49). Her first published work since *The Overhaul*, *Frissure* would appear to move Jamie's work in a different direction, as she records her experiences of surgery for breast cancer; but even in this new phase (if such it proves), questions of poetic territory remain to the fore. Describing a walk on an East Lothian shoreline, Jamie's artist collaborator Brigid Collins begins to see 'lines of every sort' in the landscape, from which she will extrapolate to the lines traced on the poet's body in surgery and reproduced in her watercolours (*Fr* 11). In the first of her short prose poems, Jamie describes receiving a get-well present of an envelope full of wild flowers, bringing with them 'the cliffs and birds' cries, a derelict village and the ever-present solace of the waves' (*Fr* 13). The borders of nation and body alike are subject to unforeseen redrawing, sometimes with traumatic consequences, but the landscapes that drive Jamie's art lend themselves to drawing, redrawing and transplantation, giving the slip to the restrictive imperatives of territory and territoriality. The various political 'lies of the land' reveal the transience of politico-cultural arrangements, but out of the 'benign indifference of the world' Jamie conjures the truer lies of art, inscribing the map with lines not of 'defence' but 'defiance' (*Fr* 3, 17).

WORKS CITED (SEE ALSO BIBLIOGRAPHY)

Bishop, Elizabeth, *Collected Poems* (London: Chatto and Windus, 1991).

Crawford, Robert (ed.), '*Heaven-Taught Fergusson*': *Robert Burns's Favourite Scottish Poet* (East Lothian: Tuckwell Press, 2003).

Crawford, Robert (ed.), *Apollos of the North: Selected Poems of George Buchanan & Arthur Johnston* (Edinburgh: Polygon, 2006).

Dunn, Douglas, introduction to *The Faber Book of Twentieth-Century Scottish Poetry* (London: Faber and Faber, 1992).

MacDiarmid, Hugh, introduction to Robert Henryson, *The Testament of Cresseid and Other Poems* (Harmondsworth: Penguin, 1973), p. 7.

Mahon, Derek, *Selected Poems* (Loughcrew: Gallery Press, 1991).

Muir, Edwin, *Selected Poems* (London: Faber and Faber, 1960).

Ní Chuilleanáin, Eiléan, *Selected Poems* (London: Faber and Faber, 2008).

Tacitus, *Agricola* (Cambridge, MA: Harvard University Press, 1970).

Yeats, W. B., *Collected Poems* (London: Macmillan, 1982).

NOTES

1. 'Author, author: Kathleen Jamie on writing a book' (2012).
2. Bishop, *Collected Poems*, p. 3.
3. Ibid., p. 94.
4. 'When all this is over, said the swineherd, / I mean to retire', Ní Chuilleanáin, 'Swineherd', in *Selected Poems*, p. 16.
5. Jamie, 'The Spirit of Bannockburn'.
6. Herbert, *The Laurelude*.
7. Muir, *Selected Poems*, pp. 97–8.
8. Mahon, *Selected Poems*, pp. 58–9.
9. Tacitus, *Agricola* XXX, p. 80.
10. Jamie, 'At Robert Fergusson's Grave'.
11. Dawson, *Don: A Poem*.
12. Dunn, introduction to *The Faber Book of Twentieth-Century Scottish Poetry*, p. xlii.
13. McGuire, 'Kathleen Jamie', p. 144.
14. Cf. Borthwick, '"The tilt from one parish / into another"'.

15. Panel on Kathleen Jamie, British and Irish Contemporary Poetry Conference, University of Manchester, 13 September 2013, cf. Peter Mackay's essay in this volume.
16. McGuire, 'Kathleen Jamie', pp. 146–7.
17. Jamie, 'A Lone Enraptured Male'.
18. Johnston, 'Shadow-play with the Soul'.
19. Yeats, *Collected Poems*, pp. 210–11.
20. Ibid., p. 168.
21. Ibid., p. 275.
22. Ibid., p. 392.

6. 'An Orderly Rabble': Plural Identities in *Jizzen*

Timothy L. Baker

In a recent discussion of W. S. Graham, Natalie Pollard highlights what Graham terms the 'difficulty of speaking from a fluid identity', arguing that he 'depicts a world in which words are not obediently representative, and language neither serves as a vehicle for self-expression, nor lends itself to autobiography'.[1] While a similar sense of flux and indeterminacy can be found throughout Jamie's work, it is especially visible in *Jizzen* (1999). Like *The Queen of Sheba*, *Jizzen* has often been approached in terms of its clear parallels between national and individual identity, particularly in relation to its focus on birth and development. Helen Boden, for instance, argues that the 'significance of Jamie's work lies in its skilful renegotiation with the ways the nation is and has been represented'.[2] In *Jizzen*, however, Jamie not only ironises or renegotiates ideas of self and nation, as in her earlier work, but further challenges any concept of stable identity. Throughout the volume, as can be seen in relation to Jamie's use of intra- and intertextual reference, she presents individual and collective identity not in terms of unity but rather, in the worlds of 'Lucky Bag', as an 'orderly rabble' (J 42). Identity is figured not simply in terms of shared experience, but also through what might be termed a politics of difference, whereby the nation and the self are both seen in terms of individual relation.[3] In *Jizzen* Jamie examines the complicated relation between language and identity: both the poems and the identities depicted in them highlight the relation between different registers and voices. This approach is exemplified in the collection's structure, where the juxtaposition of tonally and linguistically diverse poems suggests a concept of identity founded on difference rather than unity.

Jamie's 'orderly rabble' is exemplified in the sequence 'Ultrasound', whose seven poems addressed from mother to infant are each tonally and linguistically distinct. The paralleling of an infant or soon-to-be-born child and a soon-to-be-born Scotland appears in other contemporary volumes such as Robert Crawford's *Masculinity*. In 'Loganair', for instance, Crawford aligns the diversity of Fife seen from the air with 'the scan of our unborn child', while elsewhere the infant is placed in relation both to specific locations and the Scottish judiciary.[4] This combination of universal experience with geographic and cultural specificity finds an echo in Jamie's 'Bairnsang', a lullaby in which each of the four stanzas repeats the same reassuring structure (J 15–16). Each stanza begins with an address to the child himself, 'Wee toshie man' or 'Peedie wee lad', followed by an offset line describing an element of nature, ranging from the specificity of 'gean tree and rowan' to the expanse of 'sternie an lift'. The poet then speculates on a future where the child will be able to stand, run, sing and dance; as he cannot, he must remain in his mother's arms. Each stanza ends with a mention of a Scottish place, moving from east to west and south to north, from Gretna Green to the northernmost isles of Shetland. The move from a particular individual to a Scottish location, through speculative action and familial emotion, can also be found in many of Crawford's poems. Placed elsewhere in the collection – alongside the juxtaposition of 'a new-born Kirkcaldy / baby-gro' and 'a Free State' in 'Lucky Bag', for instance – the poem might be seen to have a particular cultural significance (J 42). However, 'Bairnsang' is the fifth poem in 'Ultrasound', which as a whole moves from the general to the specific and back again; natural and geographic references are both related to larger questions of life and art.

'Ultrasound' opens with a poem of the same name that invokes artistic and folk-loric representations of the supernatural. The ultrasound reveals a 'wee shilpit ghost / summonsed from tomorrow', juxtaposed with allusions to M. R. James and second sight (J 11). The child is a 'secret' and a 'ghoul', inherently immaterial, and is linked to the mystery inside Pandora's box as well as, curiously, a herring in a net. The ultrasound reveals not a potential future, as in Crawford's 'Loganair', but is tied to the past and questions of knowledge; the child is presented in relation both to literary traditions and to supernatural experiences that defy concrete representation. Not yet born, the foetus cannot be viewed in terms of a stable individual identity, but resists definition. As the speaker queries in the next poem in the sequence, 'Solstice', 'To whom do I talk, an unborn thou, sleeping in a bone creel' (J 12). Here the womb is likened to a room, and a possible future of 'stars, milkbottles, frost / on a broken outhouse roof' is posited, but the child nevertheless remains unknown and unknowable. In the world before birth, which Jamie characterises in 'Thaw' as the experience 'before we were two, from my one', communication is necessarily generalised and internalised; speaking to the child is speaking to the self (J 13). 'Thaw' and 'February', set after the child's birth, bring both child and speaker into the world of immanent materiality, whether it be 'a chopping block [and] the frost- / split lintels' or a 'heap of nappies' (J 13, 14). In these poems the interior, domestic world is connected to the exterior and natural: the stars the speaker sees outside her house remind her of the ones on the ceiling of the hospital, while washing nappies is paralleled with the flight of swans and spring's first snowdrops. Throughout these first four poems the world is in a continual cycle of expansion and contraction; each moment is known as it relates not only to individual pasts and futures, but also to a more universal and even mythic level of experience. This is equally true of individual identity: although the child is the subject of each of these poems, he is primarily an other in relation to whom the speaker is formed. Here Jamie describes a physical embodiment of Paul Ricoeur's notion of selfhood, which he describes as an intimate otherness in which 'one passes into the other'.[5] The speaker and the subject are made distinct only through their interrelation: each can only be known in relation to the other. The child's birth is a process of separation that allows both mother and child to be known as individuals.

This, then, is the setting for 'Bairnsang'. In this context the mentions of diverse physical, chronological and geographic experiences should be thought of in terms of a continuing separation between the speaker and the child, a separation that has not yet happened. In considering the child's future, the speaker is more fully able to imagine her own present. The effect of future separation is also addressed in the sequence's final two poems. In 'Sea Urchin' the speaker compares cradling the child's head to lifting a sea urchin from a rockpool, 'with no premonition / of when next I find one' (J 17). The next sea urchin may be broken or whole, or may never be found at all; similarly, the child's own development is subject to chance, and cannot be controlled. The sequence ends with 'Prayer', a brief poem of three rhyming couplets in loose five-stress lines. The child, at sixteen weeks, has begun to be distinct, his heart 'a fluttering bird' that leads the speaker to think of St Kevin, allowing a bird to build its nest in his outstretched hands (J 18). The story, familiar from many accounts, is most famously told in Seamus Heaney's 'St Kevin and the Blackbird', where the saint's action begins in pity and his recognition that he is 'linked / Into the network of eternal life'.[6] Heaney invites the reader to imagine Kevin, 'since the whole thing's imagined anyhow', and ends the poem with a depiction of complete self-abnegation:

A prayer his body makes entirely
For he has forgotten self, forgotten bird
And on the riverbank forgotten the river's name.[7]

In Heaney's poem pity leads to a loss of self, language, and memory, a loss that nevertheless must be reconstituted through the language and the idea of self. The reader must actively imagine passivity, while the poet must constitute in words what cannot be spoken. As in Ciaran Carson's early 'St Ciaran's Island', where the isolated speaker must 'lose the written word' and 'learn to grow in silence' with the 'green things of the world', Heaney's Kevin must wilfully abandon the idea of self and language until even the idea of will is forgotten.[8] For both poets unity with nature necessitates the abandonment of individual identity, or what Wallace Stevens, following Simone Weil, calls decreation.[9] For Jamie, however, the story of St Kevin points to a loss of identity that affirms the self. The poem ends 'I prayed: this new heart must outlive my own' (J 18). Although the speaker envisions a separation between herself and her child, culminating in her own death, she remains central to the equation: the poem ends not with the other, but with the self. As much as the sequence is addressed to the child, it also functions as a foundation for the self. The speaker's identity is formed in terms of separation from an other who was once part of her.

'Ultrasound' is followed by 'The Tay Moses', which functions as a coda, condensing many of the sequence's themes. The speaker again envisions her eventual separation from her child, when he will 'change hands: tractor-man, grieve, farm-wife / who takes you into her / competent arms' (J 19). While the speaker can offer the child access to the natural world, whether in terms of an oriole's nest or her favourite hills, as the child grows he will enter a human, social world over which she has no control and in which she plays no part. At the poem's end, however, the speaker renounces this separation, 'crying / LEAVE HIM! Please, / it's okay, he's mine' (J 20). As in 'Ultrasound', the speaker is able to voice her own identity in terms of an anticipated distance from her child: this relation is what allows her to speak as an 'I'. The evocation of an individual identity based on separation from another is not limited to these poems of motherhood, however. Instead, 'Ultrasound' and to a lesser extent 'The Tay Moses' can be read as representative of *Jizzen* as a whole, both thematically and stylistically. 'Ultrasound' not only focuses on an idea of relational identity, but enacts it through its juxtaposition of diverse styles and forms. Each poem is written in a different stanza form, including couplets, tercets, octaves, stanzas of mixed length, and in 'Thaw' no stanza division. Line length is regularised in some poems but not others; rhyme is similarly employed only in certain poems. Poems are presented in English, Scots or a mixture of the two. The register changes dramatically not only between but within individual poems. The voice of the speaker, and the unity of the sequence, is made possible only by this stylistic diversity. The coherence of the sequence rests not on repetition, but difference: by opening up a space for a fluid or even prismatic identity, in which the voice of the speaker changes in every poem yet remains consistent, Jamie suggests a possibility for thinking of identity in a less rigid way.

While *Jizzen* can perhaps be seen as a turning point between questions of national identity and a focus on a world that is more than human, and not restricted by traditional identity rubrics, the questions of how identity is formed are most fully expressed in the collection's opening poems, each of which addresses a different idea of a speaking, and remembering, 'I'. The first poem in the collection, 'Crossing the Loch', navigates the boundaries between individual and collective identities and memories. The poem begins with an address to an unidentified listener: 'Remember how we rowed toward the cottage' (J 1). This listener is not even identified by a 'you'; rather, the speaker alternates between her own uncertain experience – 'I forget' and 'I was scared' – and a more stable collective one: 'Our jokes' and 'we live'. The moment is shared between people, but the speaker never clarifies the nature of this 'we'. Instead, the individual speaker, removed from the experience in time and space, frames her memories as a series of questions:

Who rowed, and who kept their peace?
Who hauled salt-air and stars
deep into their lungs, were not reassured;
and who first noticed the loch's
phosphorescence [. . .] ? (J 1)

The moment described is precise but inaccessible: the speaker takes part in all of these experiences and none of them. The poem posits a form of collective memory that cannot be possessed by one individual. Both the presumed audience and the unnamed other or others in the boat are necessary to the constitution of the speaker's self, but remain silent. Instead, the speaker in this stanza recasts and repeats images from the previous stanza in a manner that both strengthens and destabilises her memories. The statement 'I forget who rowed' becomes simply the question 'Who rowed', while 'I was scared' leads to 'were not reassured', the clause curiously lacking a grammatical subject but implying an absent 'they' or 'we'. The poem fluctuates between a defined location of a 'sickle-shaped bay' and 'ticking nuclear hulls', a traditional set of images including 'an astonished / small boat of saints', and common experiences that the reader might also share: 'we watched water shine / on our fingers and oars'. Even as the poem ends with a declaration of a more stable present, where 'we [. . .] even have children / to women and men we had yet to meet', the speaker constantly reconstructs the past in a way that demonstrates the fallibility of her own memory. Without access to the historic 'we', the individual speaker must provide a partial, destabilised recollection; throughout the poem the speaker attempts to identify and reconstitute a collective identity that is now displaced.

In opening the collection with an address to an unspecified 'we', Jamie highlights a fundamental aporia. As Jean-Luc Nancy writes, 'What is produced is a gap, a rupture from what could have remained within an inherent, closed identity [. . .]. Rupture opens identity by way of difference.'[10] For Nancy this rupture is an opening that allows a move from individual identity to what he terms an 'adoration' of the world. As others have noted, in Jamie's work this migration is often framed in ecological terms. Commenting on 'Ultrasound', for instance, Matt McGuire argues that 'everyday speech differentiates us, and creates an artificial barrier between ourselves and the world'.[11] For McGuire, Jamie's work from *Jizzen* onwards can be characterised as an attempt to create an intimacy between self and world that breaks down this process of differentiation. While this is certainly true of poems such as 'Meadowsweet', discussed below, in 'Crossing the Loch' Jamie foregrounds the way language differentiates the self not only from the world, but also from other people. Being able to speak solely as an 'I' highlights a rupture where the failures of a closed individual identity can be recognised but not overcome.

In the following poems, Jamie focuses on the idea of historical rupture. The speaker in 'The Graduates' views herself as an emigrant from a land she never left, as the stories and language of 'the old country' have been forgotten by a new 'mono-glot' generation (J 3). 'Forget It', meanwhile, combines several voices to examine the difference between history as it is taught, experienced, and remembered. While the primary speaker wonders 'how come / we remember the years / before we were born' and sees the past as 'not yet done', she is unable to reconcile a school lesson on 'the slums' with the immediate experience of long, driech streets and limp wallpaper (J 5–7). These disparate perspectives can only be reconciled through the construction of narratives. Stories are posited not only as the way to preserve a given culture, but to navigate between individual and collective experience: stories 'are balm, / ease their own pain' (J 7). In both poems the need to forget and the need to remember are posited as equally pressing and equally common. As Adriana Cavarero argues, the narrative work of memory 'continues to tell us our own personal story' precisely because it is dependent not on a conscious act of remembering but on 'the

spontaneous narrating structure of memory itself [. . .] What is essential is the familiar experience of a narratability of the self, which, not by chance, we always perceive
in the other, even when we do not know their story at all.'[12] Narration, Cavarero
argues, provides access to a fleeting, insubstantial self that is always dependent on
the other. This is precisely the act found in *Jizzen*'s first three poems, where the
respective speakers try to tell stories about either their own pasts or the pasts of
their families in order to constitute themselves as selves in the present, and in relation to others. In each of the three poems this action cannot be completed: a full
story cannot be enunciated by an individual self, and always requires a response the
poem itself cannot provide. The combination of these different speakers and stories,
however, highlights the importance of narration as a path to opening the world.

The three poems that follow, preceding 'Ultrasound', as well as several there-
after, present less complicated ideas of narrative, but nevertheless demonstrate
the extent to which a given story can navigate between multiple identities. 'The
Bogey-Wife' is presented as both 'like the yeti' and 'charming when cornered'; she is
simultaneously mythic and modern (J 10). 'Mrs McKellar, her martyrdom' similarly
juxtaposes scenes of a quotidian domestic disharmony with the 'Medieval' agony
the titular individual sees herself as enacting (J 24). Both poems, like 'A Miracle',
blend ancient and contemporary perspectives to at least partly comic effect. As
David Borthwick argues, Jamie's 'dialogic mix of the local and the mythic is [. . .] a
means of forcing her readers to look beyond the limitations of "ordinary" cultural
convention.'[13] Jamie both defamiliarises everyday life and elevates it. More importantly, however, the combination of these fanciful portraits suggests a perspective
on identity that the individual poems themselves cannot contain. Mr and Mrs
McKellar are occupied with questions of 'Who mentions, who defers to whom', and
communicate solely through silent resentment, and yet their frustrations are articulated by an outside observer (J 24). The bogey-wife, similarly, is presented as one
individual when seen, and another when she speaks. Both third-person narratives
concern isolated individuals, but in telling their stories the poems open the space
for dialogue. Moreover, the combination of these individual stories, interspersed
throughout the collection, begins to suggest a relational and fluid concept of collective identity predicated on difference. The reader's perception of collective identity
is determined not by similarities between poems and speakers, but rather the way in
which different individual voices become more distinct when placed in relation to
each other.

This concept is most clearly shown in 'Lucky Bag'. The poem lists various constit-
uent aspects of what might be seen as a Scottish identity, ranging from the mundane
('Tattie scones') to the iconic ('a chambered cairn'), and from the specific ('a poke
o Brattisani's chips') to the general ('computer bits, / an elder o the wee free Kirk')
(J 42). These elements are freely mixed, as in a lucky bag of sweets, without any
preference or explanation. The list of incongruous national elements is familiar from
Carol Ann Duffy's 'Translating the English, 1989' in which the speaker welcomes
the reader to his country with the promise of 'The Fergie / The Princess Di and the
football hooligan', aligning 'Fish and chips and the Official Secrets Act'.[14] Both
poets present an ironic view of the superficially representative elements of national

identity, juxtaposing the praised with the reviled or dismissed. 'Lucky Bag' immediately follows 'Interregnum', in which the speaker navigates between rooms with a tray advertising McEwan's ale at the same time that she moves between signifiers of British and Scottish identity, considering Windsor Castle, *Prime Suspect*, haggis, and the SS *Balmoral*. 'Lucky Bag' initially appears to be a more celebratory version of the earlier poem, where instead of various cultural artifacts existing in isolation, they are brought together to form a new whole. Its various components are linked only by a repeated 'o' sound, but nevertheless exist in a rough harmony. Unlike Duffy's poem, however, or the more obvious political references in 'Interregnum', 'Lucky Bag' is largely devoid of explicit national indices, and does not need to be read purely in political terms. Even the final line, offering the only overview, is destabilised: 'please form an orderly rabble' includes a large space between the final words, such that 'rabble' is entirely offset from the body of the poem (J 42). Jamie's non-hierarchical ordering allows readers both to recognise the separation between these elements and to recombine them in different ways to form new stories. Like the collection as a whole, 'Lucky Bag' offers different identities not as a means to understand a stable collective identity but rather as a way to foreground the arbitrary and necessary relation between different ways of being.

This principle is established in a sequence of three poems set in Canada. 'Hackit' portrays an unnamed woman who is made to represent the immigrant experience. As in 'Crossing the Loch', the woman's stories combine the specific and universal; her Scottish accent can only be recognised when she tells an audience 'about surviving // their first winter' (J 33). Although she is individualised, the experiences she recounts are general and almost mythic. However, the reader has even less direct access to the speaker's life than in 'Crossing the Loch' or 'Forget It': the woman speaks to an unidentified 'they', and her speech is not represented on the page. In 'Pioneers' individual experience is reduced still further, such that the immigrants' arrival in Canada 'not long ago' can now only be accessed through photographs and 'remains now strewn / across the small-town / museums of Ontario' (J 34). Finally, 'Suitcases' reveals these remains 'Piled high in a corner of a second-hand store / in Toronto' (J 35). The sequence thus moves from a representative individual mediated through language to unnamed immigrants mediated through technology, to purely material remains divorced from any human narrative. Similarly, the sequence appears to chart an erasure of identity: the individual is subsumed in the collective, who are finally seen only in light of 'an immigrant country' (J 35). At the same time, however, as elsewhere in the collection, this separation and erasure allows for the birth of a new individual identity: in the final five lines of 'Suitcases' the reader suddenly encounters a first-person speaker. Even though the speaker leaves the second-hand shop 'headed for home, / bored, and already pregnant', the possibility for a reestablishment of identity remains. As Cavarero notes, 'narratable identity is linked to an explicit desire for narration from another's mouth'.[15] Though the speaker may dismiss this story, her experience with its remnants may permit her to speak her own, as in 'Ultrasound'. As in the collection's earlier poems, this sequence simultaneously gestures to remembering and forgetting as central aspects of the formation of identity. Identity, either personal or national, cannot be represented by one speaker or within one poem. Each exposure to a different speaker, however, creates an opening for a concept of identity that cannot be directly enunciated.

The importance of a destabilised collective identity that cannot be voiced by a single speaker is demonstrated in 'Bolus', near the collection's end, which again invokes the image of mother and child. Presented as a single grammatically complex sentence, the poem suggests that our knowledge of the world is not innate, but rather passed from mouth to mouth ' – like words, or the bolus / of chewed bread' a mother presses on to the tongue of her infant (J 47). Here language, and the world itself, is framed as a material object passed between individuals. Identity, similarly, can only be established in the passing of one to the other, or one through the other. The gift, recalling Marcel Mauss and Claude Lévi-Strauss, exceeds traditional economies and systems of relation; for Jamie, the idea of the gift suggests what might be called a physical dialogue, where individual relation is known through free exchange. Understanding of the world comes neither from language nor direct experience, but from the exchange between individuals. 'Bolus' can be seen as a precise demonstration of Hans Ulrich Gumbrecht's claim that poetry 'is perhaps the most powerful example of the simultaneity of presence effects and meaning effects'.[16] Both presence and meaning can, in Jamie's poem, only be seen in terms of relation. No object, word, or identity is significant on its own; it is only in their combination and exchange that they begin to open the world.

This potential opening is clearly illustrated in the final lines of 'Meadowsweet', with which the collection ends. The poem opens with the burial of a woman poet, buried face down, according to tradition. Although symbolically silenced, in burial she is surrounded by summer plants slowly growing to the sun, teaching her 'how to dig herself out – [. . .] full again / of dirt, and spit, and poetry' (J 49). In both 'Bolus' and 'Meadowsweet' language lies in the mouth: it is the opening of communication, or the preparation for communication, but not communication itself. Both poems, like 'Crossing the Loch', await an audience. While Rhona Brown argues that 'Meadowsweet' 'emphasises the enduring nature of ancient Scottish poetry by women', the poem also suggests a new role for language itself.[17] Language, in Jamie's work, creates a common world. 'Meadowsweet' ends with the promise of a new poem to come, a form of poetry that transcends individual experience and yet is rooted in immanent physicality. As a whole, then, *Jizzen* moves from an explicit questioning of identity to a series of poems that consider identity in terms of separation and relation, culminating with the suggestion of a poetics that transcends stable ideas of voice or language. As much as the collection is concerned with questions of self and nation, these are ultimately subsumed in a vision of poetry that highlights difference rather than unity. Language is not used simply for self-representation, but instead can be seen as a gift that passes between the self and the other, between the human and the world, and between one poem and another.

WORKS CITED (SEE ALSO BIBLIOGRAPHY)

Brown, Rhona, 'Twentieth-Century Poetry', in Glenda Norquay, *The Edinburgh Companion to Scottish Women's Writing* (Edinburgh: Edinburgh University Press, 2012), pp. 140–51.

Carson, Ciaran, *Collected Poems* (Oldcastle: Gallery Press, 2008).

Cavarero, Adriana, *Relating Narratives: Storytelling and Selfhood*, tr. Paul A. Kottman (London and New York: Routledge, 2000).

Crawford, Robert, *Masculinity* (London: Jonathan Cape, 1996).

Duffy, Carol Ann, *New Selected Poems, 1984–2004* (London: Picador, 2004).

Gumbrecht, Hans Ulrich, *Production of Presence: What Meaning Cannot Convey* (Stanford: Stanford University Press, 2004).

Heaney, Seamus, *The Spirit Level* (London: Faber, 1996).

Nancy, Jean-Luc, *Adoration: The Deconstruction of Christianity II*, tr. John McKeane (New York: Fordham University Press, 2013).

Rancière, Jacques, *Dissensus: On Politics and Aesthetics*, ed. and tr. Steven Corcoran (London: Continuum, 2010).

Ricoeur, Paul, *Oneself as Another*, tr. Kathleen Blamey (Chicago and London: University of Chicago Press, 1992).

Stevens, Wallace, *The Necessary Angel: Essays on Reality and the Imagination* (New York: Vintage, 1951).

Weil, Simone, *Gravity and Grace*, tr. Arthur Wills (Lincoln, NE: University of Nebraska Press, 1997).

NOTES

1. Pollard, *Speaking to You*, pp. 41–2.
2. Boden, 'Kathleen Jamie's Semiotic of Scotlands', p. 27. See also McCulloch, 'Women and Poetry', p. 69, where she examines personal and national identity in terms of the 'power of the speaking voice'.
3. As Jacques Rancière writes: 'Politics cannot be defined on the basis of any pre-existing subject. The "difference" specific to politics [. . .] must be sought in the form of its relation.' Rancière, *Dissensus*, p. 28.
4. Crawford, *Masculinity*, p. 59.
5. Ricoeur, *Oneself as Another*, p. 3.
6. Heaney, *The Spirit Level*, p. 20.
7. Ibid., p. 21.
8. Carson, *Collected Poems*, p. 23.
9. See Stevens, *The Necessary Angel*, pp. 174–5 and Weil, *Gravity and Grace*, p. 78; both authors define decreation as the pass from the created to the uncreated, as opposed to destruction, where something created passes into nothingness.
10. Nancy, *Adoration*, p. 15.
11. McGuire, 'Kathleen Jamie', p. 146.
12. Cavarero, *Relating Narratives*, pp. 33–4.
13. Borthwick, '"The tilt from one parish"', p. 138.
14. Duffy, *New Selected Poems*, p. 68.
15. Cavarero, *Relating Narratives*, p. 137.
16. Gumbrecht, *Production of Presence*, p. 18.
17. Brown, 'Twentieth-Century Poetry', p. 146.

7. 'Sweet-Wild Weeks': Birth, Being and Belonging in *Jizzen*

Juliet Simpson

'To the day of St. Bride, / the first sweet-wild weeks of your life / I willingly surrender': the last tercet of Jamie's 'February' concentrates a fiercely tender chiaroscuro of birth and being, which is arguably the pulse-beat and enigma of Jamie's 1999 collection, *Jizzen* (J 14). The collection's guiding theme of 'birth', figured in 'February' as a plenitude of the ordinary, is charged with an abrupt luminosity of extraordinary connection that patterns the animal and earthy, 'the hare in jizzen' with the bodily and cultural ('women's work') and other resonant 'deliveries' and discoveries of being and birthright (J 45). This essay takes Jamie's treatment of 'birth' in *Jizzen* as a starting-point for exploring its multi-faceted physical, poetic and aesthetic potency as an event unfolding oblique supernatural insight – the baby's heart 'nesting' in St. Kevin's arms (J 18) – and as unfolding a broader dynamics of cultural belonging. It will argue that the power of voice in Jamie's *Jizzen* derives from an encounter with native land, people, landscape and 'mother' tongue, ostensibly non-mythic and banal, but which engages with a more complex figuring of what it might mean to belong beyond national stereotypes of land, language and culture.

Jizzen's most compelling innovations are to be found arguably in this questioning: in a rich interweaving of birth as intensely particular and personal and its force in shaping a further growth into self, culture and their immanent potential. Indeed, a springboard for *Jizzen*'s poetics of connectedness and its distinctive poetry of both birth and being may be found in a broader dynamics of 'gravity and grace' which Simone Weil places as a touchstone of poetic insight itself. What Weil pinpoints is that recognition or transformation of experience, galvanising an inward vision beyond the scope of immediate, particular apprehension. In this way, Weil sees poetic 'grace' as a pressing back, a countervailing weight or tension, pulling against the accepted normal or real towards other possibilities and connections, 'tilting the scales of reality towards some transcendent equilibrium'.[1] Seamus Heaney's further gloss on this idea in stressing poetry's 'redressing' force gives to Weil's suggestive poetic gravity an even denser, physical relationship with everydayness and actuality. His poetic 'redress' is offered as a necessary redirecting of insight and experience towards 'a glimpsed alternative, a revelation of potential that is denied or constantly threatened by circumstances'.[2] The significance of both these perceptions here is their suggestive force – through Weil's 'gravity and grace' and Heaney's 'glimpsed alternative' – in offering approaches to Jamie's *Jizzen* that allow for its innovations and tensions of voice, craft and poetic metaphor to be understood, or better, 'glimpsed', as a more complex exploration of its urgent preoccupations: birth, being and belonging.

I   BIRTH AS MATTER AND INSIGHT

It is indeed birth's force and weight that becomes the fulcrum for deeper patterns in *Jizzen*: between connected and opposing ideas of gravity and light, domesticity and wildness, homing and exile, that make perceptible birth's effects as both a weight and grace of being and belonging. Yet Jamie's evocation of the force of birth also inverts an expected order of things in a paradoxical movement from almost weightless, ghostly glimpsing to newly earth-bound potencies. From the sequence of 'birth' poems forming the opening of the collection to the emblematic epilogue of 'Meadowsweet''s life-in-death regeneration, birth, genesis, creation are driving impulses throughout; they are *Jizzen*'s matter and substance. That matter is arguably most urgent in the poems explicitly about birth: 'The Barrel Annunciation'; the seven short pieces comprising 'Ultrasound'; 'The Tay Moses' and 'St Bride'. In these works, intimate scale and domestic detail counterpoint natural analogues in patterning life's first stirrings to fully-fledged birth as a weft of connections between matter, ordinariness and miracle. In 'Ultrasound''s 'mothy flicker', for instance, is glimpsed 'an inner sprite'; a 'ghoul's skull, punched eyes / is tiny Hope's' (J 11). 'Solstice' is an intimate address to 'an unborn thou' in dainty limbo 'sleeping in a bone creel' (J 12); transfigured, in 'February', a 'heap of nappies / carried from the automatic' offers a heady wildness – 'hoisting the wash, / a rare flight of swans,' a rush of bracing possibilities, glimpsed in 'hills still courying snow' (J 14). In a similar vein, the baby's head in 'Sea Urchin' images a toughness and fragility of its watery double, emerging as 'tenderly . . . / freighted' 'drawn / treasure' 'from a rockpool' (J 17), as too, the poignant, pulsing being flickering to life in 'Prayer': 'a fluttering bird, held in cupped hands' (J 18), evoking a weight and sweetness of *felt grace*, a Heaney-esque felicity in a sudden yielding to the marvellous.

Birth's power is revealed in the striking simplicity and force of these domestic and natural analogies, figuring a beauty of imaged, sensed and spiritual genesis, linking a poet's and painter's eye for detail. They make vivid and immediate, but from a woman's experience, Heaney's 'glimpsed alternatives': that the ordinary and earthy is indeed freighted with 'treasures' – nappies, washing baskets, outhouses, pegs, creels, sea-urchins and rock-pools – as vessels of insight. Yet Jamie's innovations here also depend on a sparseness of effect, image and poetic metrical structure. Indeed, what is perhaps most striking about the Ultrasound sequence is its rejection of a Romantic, sentimental or folksy register, to evoke, yet refigure a much older tradition of early Gaelic, Irish and Scots poetry (with its linguistic richness and spiritual-nature complexities), finding echoes rather, as in 'Prayer', in early Irish nature poetry and its concentration of a spiritual potency of new awakening within the single nature motif (the blackbird) (J 18). This idea of 'invocation', a calling forth of a nature into being, is particularly notable in medieval Gaelic, Welsh and Irish 'praise poetry', with its use of startling juxtapositions of familiar images to stimulate unexpected insights of nature–spiritual connections. [3] Something of this comparable freshness of tone, close observation and immediacy of visual effect – as invoked, for example, in the early Gaelic Albanach's praise of his patron-lord, Crobhdherg:

His reign has put grain in the ground
brought blossoms through branches tips[4]

– is heard in the intimacy and deliberate archaism of 'Solstice''s first-person address to 'an unborn thou', called to

stars, milk-bottles, frost
on a broken outhouse roof

and to days 'opening / to admit a touch more light' (J 12). And it is in this deceptive simplicity of utterance and visual immediacy that Jamie's originality finds its force, harking back on the one hand to the complexities of medieval Celtic poetic inheritance, yet on the other, recreating it through startling shifts between apparently unredeemed banalities of life, birth and especially 'women's work' and their transformations as bearers of oblique supernatural states of connection and insight. Particularly effective in this respect are 'Barrel Annunciation' and 'The Tay Moses'. While 'The Barrel Annunciation' re-imagines humble domestic and loveless objects – the 'pail', 'blocked kitchen rhone', [water] 'butt', the 'dull coin' and 'barren at her cottage door' – as birthing vessels and mediums, freighted with a glimpsed power of miraculous potency sensed in the butt's 'plunging rain . . . / held in its deep hooped belly / and triggering' 'some arcane craft . . .' (J 9) – and its darker echo of the 'ducking stool'. In 'The Tay Moses', this agency and suggestive witchcraft of the bearing vessel is reversed. It is emptied in the poignant 'woven / creel of river – ', undone by its flow in a rush of loss:

when the water will birl you to snag
on reeds, [. . .]
'Name o God!' and you'll change hands (J 19)

Like Heaney's vessels, his schoolbag 'word-hoard' and 'handsel',[5] his 'tree-clock of tin cans / The tinkers made',[6] here, the power of Jamie's poetic craft lies in a similar juxtaposition of image as tool and insight to spark moments of unlooked-for poetic, emotional and spiritual growth, as does Heaney's 'tin-can' revelation: 'it took me until I was fifty to credit marvels'.[7] Yet there is also a difference in the force and agency by which in both 'The Barrel Annunciation' and 'The Tay Moses', the 'vessel' as bearer carries a density of word and sensory texture, intimately evocative of a physical and spiritual birthing. Jamie does this through heightening the register of birth's sensuous connections with woman's body in an embodied poetics of birth as experienced grace and pain; borne, abject, blessed: as bound up with the very textures and weight of being. This is birth, sensed and as metaphor in the 'water slopping from pails'; conjured/spun in the hoisted pail to the butt's 'oaken rim seven / or nine times in that spring storm;' felt in the engorged shape and unseen depths of the butt's 'hooped belly' (J 9). And, when the vessel is empty in 'The Tay Moses', it is experienced in a wrenching fullness of unexpected loss – like a salmon leap in 'that / slither of body as you were born' (J 19), as a movement of matter or an echo of a more ancient biblical flight, into a fuller connection of body and nature as vessel and process.

2   BEING AS LANDSCAPE

Both poems are striking for ways in which their birth themes are also suggestively interwoven with a poetics of landscape and the natural world as evocative of new states and tensions of being. In turn, these are mediated by the possibilities of a further re-patterning through language and 'birthright'. 'The Tay Moses' develops such associations in its series of connections and re-workings of the pain and pleni-tude of afterbirth's emotional turmoil through elemental forces of nature – 'tide and 'flow', 'ebb' and 'birl'; 'wisdom / and guts' – as both protectors and takers of life (J 19). At times, this nature imagery has a familiar, Romantic sound to it, the 'woven / creel of river- / rashes, a golden / oriole's nest' recalling such intimate yet intense earth-heavenly analogies as John Clare's 'thrush's nest', 'her shining eggs, as bright as flowers, / Ink-spotted over shells of greeny blue'.[8] Yet even here the arresting choice of species, not 'thrush', but 'golden oriole', captures a mood at once domesticated (in its nested presence) and rare; protecting and wild – in the oriole's bright passage: an exotic migrant to Tay shores – which is distinctively Jamie's voice. Such effects are intensified by the poem's sparing use of Scots words such as 'birl' (to spin) and vernacular cadences '"*Name o' god!*"', neither ornamental nor tokenistic, but which emblematise a double utterance, tracing in movement and cry the poem's conflict-ing impulses of renewal and flight.

In 'Thaw', the third of the Ultrasound sequence, the intertwining of birth and being as landscape is even more boldly drawn. Here, Jamie seems to borrow from a more pantheistic poetic tradition of nature as a source of spiritual solace, only to reinvent it by means of a lean, elemental counterpointing of land with altered states of being, perception and reconnection. The stress, therefore, is not so much on picture-making, picturesque localism or even on nature as myth-making, but on qualities and insights that harness domesticity and wildness; the unexpected and tamed; the unyielding and intimate in the poem's movement through the extended sixteen-line opening sentence, from nature into birth and *vice versa*, as a process of primal reconnection in a 'difficult giving' (J 13). That this 'difficult giving' is intimately bound up with a sense of place as an analogous, emerging condition of physical identity and of self, is intimated in a series of sharp contrasts: the seeming endlessness of the 'steel-grey thaw', the 'river sealed', counterpointing a wild sweetness of the newborn's return, glimpsed in familiar objects: 'a chop-ping block, the frost- / split lintels;' – and the yielding of obdurate winter weather, stone, hillside and water, to tender, homely things, 'the spiral / trunks of our plum trees, the moss, / the robin's roost in the holly'. 'Chopping-block[s]', 'lintels' and 'roost[s]' are plangent in making sensible rituals of remaking and crafting 'home'. Like Heaney's work-worn objects of field and hearth, the plough's 'sweat-cured haft',[9] 'unshowy pewter'[10]; the smoothing iron's 'compact wedge', riding 'the back of the stove / like a tug at anchor',[11] it is in a recurrence of the usual that Jamie, too, perceives a potency and depth of connected being and histories, as Heaney puts it, 'dragged upon / And buoyant':[12] as both rooted and luminously charged. Yet in Jamie's 'Thaw', such things of home have equal power as un-homely. They stand out as presences within an elemental landscape to which they relate and sugges-tively belong, as herms: boundaries – spirit guardians – as gate-keepers of wildness both within and outside. Indeed, the link is forcefully incarnated in the closing eight-line sequence's actual and emblematic birth into culture and 'nature'. Here, shadowing the conceit of the constellation as abstract 'birth' of poetic inspiration (traced in Ted Hughes's transferring imprints of star-animal to human),[13] Jamie's starry transposition reinvests the abstract figure and its occult gendering as 'mascu-line', as an agency of female creative becoming. Morphing, 'ablaze with concern', to the arcing glare of hospital theatre lights, Orion's trace thus reappears, sum-moned as if by some unseen force of supernatural midwifery to 'that difficult giving': a giving threaded to the transcendent in being hard-won from the unbounded pain of body and being (J 13).

If 'Tay Moses' and 'Thaw', in contrasting ways, are both about the power and celebration of birth to recharge and rediscover connections with landscapes of body, history and spirit, 'Hackit' explores the other view: of a state of being as a landscape – unlovely, gritty, alienated yet poignant. The very word is borrowed from vernacular Scots slang for 'ugly woman' – 'see her she was right "hackit"'. But its etymology, deriving from both the Old Norse and Old English 'hack' ('heck'), carries with it a rich and expressive force which yokes an immediacy of scored or pitted appearance with felt physical pain, in referring to jagged flesh cuts or deep gouges such as wreaked by grinding work or bitter weather. Equally, the poem unfolds 'hackit' as a powerful metaphor for the woman's plight as a migrant, bound up with larger disconnections: of dispossessed hope, country and a woman's states of being. These relationships of the near and distant, pain and poignancy, of plenitude and loss, are foregrounded in the poem's epigraph. Inspired by a woman's ruined face staring from a photograph of Scottish émigrés in the Museum of Sault Ste Marie, Ontario, the image triggers a deeper explora-tion of the condition of the Scots woman pioneer, one which disturbs the tem-poral, geographical and physical distance of the ethnographically constructed and controlling view:

For every acre cleared, a cairn's raised:
a woman staggering, stone
after stone in her hands. Desire's

wiped from her eyes,
who once touched to her face
all the linen a bride might need (J 33)

Again, Jamie's minimal landscape elements – 'acre cleared', 'cairn's raised' – evoke
no pleasingly rugged scene, no encounter with wilderness as mythic overcoming;
rather, they bring into sharp relief sites of struggle with identity, land and crafting
lives. Making a new beginning, the New World hope of the waves of Scots emigrants to Canada from the late eighteenth century – by far the largest of Scottish
transatlantic diasporas,[14] yet negotiating a connectedness of two cultural worlds – is
evoked here as an intensely difficult coming into being and habituation. What is
more, this image from a collective past, one fraught with narratives of severance,
disconnection and isolation, is brought painfully close and physically present
through Jamie's exploitation of the camera's power to 'frame' a viewpoint to tell a
larger story, conflating near and far in a focalised close-up on the woman's life. But
Jamie's innovation is also to turn the power of the lens from one of control to one of
exposure. Like the uncompromising bleakness which confronts us in Walker Evans's
photographs of the un-heroic face of 1930s American migrants, which is perhaps
at its starkest in 'Mrs Burroughs' Hale' (Hale County, Alabama: August 1936),[15] in
'Hackit' the camera-eye view becomes as if a silent witness to, and presence in, a
hidden language of suffering and isolation. It lays bare a woman's anonymous, back-
breaking toil as she staggers 'stone / after stone in her hands' (J 33), weighted with
her hack-bearing burdens, to the point where youthful hope and desire, tenderly
preserved in the touch of bridal linen, have become overwritten and effaced by the
landscapes of her exile. And the poem heightens this association – of ageing woman
and borrowed land – in a movement of both pain and potency, calling again to mind
Heaney's 'glimpsed alternative' of poetry's 'redressing' effects, of a re-directing of
truth,[16] in evoking the *hackit* woman's face suggestively unrecognisable as a hacked,
striated surface, yet as visible bearer and landscape of her unseen, voiceless history,
now revealed in the living eye, ear and imaginary of its beholder:

She stares from a door,
fingers splayed, face

Hackit
under the lace mutch
brought from her box. (J 33)[17]

In these very small, spare yet telling contrasts, a great deal is being said which cannot
be told by the poetic subject. Their power lies in the almost unbearable poignancy of
their oppositions: of roughened face and its dainty frame ('lace mutch'– headscarf);
obliterated identity and familiar accent; of harsh land and intimate touch, resonating in the final line's fragile valediction and blessing – 'the last herring, small as her
hand'. In this way, the poem exploits to brilliant effect a minimal poetics of the intimately personal, interweaving the remainders of a woman's life, her few, cherished

'mindings' (souvenirs), with a more overarching revelation of dispossessed women-folk, their youth and identity; of birthright, place and personhood.

But the poem's most striking innovations are arguably in the use it makes of the constraints of the villanelle verse form to make vivid these tensions, as well as its sparing use of Scots dialect words to complicate and enact, in a Rilkean sense,[18] the density of things, suggesting, too, many simultaneous meanings, visual, aural and tactile, which take the weight and *telling* of layered histories and lived experiences. Here, Jamie's economy of means is also distinctive. On one level, this exploita-tion of individual words and cadences of vernacular Scots to articulate patterns of connected worlds and stories across histories, lands and individualities hinted in the title-piece, 'Jizzen' (old Scots, meaning 'childbed'), links her in a movement extending from Hugh MacDiarmid's 'synthetic' Doric Scots[19] to Robert Garioch and Liz Lochead in the 1980s and 1990s in reconnecting with the energy and agency of 'native' voice, or as Douglas Dunn puts it, galvanising 'a language inter-rupted by history'.[20] On another, Jamie's sparing, often tongue-in-cheek Scots, as in 'Bairnsang' (Lullaby / Child's song) or 'Lucky Bag', is in no sense either overblown or overtly about myth-making through language – as it was for MacDiarmid, pow-erfully linked with political and mytho-poetic renewal of national Scots identity, incarnated at its satiric best in *A Drunk Man Looks at a Thistle*. Jamie instead exploits the potential of Scots dialect speech for its intimacy, revelling, as she insists, in 'the feel of it, the texture of it in my mouth,' using words as food for an insightful poetics of ordinariness.[21]

If 'Bairnsang''s play with 'mither' (mother) tongue in its crooning chains of affec-tionate Scots diminutives: 'Peedie wee lad / saumon, siller, haddie' (tiny little boy / salmon, silver, haddock), 'peeswheep an whaup' (lapwing and curlew), nods teasingly to the dialect/verbal colour and inventive excess so characteristic of MacDiarmid's early poetry, as in 'The Bonnie Broukit Bairn' (bonny neglected baby), it does so more self-consciously. It points less to a nation as world-vision invented and constructed through language, MacDiarmid's conceit of the earth as a 'bairn' that 'greets' (cries) to drown out a celestial 'wheen o' blethers' (pack of nonsense),[22] than to a multiple, oral play of both sense and nonsense with words as labile entry-points to other creative possibilities, implied in the nascent evolutions spun from sound of 'saumon / siller / haddie'/ . . . an greetna, girna, Gretna Green', of being, nature and place. Likewise, Jamie's use elsewhere of Scots dialect words – 'hackit', 'birl' (spin), 'coury' (hide, cower) 'shilpit' (puny, feeble) – suggest, rather than tokens of political or linguistic nativism, oblique points of linguistic difference and complexity. They make palpable an almost pre-linguistic urgency of need – the baby's basket, snagging and 'birling' in the Tay's current ('Tay Moses'); in 'Ultrasound', the tenderly tough 'shilpit' ghost; the endured ravages of 'Hackit'– and nuance many-layered agencies of being and transformations. And such transformations also acknowledge yet liber-ate the often oppressive, parochial realities carried by words so freighted as 'hackit' (the same may be said of 'dreich', 'glaikit' or 'thrawn': dreary, stupid, stubborn), pat-terning a manifold potential to belong to different linguistic realities, and layered, sometimes, alien worlds, to question an association of language with a mythic or univocal expression of being, identity or belonging.

3   BELONGING AND 'BIRTHRIGHT'

'Hackit''s complex strata of woman-being-exile-home, alienated voice and familiar accent bring us to significant ways in which *Jizzen*'s central dynamics of birth engage – through multiple registers of being, place and language – with broader re-encounters with 'foreign-ness' and 'belonging'. Birth acquires a multifarious intensity in *Jizzen* as a stimulus for a growth in personal perception and embodied insight, and as a dynamics that re-imagines borderlines and meanings of home and birthright. The theme, a recurrent preoccupation throughout the collection at a psychic, cultural, collective level, does not allow for what Heaney worries over in MacDiarmid's recidivism, namely its prey to a virulent 'nativism'.[23] Equally, Jamie resists a movement towards an over-determined mythic synthesis which makes personal birth, or its intimate interweaving with a renegotiating 'of our place in the natural world', a poetics of emblematic national re-birth in the year of Scotland's new parliament.[24] Instead, personal birth is rather that fulcrum – the tilting, 'redressing' point, which allows for larger processes of seeing and becoming, for experiencing a culture as much from outside as inside, situating politics, including of self, in a larger reproductive dynamics. It enables a glimpsed reconnection with land and cultures – often contested lands and cultures – as intimately threaded through a woman's experience, with fullness and loss; exile and rootedness, but not simply, as Jamie herself insists, to do with flags that proclaim 'Scottish' or 'Scottish woman poet'.[25]

In *Jizzen*, these ideas are manifest in two important ways. First is the collection's broader evoking and re-patterning of personal birth experience with what Dunn refers to as Scotland's 'tripled' inheritance – Gaelic, Scots and English – of cultural and linguistic crossings.[26] Second is Jamie's inflection of these broader possibilities and arguments about a unitary, 'national' identity and voice, with distinctive responses to the complexities of Scots inheritance and poetic experience, calling into question what 'home' may mean through, as she puts it, 'bringing a quality of attention to the world', exposing small shifts which startle larger patterns into visibility.[27] Interwoven with *Jizzen*'s explicit 'birth' poems, therefore, is another group. They include 'Crossing the Loch', 'The Green Woman', 'The Well at the Broch of Gurness', 'Lochan', 'Meadowsweet' and, in a different key, 'Pioneers', 'Suitcases' and 'Flower-Sellers – Budapest', in which birth becomes tributary to multiple narratives of belonging as much about fluid states of natural and cultural re-encounter, and their capacities to energise agency, as of rootedness in place or custom.

Again, Jamie does this by borrowing from and reinventing early Gaelic verse themes: the voyage, saint cults, nature as bounty, roost, loss and grief; exile and arrivals, using short-line metrical structures which evoke the spare yet intimate first-person dialogues of early Gaelic and Irish monastic poems, calling forth an immediacy of the natural world as a homing-point for a grace of spiritual belonging, such as delicately summoned here in the anonymous gloss: 'Ah blackbird, giving thanks / from your nest in the thorn'.[28] While in 'Crossing the Loch', ideas of the voyage, saints as fragile shelters of human hope alluded to in the 'astonished / small boat of saints,' connect with other emblematic arrivals and findings – 'a twittering nest / washed from the rushes', 'the magic dart of our bow wave' (J 1). In 'The Well at the

Broch of Gurness', the visitation to the emblematic well, rituals of croft and hearth, their burial and unearthing in the 'broch's rubble' (J 44), as connective tissues for alternative narratives of land and human making, recall George Mackay Brown's poetic crafting of local Orcadian rhythms as permeated by larger pulses of their history and its oracular potency. Jamie's approach to using archetypes to probe a more contemporary questioning of 'inheritance' is suggestively more expansive than Mackay Brown's, arguably less tradition-centred, referencing, in the case of both 'The Well' and 'Meadowsweet''s dirt-spewing *makar*, a questing akin to Lochhead's for 'another language'[29] – a redress of silenced voices of women's occulted presence as poets within a complex cultural matrix of Gaelic, bardic and Scots linguistic and cultural intersections.

But it is in the small group of poems about exile and disconnection that *Jizzen*'s poetics of belonging is perhaps most sharply focused. Two, 'Pioneers' and 'Suitcases', make this particularly vivid and forceful. In both, Jamie harnesses an ancient theme of journeying to states of modern disconnection. In both, there is a nod to Mackay Brown's and Ian Crichton Smith's preoccupations with exile. Yet Jamie's is not that great sweep of leave-takings and arrivals in the migratory, especially Highland Scots' imaginary, achingly caught in Crichton Smith's westward blent poets, birds and ships 'like handkerchiefs in our memories',[30] 'in stubbly autumn, of sharp absences';[31] or of being 'thirled' (bound), like Edwin Muir's 'Ancestral rite and custom, roof and tree',[32] to a 'mother' land, to which being and cognition is somehow conditioned and approximate. Rather, Jamie's innovation lies again, as in 'Hackit', in her uncompromising use of close-ups to intuit hidden narratives of severance or connection, and in, as she puts it, 'a quality of attention' she brings to encounters with lives individually or collectively sundered. And these are lives seen as much through small-scale detail as the bigger historical picture.

In 'Pioneers', once again, it is the camera's-eye view that captures and exposes the facticity of migration, yet pain of exile 'to show us these wagons and blurred dogs, / this pox of burnt stump-holes / in a clearing.' (J 34) Images are things seen and not seen, found and lost; the photograph is both a reliable and unreliable record. People have become as 'stump-holes', their remains 'now strewn across the small-town museums of Ontario' ('Pioneers'). Belonging-exile may mean similar things – 'the axe and plough, the grindstone'– speak of home unmade, as does the last line's stopped knell: 'the wife by the cabin door / dead, and another sent for.' 'Suitcases' further pro-longs these home-foreign reversals as constant states of flux, although the mood is less bleak than 'Pioneers'. Here objects, suitcases, become emblematic 'migrants', vessels of transition, but in the opening line, appear freeze-framed as still lives,

> Piled high in a corner of a second-hand store
> in Toronto [. . .]
>
> all you can take is what you carry
> when you run: a photo, some clothes,
> and the useless dead-weight
>
> of your mother tongue. (J 35)

What may betoken the lure of arrivals, departures, beginnings, is not as it seems. Again, it is through a visual immediacy of apprehension, the suitcases 'piled high', in the close-up view, that the poem exposes the hidden telling, as does the jolting last-line enjambment of the second tercet, dragging out the rhyme of revealed disconnection in 'the dead weight / of your mother tongue'. Exile, here, suggestively pictured in its associated 'baggage' of the young migrant woman's experience, implies – rather than a new start – a fresh accent, a provisional condition, a seeking between cultures (and languages) at a tilting point where a different act of return becomes possible. The 'suitcases' are props, freights and bearers of fragile worlds. Their exteriors may be worn carapaces, protective armouries – 'One was repaired / with electrician's tape' – but their contents disclose an inner yielding, 'like an invitation', prurient and vulnerable, exposed and full:

> the shell-pink lining, the knicker-
> like pockets you hook back
> with a finger (J 35)

The force of these lines is in what is not only seen, but sensed, in micro-movements that finger 'an invitation' and a grace withheld, 'the shell-pink lining' of other possible beginnings and findings or retrievals. The suitcases may hold 'wraith[s] / of stale air', ghosts of other stories. But they are also evocative vessels in partum, padded with a delicate weight, made palpable in the concealing and nascent revelation of the closing departure, 'bored, and already pregnant'. Homing is thus a suggestive departure; what is lost may become another belonging. In 'Flower-Sellers', the old women in Budapest sell exotic flowers at the nodal crossroads of transit in a city in two parts, yet conjoined, in 'bus depots, termini' (J 26) that they may return home. Similarly, in 'Suitcases', as in 'Hackit', it is women who are pivot points for broader tensions of disconnection and belonging, women who do ordinary things: wear 'mutches', sell flowers, carry stones, pack suitcases, but with these, craft plangent connections in keepsakes, linen, linings, as bearers of salutations and farewells. In short, they are reminders that severance may also mean a poignant plenitude, an intuiting in what is borne or relinquished – be it cameras, photographs, suitcases, hacks or belongings – the potential to conceive home.

Both 'Pioneers' and 'Suitcases' highlight *Jizzen* as a collection which derives its distinctive force of utterance from its many-nuanced connections between birth as a subjective evolution and as a broader initiation. That initiation is bound up with a multi-faceted complexity of linguistic and cultural belonging which cleaves to no easy homogeneous cultural cliché or myth of Scottish identity, land, 'nativism' of self or language or custom. Indeed, to develop Dunn's perspectives, Jamie's innovations in *Jizzen* are arguably to be found in these perceptions: in suggestive ways in which she bypasses foregrounding a specific concern with Scottish subjects or a 'Scotch self' as requisites for poetry with claims to speak with cultural 'legitimacy' of country, birthright or nation.[33] Yet Jamie's innovations are arguably more precise and far-reaching in their implications. *Jizzen*'s idea of birth as a dynamics of provisional being and becoming patterns broader insights into women's physical, psychological and plural poetic experiences and expressions of contingency. Birth is thus suggestive of a more complex engagement with ways of being and belonging, with contradictory, *chiaroscuro* states of self and culture – not necessarily rooted, stable or 'homely', but to do with negotiations between agency and loss, homing and exile, and intuiting different, inclusive acts of reconnection. In sum, in *Jizzen*'s 'glimpsed alternatives' are both a gravity and grace of self and cultural redress. This is a gravity of connectedness generated by birth, yet through it, a grace of possible new centring in the rescuing of belonging and land from cliché, and in the rich textures, materials and sublimated voices, making the very weft of what becomes cultural being.

WORKS CITED (SEE ALSO BIBLIOGRAPHY)

Clare, John, *'I am': The Selected Poetry of John Clare*, ed. Jonathan Bate (London: Farrar, Strauss and Giroux, 2003).
Crighton Smith, Ian, *The Exiles* (Manchester and Dublin: Carcanet Press, 1984).
Dunn, Douglas, 'Language and Liberty', in Dunn (ed.), *The Faber Book of Twentieth-Century Scottish Poetry* (London: Faber and Faber, 1992), pp. xvii–xlvi.
Harper, Mary, 'Enticing the emigrant: Canadian agents in Ireland and Scotland, c.1870– c.1920', *Scottish Historical Review* LXXXIII, 1: 215, 2004, pp. 41–58.
Heaney, Seamus, *Station Island* (London: Faber and Faber, 1984).
Heaney, Seamus, *Seeing Things* (London: Faber and Faber, 1992).
Heaney, Seamus, *The Redress of Poetry: Oxford Lectures* (London: Faber and Faber, 1995).
Hughes, Ted, *New Selected Poems: 1957–1994* (London: Faber and Faber, 1995).
Kinsella, Thomas (ed.), *The New Oxford Book of Irish Verse* (Oxford: Oxford University Press, 1989).
Lochhead, Liz, *Dreaming Frankenstein & Collected Poems* (Edinburgh: Polygon, 1985).
MacDiarmid, Hugh, *Complete Poems: 1920–1976*, ed. M. Grieve and W. R. Aitken, 2 vols (London: Martin, Brian & O'Keefe, 1978).
Mackay Brown, George, *The Wreck of the Archangel: Poems* (London: John Murray, 1989).
Muir, Edwin, *Collected Poems* (London: Faber and Faber, 1960).
Owen Clancy, Thomas (ed.), *The Triumph Tree: Scotland's Earliest Poetry, ad 550–1350* (Edinburgh: Canongate, 1998).
Rilke, Rainer Maria, *Rainer Maria Rilke: Selected Poems*, tr. Susan Ranson and Marielle Sutherland, ed. Robert Vilain (Oxford: Oxford University Press, 2011).
Weil, Simone, *Gravity and Grace*, tr. E. Craufurd (London: Routledge, 1963).

NOTES

1. Weil, *Gravity and Grace*, p. 151.
2. Heaney, *The Redress of Poetry: Oxford Lectures*, p. 5.
3. See Owen Clancy, *The Triumph Tree*, pp. 25–7.
4. Ibid., p. 25.
5. Heaney, 'The School Bag', *Seeing Things*, p. 30.
6. Heaney, 'Fosterlings', *Seeing Things*, p. 50.
7. Ibid., p. 50.
8. John Clare, 'The Thrush's Nest' (1832), in *'I am'*.
9. Heaney, 'Iron Spike', *Station Island*, p. 24.

10. Heaney, 'Old Pewter', *Station Island*, p. 22.
11. Heaney, 'Old Smoothing Iron', *Station Island*, p. 21.
12. Ibid., p. 23.
13. Hughes, 'The Thought Fox', in *New Selected Poems: 1957–1994*, p. 1.
14. Principally from the Highlands, although by the mid-nineteenth century, this exodus had become associated by migrants and commentators with a highly contentious politics of landlord clearances and 'enforced exile': on this and associated nineteenth- and twentieth-century resettlement, see, for example, Harper, 'Enticing the emigrant'.
15. In the collection of the Walker Evans Archive, Metropolitan Museum of Art, New York.
16. And, glossing Jorge Luis Borges, in a 'continual need we experience to "recover a past or prefigure a future"': Heaney, *The Redress of Poetry*, p. 8.
17. Cf. also in 'Song of Sunday', the yoking of 'women's lot' with an unredeemed banality of 'tatties [potatoes] / peeled lovelessly, blinded / pale and drowned' (*Jizzen*, p. 31).
18. Notably in Rilke's 'thing-poems': see, for example, Robert Vilain's comments on Rilke's poetic 'objects' and their perceiving subjects, a relationship, Vilain argues, 'that releases the inner dynamics of both' (R. Vilain, in Rilke, *Rainer Maria Rilke: Selected Poems*, p. xxi).
19. From 1707 onwards, denoting peasant or rural speech, but in MacDiarmid's modernist usage, hybridised as a synthetic composite of Lowlands ('Lallands'), Dumfries, Perthshire and Aberdonian ('Doric') dialects as a tool for what, in Heaney's view, becomes at worst 'a kind of vindictive nativism' (Heaney, *The Redress of Poetry*, p. 119).
20. Of MacDiarmid: Dunn, 'Language and Liberty', p. xx.
21. Scott interview, 'In the nature of things'.
22. MacDiarmid, *Complete Poems: 1920–1976*, vol. 1, p. 17.
23. Heaney, *The Redress of Poetry*, p. 119.
24. Crown interview, 'Kathleen Jamie: A Life in Writing'.
25. Scott interview with Jamie, 'In the nature of things'; see also Crown interview, 'Kathleen Jamie: A Life in Writing'.
26. Dunn, 'Language and Liberty', p. xxvii.
27. Scott interview, 'In the nature of things'.
28. Anonymous, tenth-century Irish, in *The New Oxford Book of Irish Verse*, p. 55.
29. 'another language. / last week on Lewis', Lochhead, 'Inner', in *Dreaming Frankenstein & Collected Poems*, pp. 112–13.
30. Crichton Smith, 'The Exiles', *The Exiles*, p. 13.
31. Crichton Smith, 'Always', *The Exiles*, p. 15.
32. Muir, 'The Difficult Land', in Dunn, *The Faber Book of Twentieth-Century Scottish Poetry*, pp. 31–2.
33. Dunn, 'Language and Liberty', p. xlv.

Even If

It had poured and was still raining
in Lady Katharine's Wood.
Late evening and the days were waning.
Matting protected fresh growth underfoot.

Umbrella furled, I trod carefully,
intent on the path's end and a signal
to bleep back to my blocked BlackBerry,
when trees relayed a sound – half rustle,

half like a woman clearing her throat,
aware that speech meant risk.
I stepped on a twig, then stopped again,

edgy, keen to pick up any new note
– a fox or deer, say, hurrying through the dusk –
even if it seemed I only heard the rain.

Michael O'Neill

8. 'The Tilt from One Parish to Another': *The Tree House* and *Findings*

Peter Mackay

Since Kathleen Jamie started writing 'toward' or 'within' nature',[1] listening and attentiveness have been central to her aesthetic. Discussing her 2005 essays, *Findings*, Jamie states that 'Poets use language as a form of "seeing". More and more . . . I think the job is to listen, to pay attention.'[2] Certainly, in *Findings*, receptiveness is all; Jamie counsels herself:

> Sometimes we have to hush the frantic inner voice that says 'Don't be stupid,' and learn again to look, to listen. You can do the organising and redrafting, the diagnosing and identifying later, but right now, just be open to it, see how it's tilting nervously into the wind, try to see the colour, the unchancy shape – hold it in your head, bring it home intact (F 42).[3]

This receptiveness is as much linguistic and literary in Jamie's work as it is natural. In this passage, two of Jamie's characteristic formulations for the natural world appear: the Scots adjective 'unchancy' – meaning unlucky, ill-omened or dangerous – and the verb 'tilt'. 'Tilt' is a word Jamie has brought home intact, from an act of listening in to the language of J. A. Baker, the author of the 1967 book *The Peregrine*, which Jamie quotes in *Findings*: 'Baker writes, "The peregrine lives in a pouring-away world of no attachment, a world of wakes and tilting, of sinking planes of land and water." I could envy that, sometimes.' (F 36) Jamie's envy ambiguously encompasses both the falcon's experience of swoops and falls and also the way Baker eloquently creates – in his rhythms and syntax, his clauses and assonance – a correlative for the falcon's flight, for its world of 'tilting', the world in which it is perilously off-kilter. Baker's work introduces a question central to *Findings* and to Jamie's 2004 collection *The Tree House*: how humans engage with the rest of the natural world through language – especially the structured, rhythmic language of lyric poetry or poetic prose – and also the corollary, why we do this. Discussing *The Peregrine*, Jamie introduces what she calls 'the' paradox:

> here is a person who would annihilate himself and renounce his fellows, who would enter into the world of birds and woods and sky, but then in an act of

consummate communication to his human kind, step back into language and write a book still spoken of forty years on (*F* 43).

For writing to face up to the challenge of the paradox, that is, it has to live up to the sense of 'consummate communication', while also recognising the annihilation of the self, enacting a dynamic dialectic between resistance to and immersion in Nature. Though this is not the paradox of Jamie's own work – she approaches communication first and foremost as a writer, after all, not as an ornithologist – I am going to explore ways in which *Findings* and *The Tree House* do balance communication and annihilation or resistance and immersion, in the context of other recent writing about, towards or within nature.

For the trope of listening in, or being attentive to the world, and in particular to messages that are ungraspable and incommunicable – what is 'in the offing', in Seamus Heaney's phrase[4] – is common to much 'nature' writing. Rachel Carson, for example, whose *Silent Spring* (1962) was seminal in contemporary ecology, suggested in *The Edge of the Sea* (1956) that in '[c]ontemplating the teeming life of the shore, we have an uneasy sense of the communication of some universal truth that lies just beyond our grasp.'[5] Robert Macfarlane, meanwhile, in *The Wild Places* (2007), is overwhelmed in his search for wildness on the Isle of Skye by a sublime he cannot control:

> Suddenly I felt precarious, frightened: balanced on an edge of time as well as of space. All I wanted to do was get back off the ridge, back down into the Basin . . . Where had that sudden fear come from? It had been more than a feeling of physical vulnerability, more than a vertiginous rush – though that had been part of it. A kind of wildness, for sure, but a fierce, chaotic, chastening kind: quite different from the wildness, close to beauty, of Enlli.[6]

For both Carson and Macfarlane the natural world offers – in a manner reminiscent of Romantic writing – a sublime with religious overtones, or at least overtones of 'universal truth'; the writer is cast in the role of the young boat-stealing Wordsworth, who gains 'a dim and undetermined sense / Of unknown modes of being', and of 'huge and mighty forms that do not live / Like living men.'[7]

Such writing raises the question of what it is we listen in to when we 'listen in'; however, while Carson and MacIntyre reach for an unknowable truth or a 'fierce discovered wildness' – a God-in-the-Wilderness, as it were – Jamie seems to care less for result than for process. Her focus on attentiveness leads us back to Nicolas Malebranche's dictum, beloved of Simone Weil and Paul Celan, that 'attentiveness is the prayer of the soul'; certainly, in a 2002 diary entry for the *London Review of Books*, Jamie identifies her attitude with a form of prayer:

> I don't believe in God. I believe in spiders, alveoli, starlings . . . I might suggest that prayer-in-the-world isn't supplication, but the quality of attention we can bring to a task, the intensity of listening, through the instruments we have designed for the purpose. It might be the outermost reaches of the Universe,

the innermost changes at the bottom of a lung, the words on a page, or a smear of blood on a slide. I think it's about repairing and maintaining the web of our noticing, a way of being in the world. Or is that worship?[8]

Rather than 'prayer', directed at a God-in-nature, we have a 'prayer-in-the-world', in which the act is more important than the object. One is reminded of Elizabeth Bishop's comment to Richard Wilbur about organised religion: 'You really don't believe all that stuff. You're just like me. Neither of us has any philosophy. It's all description, no philosophy'.[9] As with John Burnside's notion of a 'secular / agnostic sacrality', it is the manner of the action that is important, rather than an abstract object to the action.[10] Rather than a 'theory of the "sacred"'[11], that is, what we find in Jamie's work is an ethos of respect. As Jamie suggests in a 2001 interview with Dósa, the quality of the language you use to represent the world is as much a matter of respect as of accuracy, *quidditas* or *haecceity*:

> You take notes almost like a naturalist who observes something, whether it is a flower or a street scene. It is not out of curiosity, but you almost respect what you are observing. You want to have what you observe accurately in its beauty and detail, and so it is almost like a mark of respect for it.[12]

And for Jamie, the purpose of this respect is mediation, communication – she claims that 'the role of the poet is not to be political but shamanic (it's the only word I can think of), mediating between various worlds and bringing messages back and forth between them'.[13] The question arises, however, how such mediation – respect for the world expressed through language – works, especially if it cannot be character-ised as the revelation of the divine, a God in the landscape. Within ecopoetics the relationship between language, humanity and the natural world is one commonly founded, as in the work of Jonathan Bate, on a Heideggerian notion of dwelling in the world. In *The Song of the Earth* (2000), Bate recommends Henry David Thoreau's notion of 'living deliberately', living 'with thoughtfulness and with an attentiveness, an attunement to both words and the world, and so to acknowledge that, although we make sense of things by way of words, we do not live apart from the world'.[14] And, drawing on the work of Heidegger and Ricoeur, Bate stresses the value of writing as a way of experiencing the world. Bate agrees with Ricoeur that in literary discourse we discover 'a "project", that is the outline of a new way of being in the world', and resolves an apparent disjunction in Ricoeur's work between world and word by con-flating the two to claim 'our world, our home, is not earth but language.'[15] Bate thus develops a view that poetry has a special status, distinct from science, and superior to it; he argues that '[w]hereas the biologist, the geographer and the Green activist have *narratives* of dwelling, a poem may be a *revelation* of dwelling'[16]; it may be, as in the resonant title of his book, the 'song of the earth'.

   This chimes in part with Jamie's poetic 'project'. In an interview in the *Scottish Review of Books* in 2012, Jamie spoke in terms very much in the Bate–Heidegger tradition, when she suggested that

I used to believe that language was what got in the way, and that if only we could stop thinking in language we'd have more direct access to the world, to the extent I could jump out of bed and go outdoors without getting my head into gear. But now I think that's rubbish. I've learned now through reading that language is what we do as human beings, that's where we're at home, that's our means of negotiating with the world. So it doesn't get in the way, it enables. We do language like spiders do webs.[17]

This attitude had been presaged earlier, however, in *The Tree House*, but in terms – I would argue – that are much more tentative, much less certain that 'we're at home in language'. 'The Bower', for example, is an attempt to relate a 'dwelling' in the natural world to the 'dwelling' possible in the structured rhythmic frameworks of poetry; the poem itself is a bower recreated in language, just as Baker's prose had tried to recreate the movement of the peregrine falcon. The poem is one of relatively few in *The Tree House* to use a consistent – if loose – rhyme scheme; making use of both assonance and consonance, it appears to construct a poetic structure equivalent to the bower it describes – interlinking yet loose-limbed. The poem brings together notions of speech, imaginative construction and dwelling: the bower is a 'forest dwelling', which is 'nothing / but an attitude of mind'; it is an 'anchorage / or musical box' and 'listing deep / in the entailed estate' it is 'sure only of its need / to enunciate' (*TH* 17). The poem is an evocation of dwelling in language as much as in nature: language as the means by which we dwell in the world, as our being-in-the-world. However, the poem does not end on the idea of 'enunciation' but on an image of communication as an uncertain give-and-take which is unpunctuated, open-ended, ongoing:

> But when song, cast
> from such frail enclaves
> meets the forest's edge,
> it returns in waves

The 'forest dwelling' becomes a 'frail enclave', made frail by the act of singing and the return of the song, by language rebounding off its own limits (as off the forest's edge): the notion of dwelling itself is undermined by the returning song.

More generally, however, the concept of 'dwelling' is made more complicated by much of Jamie's work. She is a writer, after all, who has spent a great deal of time deliberately avoiding the 'constrictions of home',[18] focusing on travelling, passing through and being contingent rather than on dwelling; and there is an element of Jamie's attention that is repeatedly drawn beyond the limits of human knowledge, beyond the limits of attentiveness, into death and absence, into a realm that is 'unchancy'. And because of the 'unchanciness' of the realm into which Jamie listens, I would argue that one of Heidegger's followers and critics, Emmanuel Levinas, provides in many ways a more fruitful approach to her work.

Levinas developed an ethics founded on being-in-the-world and on 'respect' for the other, but which recognised the limits of knowledge, the uneasiness of being. Although for Levinas the 'Other' was identifiable with God, here I will use his concept of the 'Other' more generally – stripped of its divinity and possible to be mapped onto other human beings as well as the unknowable in the natural world. For Levinas, 'responsibility for the Other' is what gives one 'the idea of the Infinite',[19] and for him an ethical position is an understanding and acceptance that the other 'is not unknown, but unknowable, refractory to all light'.[20] The language of light and dark is important: Levinas also opposes the Heideggerian notion of *Dasein* as the 'horror of the night' or of death: instead Levinas proposes a being-towards-death that is positive, that is a 'horror of immortality, perpetuity of the drama of existence, necessity of the *there* is', a being-towards-death that is, in effect, a 'horror of being'.[21] This is a position, however, which does not lend itself in any simple way to comfortable dwelling:

> The relationship with the other is not an idyllic and harmonious relationship of communion, or a sympathy through which we put ourselves in the other's place; we recognise the other as resembling us, but exterior to us; the relationship with the other is a relationship with a Mystery. The other's entire being is constituted by its exteriority, or rather its alterity, for exteriority is a property of space and leads the subject back to itself through light.[22]

The crucial element of this relationship with the other is an 'erotic', face-to-face seeking based not on knowledge, but on the 'caress',[23] a 'face-to-face without intermediary'[24] that is a fundamental, essential 'disorder' which is born not out of 'communion' but of 'collectivity'. There are two elements of Levinas's work, in particular, that help illuminate Jamie's: the attitude towards death and mortality figured as the 'being-towards-death', and the notion of collectivity rather than communion – the necessary stymieing of any attempt to know the 'other' and an ethics then founded on an understanding that the 'other' or others are inherently unknowable.

Mortality is a key element to Jamie's listening in to the natural world. This is not to say that she attends to the way, in Julia Kristeva's words, in which language 'is at the service of the death drive'[25]; rather, it is simply that her work engages in a steadfast focus on mortality as something that binds us to the rest of existence. She has affirmed that she doesn't 'recognise the idea of "the outdoors", or of "nature". We are "nature", in our anatomy and mortality';[26] in 2012, she also emphasised that 'I don't know about you, but I don't want to live forever, and I don't want my children to live forever. I can accept my mortality, it's what we are, we're mortal creatures'.[27] An approach towards mortality manifests itself in different forms in Jamie's work, from the clear-eyed examination of disease and histiology in *Findings*, to the throwaway reference to 'bletted fruit' (fruit that has gone through a process after ripening) in the title poem of *The Tree House*, or indeed the depiction in that poem of a life after all our choices have been made, as symbolised by the sandbanks on the Tay: 'the *Reckit Lady*, the *Shair as Death*' (TH 41). This attention to mortality also underpins her use of two words I picked out earlier – 'tilting' and 'unchancy' – as the world begins to tilt vertiginously toward the unknowable, unchancy and deathly. In 'Landfall', for example, the poet is walking, being attentive, and becomes off balance. Listening in, being attentive to the natural world leads to vertigo and a sense of death and otherness; poetry of the ear becomes poetry of inner-ear imbalance. In the poem, a swallow 'veers', but the poem itself tilts, taking us towards an apprehension of gravity and our own deaths, the mortality and worked-upon-ness we share with the rest of the natural world, towards the question, 'can we allow ourselves to fail'? This is open-ended: like 'The Bower', the poem ends unpunctuated. At some point, inevitably, we will fail; in the meantime, however, we 'veer', towards (and away from) death. The important thing here is that this is not simply mimetic or 'pure' description, or the 'irrelevant descriptions of nature' that Yeats condemned in Victorian poetry. Rather, this is description pointed towards death; and the aware-ness of mortality, the listening in to the abyss, disturbs the form of mediation the poet can undertake. If there is any form of communication – or communion – taking place between the swallow and the poet in 'Landfall', it is – whether consummate or not – definitely unchancy, tilting.

This unsettling is reminiscent of that experienced in Seamus Heaney's 'Field of Vision', where the metaphor of looking over a 'well-braced gate' to 'discover that the field behind the hedge / Grew more distinctly strange as you kept standing / Focused and drawn in by what barred the way' is used to mark the distance between the speaker and an old woman.[28] Heaney's poetry seems to hover behind much of Jamie's writing about nature in images of the poet as 'an ear to the line',[29] for example, or of standing 'still. You can hear / everything going on' in 'The Loaning'.[30] However, there is a political (rather than ecopolitical) dimension – and a sense of political risk – to much of Heaney's 'listening' that is not present in Jamie's. In 'The Loaning', for example, the poem shifts to the image of Dante snapping a twig and a voice sighing 'out of the blood', and then to an abstracted image of an interrogator in a cell (a quite different form of listening, or surveillance, has been going on). The image of Dante in Heaney's poem, in turn, takes the reader to Osip Mandelstam's response to Dante in a poem from his third Voronezh notebook. Here, listening is intoxication, and the effect of listening is to disturb and disorder the locations of political power (the 'jagged' palaces):

I hear, I hear the first ice
rustling under the bridges,
and I think of drunkenness swimming
radiant about our heads.[31]

Although listening in Jamie's poetry does not have oppressive cold-war or Stalin-era resonance, it is clearly not a straightforward or entirely successful form of mediation. Twice in *The Tree House* Jamie creates explicit images of stunted communication, one playful (while still tinged with a sense of death and mortality), one less so. 'The Buddleia' makes use of a mundane everyday setting to break any notion of communion. The consideration of 'a god' is disturbed by the speaker's 'suddenly / elderly parents, their broken-down / Hoover; or my quarrelling kids'; on another level the pantheistic appreciation of nature is disturbed – light-heartedly – both by these generational family relationships and by the unshakeable father-figure of

Christianity, the 'masculine / God of my youth' (*TH* 27). This is an engagement with (and as part of) the natural world which, *à la* Levinas, refuses communion (and communication) – the speaker ends with a memory of 'my father . . . whom, Christ, / I've forgotten to call'. There is also another miscommunication here: the title 'Buddleia' seems to be taking us towards Buddhism, and its difference from Christianity – whereas in fact it brings us to the botanist Adam Buddle, after whom the plant was named.[32]

The second image of stunted communication is more direct. The final poem in *The Tree House*, 'The Dipper', provides a symbol for the unknowable 'otherness' of the natural world, of our inability to communicate with birds. The bird is described as wringing 'from its own throat / supple, undammable song' in an act that alienates it from the speaker of the poem: 'It isn't mine to give. / I can't coax this bird to my hand / that knows the depth of the river / yet sings of it on land.' (*TH* 49) The poem denies the ability to evoke the process of carrying between realms and elements, the 'shamanic' process Jamie had identified as central to her poetry. The poem asserts our inability to commune, to be a community with nature; what we are left with is an ongoing mortal collectivity, an unstable, disordered engagement with creatures who we cannot fully know, no matter how walking-pace, how pedestrian our view.

There appears to be a sleight of hand here, however, which brings us closer to Bate's view of poetry as a way of engaging with the natural world. In denying one form of communion and communication, Jamie seems to offer up another: the description and the symbol of the 'dipper', brought home intact, perfected for us – in regular rhyme – to function as some kind of 'catharsis or consolation' (in Matt McGuire's words).[33] Is the way she figures the unknowability of the dipper's song not another example of our dwelling in the world being done through the creation of poetic symbols, poetic difference? A suggestion, in other words, that poetry can create a form of communion, dwelling or knowing while it denies the possibility of other forms of 'knowledge' of the natural world? Not necessarily. Rather, I would suggest that 'The Dipper' offers a deliberate challenge to the reader's own ability to listen in, to be attentive to literature as well as to the natural world. For if the poem is read in the light of the opening poem in the collection, the reader's approach is destabilised and ironised. 'The Wishing Tree' is as much a disavowal of literary expectations as an engagement with the natural: it stands

neither in the wilderness
nor fairyland

but in the fold
of a green hill

the tilt from one parish
into another. (*TH* 3)

The tree survives despite the physical intrusion of human longing, the coins wishfully pushed into its bark: despite this, it is 'still alive – / in fact, in bud' (*TH* 4). The tree resists the process of symbolising. It stands, but does not stand *for*; it is not a symbol or metaphor for some mystical fairyland or sublimated 'wilderness'. In fact its existence is threatened by the process of symbolising, of giving symbolic meaning – by the coins pushed hopefully into it (the small change: the 'fleur-de-lys' and 'enthroned Britannia') to represent wishes. Though the tree is the repository of human hopes – 'the common currency of longing' – it does not belong to any single human group or community: rather, it is on the 'tilt from one parish / into another', it is unsettling, vertiginous, taking it out of ourselves.

And yet, the image at the end of the poem – the tree being 'still alive – / in fact, in bud' – is the creation of another type of 'human hope', another creation of the 'common currency of longing'. So too are the poem, the collection as a whole, and the whole notion of listening in and attentiveness to the natural world, the idea of the 'prayer-in-the-world': all are born from the 'common currency of human longing'. Writing poems 'toward' nature itself is, in effect, the act of pushing coins into the bark, of pushing human 'hope' onto the natural world – and with as little hope of acting upon, knowing or truly mediating the natural world. And the more one listens in to the poems, and the more attentive one is to the poems, the less knowable they will necessarily become. We are once more in a process of infinite regress, in which knowledge is always at one step removed. This is not poetry as the song of the earth, or of a revelation of dwelling, but as a stymieing and troubling of communication. Contemporary poetry is often an art of non-communication, a resistance, a making strange: what we have in *The Tree House* is a consummate communication of this non-communion, a tilting of the world in all its unchanciness.

WORKS CITED (SEE ALSO BIBLIOGRAPHY)

Burnside, John, and Maurice Riordan (eds), *Wild Reckoning* (London: Calouste Gulbenkian, 2003).
Farley, Paul, and Michael Symmons Roberts (eds), *Edgelands: Journeys into England's True Wilderness* (London: Vintage, 2012).
Fazzini, Marco, 'Kenneth White and John Burnside', in Matt McGuire and Colin Nicholson (eds), *The Edinburgh Companion to Contemporary Scottish Poetry* (Edinburgh: Edinburgh University Press, 2009), pp. 111–25.
Heaney, Seamus, *Field Work* (London, Faber, 1979).
Heaney, Seamus, *Station Island* (London: Faber, 1984).
Heaney, Seamus, *Seeing Things* (London: Faber, 1991).
Heaney, Seamus, *Stations* (Belfast: Ulsterman, 1975).
Kristeva, Julia, 'Revolution in Poetic Language' in Toril Moi (ed.), *The Kristeva Reader* (New York: Columbia University Press, 1986), pp. 89–136.
Levinas, Emmanuel, *The Levinas Reader*, ed. Seán Hand (London: Blackwell, 1989).
Mandelstam, Osip, *The Selected Poems of Osip Mandelstam*, tr. Clarence Brown and W. S. Merwin (New York: NYRB Classics, 2004).
Spiegelman, Willard, *How Poets See the World: The Art of Description in Contemporary Poetry* (Oxford: Oxford University Press, 2005).
Wordsworth, William, *The Prelude: The Four Texts (1798, 1799, 1805, 1850)*, ed. Jonathan Wordsworth (London: Penguin, 1995).

NOTES

1. Jamie, 'Author Statement,' British Council website.
2. Scott interview, 'In the nature of things'.
3. There is a similar injunction in Jamie's 2012 essay collection, *Sightlines*: 'It was probably nothing, so I said nothing, but kept looking. That's what the keen-eyed naturalists say. Keep looking. Keep looking, even when there's nothing much to see. That way your eye learns what's common, so when the uncommon appears, your eye will tell you' (p. 82).
4. Heaney, *Seeing Things*, p. 108.
5. Rachel Carson, *The Edge of the Sea* (1956), quoted in Burnside and Riordan, *Wild Reckoning*, p. 5.
6. Macfarlane, *Wild Places*, pp. 56–7.
7. Wordsworth, *Prelude*, 1799 Prelude, II: 121–8.
8. Jamie, 'Counting the Cobwebs', p. 39.
9. Quoted in Spiegelman, *How Poets See the World*, p. 3.
10. 'John Burnside in Conversation with Marco Fazzini', *Il Tolomeo* 1 (8) (2008), p. 95, quoted in Fazzini, 'Kenneth White and John Burnside', p. 120.
11. Gairn, *Ecology and Modern Scottish Literature*, p. 158.
12. Dósa interview, 'Kathleen Jamie', in *Beyond Identity*, p. 137.
13. Ibid., p. 142.
14. Bate, *Song of the Earth*, p. 23.
15. Ibid., p. 251.
16. Ibid., p. 266. Italics in original.
17. Goring interview, 'Kathleen Jamie: The SRB Interview' (2012).
18. Cf. Gairn, *Ecology and Modern Scottish Literature*, p. 168.
19. Levinas, *Levinas Reader*, p. 5.
20. Ibid., p. 43.
21. Ibid., p. 34.
22. Ibid., p. 43.
23. Ibid., p. 51.
24. Ibid., p. 54.
25. Kristeva, 'Revolution in Poetic Language', p. 119.
26. Scott interview, 'In the nature of things'.
27. Goring interview, 'Kathleen Jamie: The SRB Interview'.
28. Heaney, *Seeing Things*, p. 22.
29. Heaney, *Field Work*, p. 36.
30. Heaney, *Station Island*, p. 52.
31. Mandelstam, *Selected Poems*, pp. 89–90.
32. Farley and Symmons Roberts, *Edgelands*, p. 137.
33. McGuire, 'Kathleen Jamie', p. 148.

9. Repetition, Return and the Negotiation of Place in *The Tree House*

Lynn Davidson

The Tree House asks how we can live more interactively and less destructively with nature. It explores the concept of place with its confluence of political, historical, communal and familial elements, and raises questions around the mythologising and division of land. My interest is in how Jamie employs poetic technique to demonstrate new ways of thinking about place: specifically, her use of intertextual repetends and how these repetitions negotiate between a connection to place and the need to advance our stories of belonging.

Jamie chooses particularly resonant words to repeat – among others: 'unfold', 'rim' and 'light'. These repeated words prompt the reader to 'hear' how there is a variation of meaning, connotation and evocation with each new placement. Meaning broadens and shifts as the repeated word or words interact with, and are infused by, their new context. These shifts in meaning and resonance allow the poems to ask, in a variety of settings, if and how human-made templates of ownership and mythology are relevant in a contemporary, environmentally compromised world. *The Tree House* foregrounds the fluid and unfinished act of poetic making as enactment of and attention to a fluid and transforming world.

Jamie employs various modes of repetition in *The Tree House*. Its theme is return and repetition: birds return to old nesting-places, people return to remembered places (sometimes tree houses), the human gaze is returned by the gaze of creatures. Song, in 'The Bower', 'returns in waves' and in 'The Falcon' a 'single peregrine . . . returns and returns' (*TH* 17, 40). There are repetitions of form – sonnets and ballads, and the return inherent in translation – some poems by Hölderlin are re-versioned by Jamie into Scots. The theme of return is also significant in Jamie's next two collections of poetry, *The Overhaul* (for example, in 'The Beach' (*O* 3)) and *Frissure* (where in 'Healings 2', she writes: 'we are returned to the wild, into possibilities for ageing and change' (*Fr* 7)). What the repetends in *The Tree House* uniquely display is the permeability of language – that is, how words can alter in meaning and connotation by their placement in a series of new semantic neighbourhoods. This is a process Don Paterson in *The Lyric Principle* refers to as 'semantic infection'.[1]

The Tree House opens with a quotation from Friedrich Hölderlin: 'But it is beautiful to unfold our souls / And our short lives'.[2] This epigraph has the first example of the word 'unfold', which is repeated in several poems through *The Tree House*. The Hölderlin passage also suggests a certain tension in its juxtaposition of an aspirational 'unfolding' of one's 'soul' with the simple fact of our 'short lives'. *The Tree House* explores this conversation between the temporal and the a-temporal in a uniquely poetic way: in the return and revision of repetition.

'Unfold' means to open out, or to release from a fold, and 'fold' has many variations of meaning. To fold can mean to bend or plait. It can mean to turn material back against itself. To be in the fold is to be gathered within a physical or religious enclosure, while to fold means to yield to pressure. When we read a book and turn its pages we fold back the read page at the same time as unfolding and revealing the unread page. Brigid Collins's representations of Jamie's mastectomy scar in *Frissure* include the fold of the book. Collins writes, 'I learned . . . to allow the spine of the page to become visible as I worked across it.' She describes this way of working across the page as an example of learning to 'value process over any sense of resolution' (*Fr* iv). While there are several 'unfolds' in the text of *The Tree House*, there is only one 'fold'. It appears in the opening poem, 'The Wishing Tree'. A wishing tree is a tree that is believed to have spiritual values and the ability to grant wishes. Traditionally, believers make votive offerings, in the case of the tree in this poem, by hammering coins through the bark into its wood. Each coin, if you are a believer, buys a wish. In the poem, this particular wishing tree has a voice and opens the poem, and the book, by giving its coordinates – or rather, the negative of that – it declares where it does not stand:

> I stand neither in the wilderness
> nor fairyland
>
> but in the fold
> of a green hill (*TH* 3)

The ideas of wilderness, with its implications of an unknown, unpeopled land, and fairyland, with its ephemeral almost-people in magical almost-places, are called to account by the wishing tree, who has suffered for both conceits. The poem, however, utilises another such conceit – the pathetic fallacy – to reveal the impulses behind this anthropomorphism. The tree uses its 'voice' to reflect back the projection onto it of human longing and wishing.

The wishing tree, which first defines its place by where it is not – not fairyland, not wilderness, not within a parish – declares its place to be in the fold of a green hill. Not in human-made territories of faith, but in the fold of the land. From this coordinate the wishing tree speaks back to those who invented it and caused it to 'hoard / the common currency // of longing' (*TH* 3). Although this tree describes itself as 'poisoned / choking on the small change // of human hope,/ daily beaten into me', it finishes with a small unfolding. In an act of generosity it asks the reader to look at it again, as a tree. It says 'look: I am still alive –/ in fact, in bud.' (*TH* 4) Just as nature renews and revises itself on the back of nature, Jamie uses the conceit of the pathetic fallacy to speak back to and revise some ancient stories of longing and belonging.

The next 'unfold' appears two poems further into the collection, in 'Alder' (*TH* 7). This time, using the technique of apostrophe, the speaker in the poem addresses the tree, asking it questions – most particularly, the question of how to live. For a moment it seems that the speaker has already answered that question, in that one could live according to the sequential laws of nature: 'first one leaf then another'. But *The Tree House* suggests there are no easy solutions or consolations for humankind, not with all our stories and mythologies and our longings to belong:

> alder, who unfolded
> before the receding glaciers
>
> first one leaf then another,
> won't you teach me
>
> a way to live
> on this damp ambiguous earth?

'Unfolded' in this poem sits between the tattered 'fairy lungs' and the history of the world with its 'receding glaciers'. Not in fairyland or the wilderness, the poem imagines the alder in the context of its evolution. However, the fact of the alder's long unfolding is little consolation or help to a human speaker who finds the earth ambiguous and one week a long time when the weather is bad. Towards the end of the poem the speaker makes a shift from imagining the long past, to imagining the near future, when the rain and the sun will make the tree sparkle 'like a fountain in a wood / of untold fountains'. This simile likens the tree to something human in scale, human-made and artful. However, the word 'untold' begins to evoke the strange (to us) concept of nature without the imprint of human presence. '[U]ntold' echoes back to 'unfolded' and suggests the ancient, untold unfolding of the earth before humankind existed and 'telling' had begun. 'Untold' draws something chill and 'glacial' out of 'unfolded' in this poem. In contrast to the wishing tree, which speaks words we may not want to hear, the alder does not speak at all. We might want to scuttle back to the wishing tree, to our tilting parishes, in the chill fact of the alder's innate unfolding.

The next unfolding happens towards the middle of the book, in the confines of a domestic garden. 'The Buddleia' opens with a rather formal reflection: 'When I pause to consider / a god, or creation unfolding / in front of my eyes –' (*TH* 27). Then there is a sudden register change to a colloquial and slightly exasperated 'is this my lot? Always / brought back'. The poem goes on to detail the domestic issues of the middle-aged, concerned with growing children and elderly parents with 'their broken-down / Hoover'. The unfolding in this poem is vague in that it refers to the unfolding of *a* god *or* creation. The possibility of finding *a* god, with its indefinite article, seems a contemporary quest with its global world context where all possibilities are available yet all somehow out of reach. The word 'Always' suggests a predictable return to something, a situation or mythology perhaps, that is not quite fitting anymore; that constant return to 'the same / grove of statues in ill- / fitting clothes'. The sense here is of things being stuck, not repeating generatively as they need to. The 'unfold' in this placement is shut down by context, rather than opened out. Faith Lawrence notes in this volume that the trope of listening in Jamie's poems allows her 'a metaphorical place to stand and receive' and that her poems 'seem to "listen"'. With poetic repetition, the repeating word is released from a site-specific context and enters a new context where it is infused by the words around it: Paterson's 'semantic infection'. The repeated word 'listens' to different encircling words, ensuring that meaning remains open, fluid and capable of change within an evolving environment.

In a reading that to some extent misses the dynamic poetics in *The Tree House*, Laura Severin suggests that Jamie's book of essays, *Findings*, is a more success-ful environmental work than *The Tree House*, and argues that Jamie's attempt to combine the idea of nature's integrity and difference with humanity's connected-ness to nature only really comes together in her later work (her essays). Of Jamie's *Findings*, she suggests 'that it is at the borders between genres that artists are able to express themselves most radically'.[3] I would argue that the poetic structures of *Jizzen* and *The Tree House*, which Severin claims 'objectify nature for human needs and purposes', are the structures that uniquely enable the conversation about nature and our place within it to remain open and dynamic. This is the territory that *The Tree House* explores deeply: the manifestation of a fluid or transforming world, using the relationship of language with context and the poetic device of repetition. Paterson describes how poetic structure can release language from certain strictures of thought. At the beginning of *The Lyric Principle* he notes that 'Language put us at a terrifically unfair advantage [over other species] in terms of forward planning'.[4] Later in the essay he writes:

> Poetry is the means by which we correct the main tool of that thought, lan-guage, for the worst of its anthropic distortions: it is language's self-corrective function . . . through the insistence on a counterbalancing project, that of lyric unity . . . We do this by singing of the larger unity of which it's merely a synec-dochic expression.[5]

Central to poetry's ability to sing of 'the larger unity' is its ability to listen and to hear shifts in meaning and connotation; what Paterson describes as a 'non-fixity of interpretation'.[6] This openness to interpretation is achieved by, and distinctive to, poetry because poetry foregrounds the permeability of language and its ability to listen to and be influenced by its environment. *The Tree House* attends to the process of continuity and change – folding and unfolding – the one enabling the other.

What is lost in looking for 'a god, or creation' in 'The Buddleia' is found via an evocation of nature. When the speaker in the poem begins to name the plants in the garden – 'the lupins, or foxgloves,' she quickly comes to the 'self- / seeded buddleia' (*TH* 27). Until that moment there is a perceived impasse in the poem between an unresponsive version of the divine and the duties of domestic life. There seems to be no room for infusion or re-vision. Language is not listening to language. However, this impasse is released by the act of attention to a new form in the garden. The buddleia in this poem is an uninvited, self-seeded plant and in the first description it seems almost devilish with its sensual 'heavy horns', but this plant is in the process of opening; the 'heavy horns flush as they / open to flower'. In this moment of attentiveness, space is made for the infusion of new elements into the garden and fluidity is achieved. The colons, semicolons and line breaks that suggest the fracturing irritations and disappointments in the first stanza '. . . in ill- / fitting clothes: my suddenly / elderly parents, their broken-down / Hoover; or my quarrelling kids?' give way to images of regeneration underscored by an alliterative music, 'these bumbling, well-meaning bees / which remind me again'. There is attentiveness to the changing environment and then there is fluidity and a place to 'stand and receive'. Like the buds on the wishing tree, these small, unscripted, unarranged unfoldings persist. The articulated and hoped-for grand unfolding of creation that the speaker implies should play out almost like a performance 'in front of my eyes –' can only actually be known by its parts, by these small unfoldings, these changing forms that sing 'of the larger unity'.

The poem 'Pipistrelles', a ballad, details the idea 'for a new form / which unfolded and cohered // before our eyes' (TH 30). Pipistrelles are a type of bat and bats are, of course, connected with stories of vampires and the underworld. But the bats in this poem emerge from a light space enfolded by Douglas firs. They are lively and quick: 'cinder-like, friable, flickering'. A cinder may be dark, but it is made from fire so 'friable' and 'flickering' also suggests the shifting of matter from one form into another, again musically underscored by an alliterative flickering of sound. The transformative possibilities of simile and metaphor suggest new perceptions. The enclosure is 'like' a vase, the vessel is 'tinted like citrine', the pipistrelles are 'cinder-like'. Here is the possibility for a less archaic way of thinking about our fellow species. However, this re-vision is subverted by the human desire to have nature reflect and demonstrate important concerns about human lives. The phrase 'before my eyes' from 'The Buddleia' is echoed in 'Pipistrelles'; the new form is described in stanza five as unfolding 'before our eyes'. The perceived performance of nature for humankind – the mythology that trees might grant wishes, or talk or listen – is implied in the question: 'is that what they were telling us?' The new form 'vanished, suddenly' at the moment of that question. The act of repetition narrated and enacted in this poem, with old forms generating new, falters, and negotiations cease. The trees which in stanza one were particular, named and interactive are reduced to generic 'trees' and described as 'mute', as though they had human language but could not, or would not, speak.

The last 'unfold' in The Tree House suggests a process in harmony with its context. It appears in the poem 'Water Lilies' (TH 34). In this poem the native water lilies unfold in the 'open / border where water / becomes air', so in that place of natural transformation where one element infuses or becomes another. This unfolding happens in the last stanza of the poem. It is observed, but not strained towards, as in 'The Buddleia', or over-thought, as in 'Pipistrelles'. In the first three stanzas the facts are presented largely without the transformative work of simile and metaphor. The leaves are furled, accurately describing their coiled or folded-away aspect. The water is 'peat-stained' and shallow – which describes the nutrient-rich environment that sustains the lilies. The first three stanzas present the thing itself, but of course not just the thing itself, because you cannot say the white water-lily flowers are 'blown' and the water 'stained' and the leaves 'rising', and then have a transformation of elements, without noting the language and imagery of Christianity. If 'The Buddleia' makes an anxious prod at concepts of divinity, 'Water Lilies' grows the language of faith organically from the poem's enactment of a shared and constantly becoming world.

The repetition of fold and unfold through *The Tree House* enacts a way of thinking about place and belonging that is not absolute, not fixed. It questions aspects of the 'old' self-defining stories by listening to words that carry significant freight, words such as 'unfold', 'rim' and 'light', not once but again and again in different semantic neighbourhoods through the book. The fold in 'The Wishing Tree' negotiates between the wilderness, fairyland and tilting parishes; the alder unfolds between fairy lungs and receding glaciers; the self-seeded buddleia unfolds quietly as humans search out creation; pipistrelles rise out of enfolding trees to make, briefly, the shape of new ideas before being shut down by old ideas; and finally, water lilies unfold in two places of transformation: in the border place 'where water becomes air', and the symbolic place where leaves become 'almost heart shapes, / almost upturned hands'.

In an interview with Atila Dósa, Jamie discusses the power of writing about uncertainty, and the possibility for uncertainty to undermine the first principals of fundamentalism: 'It's just what fundamentalism can't bear. It can't bear uncertainty.'[7] This idea of uncertainty, which could also be called fluidity, is demonstrated in these acts of repetition in *The Tree House*. In a self-correcting action, the repeated word negotiates with its new and evolving environment. The repeated 'almost' after the unfolding in 'Water Lilies' stops short of an anachronistic anthropomorphism, but, in the best actions of poetry, in the work of making connections, these 'almosts' allow for the immaterial – the soul, with its long unfolding – to call up, to remind us of our places of belonging as we take our momentary form in the world.

WORKS CITED (SEE ALSO BIBLIOGRAPHY)

Hölderlin, Fredrich, *Selected Poems*, tr. David Constantine (Newcastle upon Tyne: Bloodaxe, 1990).
Paterson, Don, 'The Lyric Principle', www.donpaterson.com/arspoetica.htm (last accessed 10 December 2013).

NOTES

1. Paterson, *The Lyric Principle*, p. 24.
2. Hölderlin, *Selected Poems*, p. 78. Quoted as an epigraph to *The Tree House*.
3. Severin, *A Scottish Ecopoetics*, p. 101.
4. Paterson, *The Lyric Principle*, p. 1.

5. Ibid., p. 14.
6. Ibid., p. 10.
7. Dósa interview, 'Kathleen Jamie', in *Beyond Identity*, p. 140.

A Man, a Former Environmental Activist Turned PR Consultant for Logging Companies, Defends His Choices

Voice:
The sky is blue. The fairybird is blue.
A great bird soars across the sky's blue dome,
its upturned bowl of brightest, brilliant blue
above the treeline and the canopy.
The canopy is closed: *dipterocarpus*,
your timber-lumber, underneath whose crowns
smaller trees grow whose limbs form scaffolding
for creepers and climbers, herbs and smaller shrubs,
for the pitcher plant and the sun fern *dipteris*
whose print is found in pre-historic fossils.

Man:
The dog barks, the cow moos, the sheep goes *baa*.
Man sizes up the cow and sheep
and clucking hen – and then puts them to use.
Look, answer me this: if a tree falls in the forest
and no one's there to see it, will it burn?
Can it be stripped and pulped, packed and exported?
Does it make props and tiles? Or does it rot?

Voice:
The sky is blue. The distant sea is blue.
The moon's torque drags that salty wedge each day
up through the mangrove forests to the east,
where a little snail will climb its tree each morning
descending at evening – not to escape the tide
but through an evolved, coincidental rhythm.
The mangrove trees drop twigs and other litter
that crabs and fungi break to phosphorus-rich

mulch for the zooplankton; bottom-feeders
who feed, in turn, carnivorous fish and birds

Man:
. . . who feed the bigger fish who then feed man,
the food chain's top banana, cream of the crop
who pens in shrimp ponds and rips out raw gas.
Glory be his brain and spinal column!
His vertebrate strength and pelvis-threatening skull!
. . . You know, I see your point, when I was young
I thought that I would live . . . *reactively*;
cultivate plots, grow only what I need
but 'need' as a concept proved prone to expand.

Voice:
The sky is blue. The flycatcher is blue.
The king quail's breast is blue. The forest hosts
dark-handed gibbon, yellow-banded snake,
the snub-nosed monkey and the flying fox
which scents, at range, the lowland fruit and blossom
crash-landing into trees to feed on nectar.
The trees grow buttresses. Some hollow limbs
house porcupines and rats whose pungent waste
is milled by the little creatures in the soil
then tilled back to the red loam of the earth.

Man:
When I was young I thought the life I'd lead
would be passionate, nomadic, self-contained
with my nine bean rows and hives of buzzy bees . . .
I'd keep a few goats, use only what I need
– but oh how the boundaries of sufficiency
shift ever outwards. That's a fact of life.
Nests must be feathered, little mouths be fed.
And from such seeds do corporations grow.

Voice:
Here every kind of crawling rustling species,
from stinkhorn fungus to the giant flower,
jostles in constant restless composition
but the tree and its mast is root and branch of all.
The tree in its cycle is gregarious
so isopod crustaceans crowd in root-tips
and convex leaves shield colonies of ants.

Man:
So the pitcher plant lures insects to its lip
and inside larvae browse over their corpses.
The nematode worm and mosquito feed like this.
The forest hosts the opportunist killer
as the fig-tree hosts fig-wasp and parasite.
When man clears the trees he makes his destiny
alongside the timber-yards and paper-mills,
and the scorch on the mountain is his signature.

Voice
The sky is blue. The endless sky is blue

Man:
The smoke hung above the chimney stacks is blue.

Voice:
The glinting fly and darting bird are blue.

Man:
The ink on my ledger's bottom line is blue.

Leontia Flynn

10. Form in *The Tree House*

Michael O'Neill

In her dealings with form, Kathleen Jamie is on her guard against anything that smacks of prepackaged comfort. Forms seem often to be calculatedly under stress, at an angle to anything conventional, as in the fine sonnet 'The Cupboard' from *The Tree House* (44). In this poem, short lines and an emphatic but unpredictable use of rhyme and off-rhyme keep the poem and reader on their toes, following the twists and turns of a poem that feels its way forward. The 'cupboard' is less symbol than wryly presented surrogate for symbolic meaning. Jamie adeptly obeys and departs from the organising principle suggested by the sonnet. The division between octave and sestet is maintained as the poem follows into two single-sentenced questions, though the octave's sentence runs over into the mock-querulous question, 'why is it at *my* place?' at the start of the sestet. The word 'place' rhymes or off-rhymes with 'us' and 'sarcophogus', and momentarily, for all the humour, rhyme is a noose that tightens round the theme of all of 'us / put together' and waiting our own cupboard or coffin; yet Jamie never states such a notion unequivocally.

The implication is of a rearrangement of furniture following some significant life-event, and of the poet's irked sense of being lumbered with a near-unmanageable object. But the final suggestion is that the object proves how little agency the poet has; the cupboard appears to find its own way 'through the racked, / too-narrow door', much as meaning enters this lyric whose own doors are 'too-narrow', and rhymes are just a little 'racked'. The sonnet is often concerned with immortality and with housing infinite riches in a little room. Jamie replays and half-ironises these themes in a poem that packs a great deal in as it moves from origins to imagined ends or endlessness, and that suggests the cupboard will stay where it is 'no doubt for evermore', a phrase that cunningly teeters between irked muttering and something more resonant.

Jamie is often a poet who balances the claims of modernity and tradition. If her diction tugs towards a toughened speech of the soil, the harassed and harvested land, it also has scope for something more literary. Two Hölderlin poems rendered into Lowland Scots serve almost as paradigms of Jamie's relationship with tradition. In each case she seeks to uncover an equivalent in Scots to Hölderlin's visionary intimations. On successive pages in Michael Hamburger's *Poems and Fragments*, 'Heimath' ('Hame' in Jamie (*TH* 28)) and 'For When the Grape-Vine's Sap' (lower-case 'vine' in Jamie (*TH* 12)) appear at a distance from each other in *The Tree House*, the latter appearing first, but anticipating the former as it moves towards a close in Jamie's rendering of the bees that turn from vine to sun: 'but when the sun beeks, / fey-like, they turn hame' (*TH* 12). In her fourteen-line work, one that seemingly to its own surprise turns into a version of a sonnet, Jamie's language is alive with strength and tenderness, the 'smeddum' and 'sweetness' given to 'men' and 'lasses', respectively. Her 'fey-like' may, to the English ear, drift dangerously towards the archaic, the 'fey', and suggests the difficulty her Scots idiom has with abstractions (Hamburger has the bees 'Divining much' for Hölderlin's 'vielahnend' – literally, 'much guessing').[1] But the reader is prepared to trust that the phrase has a living quality to it, even as he or she notes that the presaging has taken on a more ominous note than in the original, because of the conviction carried by the rest of the poem. This includes the haunting simplicity of the close where Jamie follows Hamburger by allowing the original ('darob / die Eiche rauschet') to 'rustle' in its own suggestive symbolic space, except that her lineation lets the last line float off: 'abune / the aik reeshles' (*TH* 12).

In 'Hame', Hölderlin's opening, stand-alone assertion – 'Und niemand weiß' ('And no one knows', Hamburger, pp. 532–3) – turns into Jamie's more questioning 'Wha's tae ken' (*TH* 28). Hölderlin sets ultimate lack of knowledge against, in Hamburger's translation, 'my love for you / Upon your paths, O Earth'. His lyric reaches 'heavenward' near its conclusion and finishes with a sense that, momentarily, almost magically, 'all is well'. Jamie captures the love and the longing for well-being, but she soft-pedals the rubric of final unknowingness under which the original orchestrates details of corn, trees, well-known bell, and birds, and she minimises the epiphanic singularity of Hölderlin's conclusion: the German poet refers to 'the hour when / The bird's awake once more'; she speaks of 'the oor when the birds wauken / ance mair' (*TH* 28).

Jamie's versions of Hölderlin suggest a poet inventively at ease with poetic tradition, able to summon yet subdue its resonances as she chooses. 'For When the Grape-vine's Sap' responds to the physical immediacy and symbolic suggestiveness of Hölderlin's lyric practice; 'Hame' softens metaphysical doubt in favour of eco-celebration. Both poems convey an intimate sense of affinity with the German Romantic's vision, whilst locating themselves in the present of Jamie's responsiveness to the natural world. The stance taken by her in her poems is often that of 'The Wishing Tree' in which the tree speaks of itself as the objective correlative of human desire, 'because I hoard / the common currency // of longing' (*TH* 3). That 'common currency' might describe the luggage borne by the forms of many poems by Jamie. The poet as user of form is in contact with 'the common currency' of human experience. Here, her slow-moving, brief-lined couplets conjure an unexpected affirmation at the end, 'look: I am still alive – / in fact, in bud' (*TH* 4). Jamie works her conceit – that coins embedded in the tree's bark correspond to human longing – with deliberate, even slightly dogged care. But the concluding couplet halts, turns in a different direction, delightedly reminds us that the tree is a tree in the phrase 'in bud', while allowing for the fact that such a phrase can apply to human beings, as when Herbert in 'The Flower' asserts: 'And now in age I bud again, / After so many deaths I live and write' (*TH* 36–7).² These lines might serve as an epigraph to 'The Wishing Tree', and indeed Jamie has a Herbert-like fastidiousness of attention to detail. She may not rhyme her lines here, but the assonantal movement from the tree's 'choking on the small change // of human hope' to the invitation to 'look' reprises the poem's switch from asphyxiation to a new intake of breath.

As if to express a restlessness with the poem's perspective, Jamie uses the same couplet form in the collection's third poem, 'Alder', to communicate her awareness that any meaning deriving from nature has, at least in part, to be a meaning conferred. Here, Jamie does not seek to speak as a tree, but to talk to it with a beguiling sympathy: 'Are you weary, alder tree, / in this, the age of rain?' (*TH* 7) In what sense, the reader wonders, is 'this, the age of rain'? The answer must be that supplied by the reference to the fact that the alder existed before the ice age, in a passage where the line-endings span a vast geological span of time. Jamie sustains the questioning that is a form of pleading: 'won't you teach me // a way to live / on this damp ambiguous earth', where 'ambiguous' suggests why 'a way to live' is at once a necessary and a difficult ethical discovery. The final six lines show again how Jamie can shape her couplets and questions into a poem that rejoices in its own provisional answer. The poem achieves here the status of a salute to the beauty, durability and possibilities of the natural world. The 'broken tune' might be the poet's as well as the tree's; again, Herbert comes to mind, the poet who tells us in 'Deniall', 'Then was my heart broken, as was my verse', before at the close he is able to 'mend his rhyme' (Wilcox, ed. pp. 288, 289). In Jamie's lines, the sustaining of two octosyllabic lines suggests that the 'tune' is mending itself, prefiguring the final image in which the tree becomes 'a fountain in a wood / of untold fountains': 'untold' because so many, 'untold', too, because the tale of the tree has yet to be told. As a 'fountain', it belongs to a post-glacial world and acts as an analogue for a frequent image for poetic creativity.

It is an image developed two poems later in 'The Fountain of the Lions', and *The Tree House* exemplifies Jamie's ability to link poems, interweaving motifs and themes, so that rarely is a poem simply or solely self-subsistent. Here Jamie draws on a Rilkean precedent, his 'Roman Fountain', a sonnet about a fountain in the Borghese Gardens that depicts with exquisitely cadenced accuracy the water's overflow from basin to basin. For her part, Jamie describes how the water 'overbrims' (*TH* 10). The way that in this third stanza 'dish' repeats its central sound in 'replenishes', and 'overbrims' rhymes with 'rim' and 'hymns' which are line-end words in the first stanza, gives expression to a self-generating system of filling and overfilling. This system is one 'of hydraulics'; it might be nature seen in a certain slant of light; it might be the act of attention, embodied in a poem, one conscious that its quatrains themselves 'stare // to every sorrowful / quarter of the world'. At such a moment one is aware of Jamie's readiness to fill her taut poetic shapes with verbal gestures of considerable ambition. Assonance links the fountain's leonine 'jaws' and their 'coursing' 'streams' with 'each sorrowful / quarter', as though art, if one may so allegorise the fountain, sought to supply balm for the 'sorrowful'.

Whether this seeking is endorsed or curiously pitied is left in limbo by the poem, which implies the ambiguously 'endless' nature of its activity (the streams are 'coursing endless'). That is, the streams may be 'endless', forever self-generating, or they may be purposeless, without an 'end', with no wish to make anything happen. It is an achievement to create such a balance of poise and indeterminacy, even if it is one attained by a slight straining after effect evident in the phrasing of 'the world' and in the ungrammatical 'endless' (rather than the expected 'endlessly'); Jamie's handling of the quatrain form is highly accomplished, allowing the short lines to run on, but endowing the poem's two sentences with an unportentous weight and dignity. Each takes two stanzas to complete itself, conveying information unhurriedly, shaping itself in such a way that it asks to be rehearsed again and again, its simulation of process endlessly repeated.

'The Fountain of the Lions' also invites us to consider whether Jamie's occasional reliance on grand assertions towards the close concedes that a chosen 'form' may be too frail in itself to enact larger meanings. Elsewhere, we comes across 'the tenancy of our short lives' ('Water Day', *TH* 8–9), 'our old idea of the soul' ('The Blue Boat', *TH* 19), 'The world's / mind is such interstices' ('Pipistrelles', *TH* 30–1). The first poem, 'Water Day', is written in four short-lined paragraphs, the lines containing varying numbers of stresses, the verse-paragraphs consisting of four sentences and, respectively, of six lines, eleven lines, then two of seven lines each. The first line might suggest a numerological basis for the four paragraphs: 'For four hours every eight days / our terraces' *acequias* / run with snow-melt' (*TH* 8). The thematic fit with 'Alder', the previous poem in the volume, is evident, though here the emphasis is more collective (*acequias* are community-run watercourses). From the beginning, a mode one might wish to call the descriptive–celebratory runs alongside, and at times wrestles with, a half-repressed wish to find a deeper meaning. Jamie admits yet checks this wish. She begins the second paragraph with lines that do their best to steer the writing away from merely reflective prose and follow their own increasingly descriptive idiom, only to break off at the start of the third paragraph to ask: 'couldn't we make / heavy weather of it all?' (*TH* 8)

The impulse to interrupt a possibly symbolic or allegorising reading with something self-admonishing enlivens and bedevils poetry written in a free-verse style one might associate with the practice of William Carlos Williams. Developing an image of 'old age' as a flight of birds in 'To Waken an Old Lady', Williams asks, almost self-wreckingly, 'But what?', a terse interjection that suggests a momentary discomfort with the direction that the poem is taking.[3] His poem, to its benefit, sweeps past that moment of self-questioning. Jamie tries to keep in play the dual activities of probing reflection and awareness that might all add up to 'heavy weather'. Jamie is not prepared to allow the natural object to be the adequate symbol without nudging us in the direction of how we might turn the one into the other. The challenge for a writer in this Williamsesque mode is of allowing abstraction into a poetic process whose *raison d'être* is submission to what lies at hand. Jamie takes Williams's near-slogan 'No ideas / but in things' to a bold extreme, allowing ideas to enfold themselves round things, as she does at the end of the poem.[4] She implies a switch of mode in the final two paragraphs, by constructing them out of seven and eight lines respectively, thus bringing them into connection with the sonnet form which is a presence throughout a volume that thrives, as Lynn Davidson observes in this volume, on the 'repetitions of form'. She imagines following the stream until 'it simply / quits the tenancy of our short lives' and we can 'let it go'.

'[T]he tenancy of our short lives' (*TH* 9) seems swept into an intertextual current that runs back to (and beyond) the Book of Job (compare 14: 1–2). Yet Jamie just about wrests a difficult victory from her materials, one that, despite appearances, works 'unsimply' as she permits the to-and-fro balances encouraged by her use of form to make an impact. The idea of 'life' as a 'tenancy', something leased out, belongs to the overall structure of a poem about land worked by shareholders; and the switch of subjects from 'quits' (something the waters do) to 'let' (something that 'we' do) gives the poem a freedom that derives from the recognition of necessity. It is the 'we' who 'let it' (the stream) 'go', freeing it from our demands on it (*TH* 9).

The poem, then, tests to its limits its chosen form and emerges with a highly self-aware creation that survives its own self-awareness. Mind and being tussle inevitably in any poetry of nature, especially one that has, as Jamie's does, a steadily maintained ecological vision. Mind's power over nature might show itself through the adoption of forms that assert control and dominance. As though reacting against such control and dominance, Shelley, in his 'Mont Blanc', employs irregular rhymes that disrupt any sense that the mind has the upper hand in its encounter with the mountain. Jamie may turn to forms that imply a befitting humility in the presence of large questions, but to her credit she is prepared to take risks, too, even if one might sometimes wonder whether she might push risk-taking further. In 'The Blue Boat' (*TH* 19), Jamie crosses Imagist lyric with a nonsense verse; 'The Owl and the Pussy-cat', with its 'beautiful pea-green boat', hovers in the background.[5] The poem itself 'journeys', a 'blue boat', whose 'gilded' look recalls the praise-poem 'Gilded in Arabic' at the start of 'The Fountain of the Lions'. 'How late', it begins, yet the rest of the poem tries to restore something earlier, whether a boat with a sail and 'lantern', or, in the last line, 'our old idea of the soul'. The lyric has a belated resonance, and yet that line threatens to tear down the frail fabric which houses it, to demand a different kind of poem, perhaps the more expansive lyric treatment that Wallace Stevens, say, might give the question. Where has it come from, what status does it have for Jamie, this 'old idea of the soul'? Is it just a piece of delightful spiritual bric-a-brac? The questions are not wholly confronted by the poem, and thus bequeath a sense of disquiet as well as satisfaction.

Admittedly, the 'soul' is not an easy substance for a modern poet; and certainly Jamie's lyric tact and grace have an effect of aesthetic refreshment, yet the reader may wish the poem offered a more spiritually thirst-quenching draught. The choice of form is crucial here, and one can well imagine a more sustained address to the topic. In 'Pipistrelles' (*TH* 30–1), Jamie uses quatrains – six of them, again made up of lines with between two and four stresses, employing delicate almost-rhymes in the second and fourth lines – to evoke a process of quickening awareness. The poem deals in wheelings and concentrations of attention, in the noticing of what had not been noticed, in promises of aesthetic perfection, 'a tall enclosure like a vase'; Steven's jar and Keats's Grecian urn haunt about the fringes of this opening. Its initial trajectory of latent self-reproach gives way to lines in which the bats serve as surrogates of the poet's apprehensions, 'cinder-like, friable, flickering', and 'a single / edgy intelligence, testing their idea / for a new form' (*TH* 30).

Jamie makes her quatrains spaces where thought and beings both grow; the pipistrelles, for example, change from being burnt-out ('cinder-like'), to being 'friable' (possibly with a half-pun on 'viable' flittering in the background'), to 'flickering', where they start to take on substance in a 'place hained by trees', the Scots word 'hained' meaning 'enclosed' or protected', and lending surrounding words, in context, a quality of hushed calm. The word 'quicken' at the stanza's close transmits its rhyming energy onwards to the next stanza, in which Jamie raises the stakes by turning the bats into, or seeing them as, 'a single /edgy intelligence', the line-ending adding its own raggedy edge to what might have been too totalising an adjective. Jamie uses forms to turn questions of agency inside out; instead of the bats representing an 'idea', they seem, delightfully, to take over at the poem's controls, 'testing their idea / for a new form / which unfolded and cohered // before our eyes'. Word and world briefly harmonise; a 'new form' in which human and natural world share one another's intelligence seems, such is the dexterity of the verse, to unfold and cohere 'before our eyes', those of the spectators and of the readers.

Whether the following lines press too firm-footedly beyond this unfolding and cohering is a matter of critical judgement and individual response; Jamie has a Romantic precedent for her practice – one might compare her attempt to explore 'the world's / mind' with Coleridge's question, 'And what if all of animated nature / Be but organic harps diversely framed . . . ?' ('The Eolian Harp', 44–5).[6] Like Coleridge, Jamie employs question, before she turns in her final stanza to something close to repudiation of attempted understanding and to an end of any rapprochement between nature and language. Coleridge's conversation poems long to trace a circle, yet, with restraint and grace, he often concedes that his circle-tracing triumphs are provisional. Jamie, for her part, infuses her poem with understated pathos at its close as she ends on a 'muted' rhyme between 'understood' and 'mute' and excludes the poem-making consciousness from the 'circle' it had seemed to enter.

'Pipistrelles' comes close, however, in its way to embodying as well as celebrating a 'new form', one made up of traditional materials – the quatrain, rhyme, statement, question – but seeking to be the verbal equivalent of 'cells charging with light of day', where Jamie updates and rewrites Hopkins's vision in 'God's Grandeur': 'The world is charged with the grandeur of God. / It will flame out, like shining from shook foil' (1–2).[7] Jamie's image seems more like a mobile phone 'charging' its depleted battery. Elsewhere, in *The Tree House* her poems explore the relationship between 'a new form' of consciousness, of an experience of the world, and the form she seeks to shape in her poems. As noted, the volume is intrigued by the sonnet; at once old and resilient, the form answers the needs of a poet who wishes to keep faith with the natural world and to renew or re-comprehend her vision of it.

At the same time, her poetry is post-Darwinian rather than sentimentally New Age, as can be seen in her sonnet 'Moult', which reads like a calm revisiting of Frost's 'Design', a poem equally chilled by the presence or absence of 'design'. Jamie's sonnet is sure about, though unable to know the details of, 'design', and is moved rather than menaced by it, suggesting that there is a mould behind 'moult'. Short-lined yet almost majestic in its movement, her sonnet flows onwards from the 'dead things' shed by seabirds to ask about the relationship between 'one frayed feather' and an overall pattern, and, in the concluding couplet, about 'the covenant they undertake, / wind and kittiwake' (*TH* 38). Rhyme here has the effect of proving the fact of a 'covenant'; the precision of 'kittiwake' allies itself with the specific compulsions of poetic form to hymn the particularity of the natural world. Jamie's formal skill shows in the way in which the small craft of her poem shadows the ocean-going liner that is the typical Shakespearean sonnet, only to catch up with it in the clinching rhyme at the end.

Elsewhere, form serves also as a vehicle for the holding on to a sustaining wisdom. In 'The Creel', Jamie uses three quatrains, each rhyming the second and fourth lines, to move past the almost point-scoring first line, in which 'a woman' is a point of origin for 'The world', to convey the woman's sense of carrying the world in her arms and 'her fear that if ever she put it down / the world would go out like a light' (*TH* 45). The poem's rhythms and enjambments sympathise with this 'fear', with their growing reluctance to stop, to 'put . . . down' the burden of their meaning-making. The result is a poem about care for this world that eludes the polemical impulse, covertly there in the opening. 'The Creel' enacts the effort of keeping the world going. Because the poem does have to finish, and because this finish coincides with the articulation of the woman's fear, the control of form imparts a startling charge; the reader reads the words and senses a coincidence between that fear and the linguistic moment in which the poem itself has gone out 'like a light'. That last simile has a shopworn appearance at first glance, but its function as a rhyme may prompt us, on further reflection, to see Jamie's light as akin to Wordsworth's 'light of sense' that 'Goes out in flashes that have shewn to us / The invisible world' (*The Prelude*, 1805, X. 534, 535–6).[8] This is not to suggest that Jamie is alluding to Wordsworth, though he, too, is a poet with a deep concern for what in the same poem he calls 'the very world which is the world / Of all of us, the place on which, in the end, / We find our happiness, or not at all' (X. 725–7; Gill ed., p. 476). It is to suggest that both poets find in the phrase 'go out' mixed suggestions of extinction and residual dissemination.

For all the volume's wariness of pentameters and iambs, then, the poem, like others in *The Tree House*, accommodates itself to tradition with an imperilled trust in the capacity of forms to embody a desperate hope. In 'The Puddle' (*TH* 47–8), the quatrains are at once a mirror of that force 'upright within us' that forbids us to respond to natural beauty, and the medium through which we can glimpse 'that flush in the world's light / as though with sudden love'. The 'sudden love' overrides the risk of insistence through a quality of vulnerable surrender in the phrasing and rhythm, and through its touching off-rhyme with the poem's next line, 'how should we live?'. How indeed, other than to respond unreservedly to the show of 'sudden love', and yet the poem knows metaphors and figures will never wholly reconcile the people with nature, to adapt Williams's phrasing from 'A Sort of a Song'; hence the elusiveness of that last rhyme with 'love' and 'live'. And yet 'The Dipper', the volume's following poem, as pure a lyric as any in the poem, feels like a crystallisation of aspects of Whitman's 'Out of the Cradle'. Whitman is hurt into poetry by the songs of unsatisfied longing uttered by the he-bird after its mate's disappearance. Jamie rings together her pervasive imagery of water and her preoccupation with 'supple, undammable song', achieving through her own singing, ballad-like lines and rhymes a poignant blend of incapacity ('It isn't mine to give') with a giving over of the poem's floor to the bird that finishes the poem with its displaced song; it emerges from a river, 'yet sings of it on land' (*TH* 49). Form here does the work of divination; psychopomp-like, it enables migration between one dimension (the river) and another (the land), between, if one might press harder at the point, intimations and their incarnation in words. Jamie's poems end as though only there, at their ends, is the possibility of an unfolding and cohering brought out and into the open. Occasionally, as in the elegy 'The Brooch', the ending merely confirms what the opening suggested, though, there, the delay between opening and conclusion effectively wards off that awareness for a space, at once numbly and like a brief grace, as the poet attends to the physical reality and associations of the 'agates' (*TH* 46). More often, as in 'The Buddleia', the poem uses form to take us on an unpredictable journey. Here the two verse paragraphs (nine and thirteen lines respectively) switch from musing on 'my suddenly / elderly parents' to a wittily affectionate second paragraph focusing on the father as it describes how the buddleia

>   draw
> these bumbling, well-meaning bees
> which remind me again,
> of my father . . . whom, Christ,
> I've forgotten to call. (*TH* 27)

The references to 'a god' and 'the masculine / God of my youth' give way to the humorous, mild profanity of 'Christ', and the poet has caught in the resourceful net of her associations with the father deity and insects, hinting, in a light but purposeful way, at the presence of divinity in all things: divinity as defined in the poem, namely, a quality to be found in all things viewed with a poet's unsentimental but 'sudden love'. There is playfulness, almost self-mockery, in the fact that the poet has 'forgotten to call' her father in the act of writing a poem in which many things 'remind [her] again, / of my father', lines in which the pause enforced by the ungrammatical comma obliges the reader to slow down and attend to the father.

Form, Jamie's *The Tree House* implies, is a mode of attention. It works as the means by which precise awareness of being and mind is attained. It is glove to the content's hand, and also the tendons and digits of that hand. It is an undemonstrative showing forth that, every now and then, shines. Short lines, couplets, quatrains, sonnets, the virtual absence of resonant pentameters: all bear witness to an artist who neither spurns nor is in thrall to tradition, who, in Peter Mackay's words, 'resist[s] the process of symbolising', even as she is drawn to it.[9] What is striking about Jamie's formal artistry in *The Tree House* is its constant ability to transcend limits precisely by working uncomplacently within them.

WORKS CITED (SEE ALSO BIBLIOGRAPHY)

Coleridge, Samuel Taylor, *The Complete Poems*, ed. William Keach (London: Penguin, 1997).

Herbert, George, *The English Poems of George Herbert*, ed. Helen Wilcox (Cambridge: Cambridge University Press, 2007).

Hopkins, Gerard Manley, *Poems and Prose of Gerard Manley Hopkins*, ed. W. H. Gardner (Harmondsworth: Penguin, 1963).

Hölderlin, Friedrich, *Poems and Fragments*, tr. Michael Hamburger, 3rd bilingual edition (London: Anvil, 1994).

Lear, Edward, *The Complete Nonsense and Other Verse*, ed. Vivien Noakes (London: Penguin, 2007).

Williams, William Carlos, *Selected Poems*, ed. with intro. Charles Tomlinson (Harmondsworth: Penguin, 1976).

Wordsworth, William, *21st Century Oxford Authors: William Wordsworth*, ed. Stephen Gill (Oxford: Oxford University Press, 2010).

NOTES

1. Hölderlin, *Poems and Fragments*, pp. 534–5.
2. Herbert, *Poems of Herbert*, p. 568.
3. Williams, *Selected Poems*, p. 38.
4. Williams, 'A Sort of a Song', *Selected Poems*, p. 133.
5. Lear, *Complete Nonsense*, p. 238.
6. Coleridge, *Complete Poems*, pp. 87–8.
7. *Poems and Prose of Hopkins*, p. 27.
8. *21st Century Authors: William Wordsworth*, p. 390.
9. See Mackay, 'The Tilt from One Parish to Another', in this volume.

11. Nature and Embodiment in *This Weird Estate*

Lucy Collins

In an essay entitled 'Pathologies', first published in Granta's 2008 volume *The New Nature Writing*, Kathleen Jamie reflects on the role of the microscopic other in endangering human well-being and continuing life. Reconsidering her understanding of the term 'nature' in light of these thoughts, Jamie acknowledges the need to conceive of the body itself as a form of ecosystem: 'It's not all primroses and dolphins . . . [t]here's our own intimate, inner natural world, the body's weird shapes and forms, and sometimes they go awry.'[1] This 'inner natural world' is both complex and contingent, and developments at the interface between creativity and technology have for some time problematised the concept of the body as singularly 'human' in character: 'my "own" body is material', Jane Bennett writes, 'yet this materiality is not fully or exclusively human . . . In a world of vibrant matter, it is thus not enough to say that we are "embodied". We are, rather, *an array of bodies*.'[2] Jamie's engagement with the intricacy of bodily experience and representation, in particular with notions of the 'other within', is memorably explored in a short sequence of poems published as *This Weird Estate* in 2007. These poems were written in response to anatomical representations from the nineteenth and early twentieth centuries.[3] This essay will explore these poems in detail and situate them at the interface of the poet's engagement with generational change and ecological responsibility.

Jamie's perception of the otherness of the human body not only calls into question the notion of a singular subjectivity but also challenges both the perception and representation of the body as a defined and unitary entity. In this respect it is the interrelationship of different forms of matter, as Bennett explores in her study, which determines both the energies of the living and our understanding of the complex and connected character of all life:

> Each human is a heterogeneous compound of wonderfully vibrant, dangerously vibrant, matter. If matter itself is lively, then not only is the difference between subjects and objects minimized, but the status of the shared materiality of all things is elevated.[4]

As Bennett indicates here, the energies that inform both human and non-human materiality fundamentally alter any existing perception of the relationship between subject and object. She cites Lyotard's view that the human is characterised by a particularly rich and complex set of materials, within which consciousness and language have a significant role.[5] There are certain contexts, however, in which this complexity demands very particular scrutiny; medical discourse and imagery both elevate the human through the importance they place on the improvement and prolongation of the individual human existence, while at the same time revealing the human body to be materially linked to other forms of life.

Jamie's first documented encounter with the objects of medical study occurred in the essay 'Surgeons' Hall', which appeared in her 2005 essay collection, *Findings* (128–45). In this piece Jamie reflects on her visit to the Royal College of Surgeons in Edinburgh, where she views preserved specimens – parts of the human body once used to teach students anatomy:

> Many of the specimens are beautiful. One of the earliest is what looks like bracket fungus, but it is actually a fine slice of kidney into which the then preservator has introduced mercury. Silver threads of mercury fan through the tissue, illustrating its blood vessels. It is quite lovely; one could wear it as a brooch [. . .]
>
> We consider the natural world as 'out there', an 'environment', but these objects in their jars show us the forms concealed inside, the intimate unknown, and perhaps that is their new function. Part art gallery, part church for secular contemplatives. 'In the midst of this city, you think you are removed from nature', they say – 'but look within'. (*F* 140–41)

Jamie's awareness of the combined beauty and strangeness of these objects is the result of careful scrutiny – 'For two, perhaps three hours, I have been gazing in silence.' (*F* 131) She likens this 'act of unhurried, unmediated examination' to the interest one pays to a lover or child, much as in *A Lover's Discourse* Roland Barthes connects the attentive gaze to desire: 'I catch myself carefully scrutinizing the loved body . . . I am searching the other's body, as if I wanted to see what was inside it.'[6] In Barthes's case, the erotic searching look does not view the body as an organic whole, but rather as a series of parts – any one of which may yield a sudden and transformative insight.

This fragmentation of the body confirms the instability of human subjectivity, representing an endless fluctuation between the position of subject and object. To bear witness to these once-living things has an intellectual and a moral dimension, and Jamie's sensitive description of the encounter is an important record of the changing mood of the observation and its effects on her creative process: 'I do still believe that there is value and worth in trying to move towards something which is true or good in the arts. All the arts ought to act as a conscience, a human conscience.'[7]

The act of questioning initiated here takes a different form in Jamie's later essay 'Pathologies' (*S* 21–42). Jamie begins this essay by recording her response to the death of her mother: an experience that prompted her to rethink her understanding of the term 'nature': 'What was it, exactly, and where did it reside? I felt *something* at my mother's bedside, almost an animal presence.' (S 23) Jamie went on to spend some time in a pathology unit, observing its practices – an experience that marked the beginning of an important period of enquiry for her, and one that would yield a number of diverse creative works. The first effect of this research process was to prompt Jamie to begin to see parts of the body in new ways. Here she describes a section from a colon: '[the] surface was pale yellow-brown, and ribbed like a beach at low tide. It was a natural artefact alright, but far from elegant, and if I hadn't been told I couldn't have said whether it belonged to an aquarium, a puppet theatre, or a bicycle repair shop.' (S 26) This diverse array of contexts heightens the strangeness of the normally unseen body part, even though Jamie's first inclination was to situate it in a descriptive landscape that would be familiar to her readers. The same experience was to generate a poem, commissioned for a volume called *Signs and Humours: The Poetry of Medicine*.[8] Jamie's contribution to this collection adopts the perspective of a pathologist, drawing implicit links between that role and the position of the poet in her own act of scrutiny. Though she again sees human tissue as a part of the fabric of nature – likening it to a marine-dwelling animal – the human being from whose body it comes remains of the utmost importance. The patient whose tissue is under scrutiny is addressed directly in the poem, so that it preserves both the clinical distance of the pathologist's perspective (he prefers 'to work quietly, at one remove') and the intimacy of the poet's, who is concerned with the fate of the human individual. This doubleness of perspective is reflected in Jamie's essay too:

> I kept having to do a mental exercise, every so often, to unhook myself from the colon being cut up in front of me, which was not a beautiful object of contemplation, and consider what it meant. To think upstairs, I mean, to that person lying ill and frightened, and anxiously awaiting 'the results from the lab'. (S 29)

Yet the poem shows how the scientific gaze, now brought to bear on the normally concealed organ, is able to 'read' a world of interpretation into this small amount of matter:

> See: through a microscope
> How a smear of tissue
>
> drawn from your small intestine
> contains great kingdoms:
> like an airman, I look down
> on promontories, fiords,
>
> miles of hinterland[9]

This observation must be seen in parallel with Jamie's first response to looking at liver cells through a microscope: 'I was looking down from a great height upon a pink countryside, a landscape. There was an estuary, with a north bank and a south.

In the estuary there were wing-shaped river-islands or sandbanks, as if it was low tide.' (S 30)

The visual awareness that inflects both the prose and poetry that Jamie wrote about this experience was to be further developed in her next creative project. For this she was commissioned to write poems in response to a series of anatomical representations from the first half of the nineteenth century, and one from the early twentieth; these were later printed – together with the images that inspired them – in a volume called *This Weird Estate*. This publication emphasises the dialogue between image and word, and also between different ways of coming to terms with what lies beyond our existing body of knowledge. The work grows directly from Jamie's interest in a reading of 'nature' that extends beyond what we can apprehend with the naked eye, moving towards microscopic processes (mutating cells, encroaching diseases) that are damaging to humans. These processes not only threaten our sense of supremacy but also fundamentally trouble the boundary between human nature and non-human nature. This volume shows a preoccupation with loss of life, and reveals Jamie's concern to link environmental destruction with the most minute, particular and personal manifestations of it.

The interior of the human body has always been a significant preoccupation both for scientists and creative artists. In earlier centuries, however, such an investigation would be judged to transgress the natural boundary between exterior and interior – the former being the realm of art, the latter of science.[10] Andreas Vesalius (1514–64) was among the most influential of early anatomists, and his volume *De humani corporis fabrica* is illustrated with detailed drawings showing skeletal and muscular structures of the human body, often with allegorical elements. Such peculiarities of representation would be common in anatomical drawings for centuries to come:

> from sixteenth-century diagrams to early nineteenth-century frontispieces, the dominant tradition of anatomical illustration is strangely dynamic and expressive, often implying or following an unfolding story: skeletons who stride through pastoral landscapes; deeply dissected corpses who nonetheless smirk seductively; cadavers who assist in their own dissection, gazing raptly into their abdominal cavities.[11]

The contest between realistic and expressive forms of representation was a subject for debate. John Bell, a Scottish surgeon writing in 1810, noted that '[e]ven in the first invention of our best anatomical figures, we see a continual struggle between the anatomist and the painter; one striving for elegance of form, the other insisting upon accuracy of representation'.[12] He went on to accuse anatomists of being 'arbitrary and loose in their methods; not representing what they saw, but what they themselves imagined'.[13] This criticism obscures the difficulties faced by physicians in their attempts to advance this branch of medical learning, however. Until the middle of the nineteenth century, anatomical study was the subject of widespread disapproval. Prior to the passing of the Anatomy Act in 1832 the only bodies made available for dissection were those of criminals who had been condemned to death and dissection by the courts. The difficulty in procuring cadavers and the transgressive implications of portraying them made anatomical drawings revolutionary, both for the intellectual and the aesthetic advances they represented.

Anatomical texts also foreground the acquisition of knowledge; they are part of a process of education that has shaped the medical practices of today – 'A high evidentiary value is thus attributed to images of anatomy: it is in seeing the interior of the body that we see its truth.'[14] Jonathan Sawday's comments on the practice of dissection confirm this: 'in lieu of a formerly complete "body", a new "body" of knowledge and understanding can be created. As the physical body is fragmented, so the body of understanding is said to be shaped and formed.'[15] The process of dissection is significant in this respect: at the same time as it signals the potential loss of bodily integrity it marks a desire for knowledge that exceeds the normal extent of observation, since what is within the body is not available to the gaze and is rarely a fitting subject for scrutiny. The earliest anatomical texts mark a transition from the practice of touch to that of sight, though – as Phillippe Peu, author of a seventeenth-century treatise on childbirth, affirmed – this did not necessarily promote realistic description of the internal organs, but rather encouraged the production of new knowledge through the ease with which such information could be practically applied.[16] The drawings are not an end in themselves, therefore, but part of a larger process of discovery. For Jamie, this creative project is on a historical frontier of knowledge, combining science and art in a way that deepens the investigation of the relationship between the human body and non-human nature.

Many of the surgical illustrations included in *This Weird Estate* seem strange to the twenty-first-century observer, not primarily because of their inaccurate rendering of anatomical fact, but rather because much medical detail remains puzzling to the untrained eye. The tendency to represent the abnormal by means of visual representation is one reason why this estrangement persists, yet the combined force of text and picture plays an important role in the explication of medical detail.[17] William Hunter, in his 1774 introduction to *The Anatomy of the Gravid Uterus Exhibited in Figures*, affirms the instructive role of the visual representation:

> The art of engraving supplies us, upon many occasions, with what has been the great desideratum of the lovers of science, an universal language. Nay, it conveys clearer ideas of most natural objects, than words can express; makes stronger impressions upon the mind; and to every person conversant with the subject, gives an immediate comprehension of what it represents.[18]

The important interaction of image and word in *This Weird Estate* testifies to the power of the visual not to replace language but rather to extend its potential to represent what might otherwise prove unrepresentable. In each of the poems Jamie adopts a strikingly different perspective and creative method. The first addresses an engraving by Antonio Scarpa showing the arteries of the brain.[19] Written in Scots, the poem imagines traversing this landscape, which is as strange as a dream-kingdom.

> The kintra drawn on this auld cairt
> s'nae sae fremmit as it seems,

but a kingdom ye micht gang tae
in Elfyn-ballads an dreams (WE)[20]

This interpretation speaks not only to the drawing, which resembles an unusual terrain with bifurcating and dead-end paths, but also to the metaphorical significance of the mind as the originator of thoughts and dreams. The choice of language is important here: for most readers it is not the language of everyday speech and this contributes to the 'otherness' that marks the experience of reading the poem. Jamie has said that the image reminded her of the journey in Thomas Rymer's 'Queen of Elfland', and the complex textual resonances of this association are important to the reading of the sequence as a whole.[21] In the environment of Jamie's poem, years might be spent traversing the pathways between the 'briars an thorns' before reaching a clearing, or a space of reflection and reassessment. This is an important text with which to begin the collection, since it invites the reader to contemplate the strangeness of these anatomical landscapes, and to enter this imaginative world fully. The process by which the speaker comes, in the final line, to understand himself as 'laird o this weird estate' is one requiring effort and commitment.

This conflation of the strange representation of the hitherto undiscovered terrain of the human body with a voyage of discovery is altered radically in the next poem, written to accompany a plate from John Lizars's *Observations on Extraction of Diseased Ovaria*, published in 1825. Jamie explains,

I wrote the poem after reading the case notes which accompany the illustrations. They are hair-raising, but also heroic in their way and they give us a glimpse of the real people involved. In this poem, all the phrases in italics are taken verbatim from the case notes [. . .] The poem [is] spoken as if by Janet herself, but I was interested also in the tumour as an object, a sculpture almost, its strange otherworldly shape, the rather lovely colours it was etched in. I'm impressed by the surgeon–artist's ability both to treat their patients with compassion, and also to look so hard and dispassionately at what they find within us.[22]

Here the woman responds directly to the act of representation itself – 'Here, at *true size*, / is shown the object / I bore within me'. Her understanding of her experience is fundamentally altered by what she now knows of its cause. She likens the tumour to a lengthy pregnancy, without the joy of giving birth, and sees the growth as a living thing – the 'black pearls' of its 'eyes or buds' making it appear similar to an oyster. Up to this point the metaphors have been familiar ones but soon, in suggesting that 'its bulk, its / turning away, suggests / a minotaur's shame', she shows amazement at the mutations of the human body entering the world of myth – a sight almost beyond the capacity of the human mind to imagine. Yet this woman's unswerving consciousness is one of the most striking features of the poem.

Of course, I was awake
throughout. It's May now,
ten weeks. The scar

concealed, I again *bind*
shoes for a living.
I am *daily mending.*

Her experience of the excision is at once dramatic and unremarkable; her resump-
tion of her job binding shoes allows for the double meaning of the final line: she is
herself 'mending' – her health restored after the ordeal – and mending the belongings of others.

An important dimension of the sequence as a whole is the close links it forges
between the concealed aspects of the human body and the representation of the
natural world. The third picture, also from a text by John Lizars, is made up of nine
drawings in all.[23] Each depicts a stage in foetal development that Jamie uses to consider the vulnerability of the earth itself.

Little man, homunculus, revealed
within your rind; your blinds and veils
are drawn gently aside, but you don't see us
examine you in your privacy: eyes

closed fast, you're asleep. Oblivious –
a nut tucked in its shell, seed in a pod,
you grow steadily, curled in the coracle
which carries you downriver to your birth.

So it must have been for each of us,
tissue-wrapped in nature's layers and folds,
precious cargoes, nourished through a cord.

Perhaps, aeons ago, this very Earth
– planet of tundra, mountains, oceans, glens,
formed thus inside her mother, then was born.[24]

The poet draws attention to the power of the gaze both as an agent of scientific
knowledge and as a means of interpretation in the poem. By figuring the unborn
child as a diminutive adult, one asleep and oblivious to observation, she emphasises his agelessness and vulnerability.[25] From the beginning she combines images
of man-made coverings ('blinds and veils') with natural ones ('rind', 'a nut tucked
in its shell', 'seed in a pod'). Direct address and simplicity of form add to the
immediacy of effect here, but this poem is tightly wrought: the internal rhyme
of 'rind' and 'blinds' and the repeated imagery of sight – 'you don't see us', 'eyes
// closed fast' – create an organic wholeness more powerful than our knowledge
of the medical problems these illustrations depict. Jamie implicitly considers the
beginnings of all natural life as an act of birth: 'So it must have been for each of us
/ tissue-wrapped in nature's layers and folds'. It is clear from the illustration where
this idea is developed from – the largest representation of the series is of the inside
of the ovary, depicted like the earth itself. This globe is not only the site of new

birth, but itself emerged from the void, undergoing the same process as the 'little man' of the poem's first line. The vulnerability of the unborn child suggests that the world itself is a threatened life form – the threat to the individual, and to the whole, bound together.

The next picture in the sequence is the first to depict a recognisable human body framing the interior organs, and in doing so it introduces a new perspective on the relationship between the public and private spaces of the body. Sander Gilman has noted a model for the use of illustration that stresses the artistic medium itself and the internal iconographic tradition of the work of art.[26] Here, the limbs, and hands, are elegantly drawn – the latter depicted gently overlapping, bound together with threads above the eviscerated abdomen. The oval pictorial space is perfectly centred on the page, so it is perhaps unsurprising that Jamie chooses to focus in her companion poem on the concentration involved in the act of illustration itself. She depicts it as a solitary process, as a kind of communion between artist and subject: 'Bar my own breath / and the pencil's scratch / I draw in silence' (WE). Likening the opened belly to an animal's lair, she sees the act of representation as akin to physically entering the space of the body, or the home or centre of animate life. The artist, who is also the doctor, marvels at the absence of the heart from this scene: 'See – at the human core / lies not the heart // but a forked stick'. The missing heart suggests the artist's own lack of emotional response to his task but the clarity of language and line in this poem – like the precision of the surgeon's art – expresses not lack of feeling, but an appropriate sublimation of emotion to craft. This cleft stick is indicative of the moral dilemma suggested by even this reverend investigation of the body in death – a body whose 'poor ligatures' hint at the class distinctions between the dead boy and the living men in pursuit of medical knowledge. Here the moral imperative becomes exactness, the representation of the body in its natural state, the value of the artist as a recorder of the real.

From the unity of this depiction comes the multiplicity of the next – another set of illustrations by Richard Quain, thirteen in all, from the second volume of *The Anatomy of the Arteries of the Human Body*, published in 1844. These painstaking repetitions draw out the extraordinary variety of the human anatomy, but hint too at the mechanical dimensions of such repeated representation. The perspective adopted in the poem is more obscure than elsewhere in the series: 'Human, when you were seized / With the need to know / What coupled your hearts [. . .] to your calculating heads' (WE). It addresses the human quest for knowledge directly, and this time it sets the relationship between emotion and intellect at the centre of the enquiry. It concludes that the drive to understand this relationship has led humans to open the most private space of the 'other' – the interior of their bodies. Again the hierarchies of power are hinted at: the doctor, dissecting and displaying, renders the other human being as an object of the gaze, removing its individuality and its emotional potential. To counter this dynamic, it is the heart that is treated most expansively here – 'shattered one day / ablaze with love the next' – while the 'calculating head' remains within its own boundaries. The plea for freedom in the second stanza is ambiguous, however. Beginning 'Please, now we're free', the 'we' seems to refer to the multiple illustrations of arteries depicted here. It is posited as different from the 'Human', to whom the first stanza is addressed, and is grouped with, yet clearly differentiated from, animal life. The suggestion that these living objects will spend their lives as 'corals, perhaps, or shy deer – ' reveals how the details of visual representation are used by Jamie as imaginative prompts – the pictures loosely resemble coral formations, and the narrow tubular networks could be mistaken for antlers on the heads of deer. Here the body becomes a 'dark machine / pulsing, pulsing', its parts condemned to endless service of the whole.

The final poem in the series – in keeping with the twentieth-century origin of the picture – invokes a more personal response. From a German source this time, the image is an X-ray of a small baby, its skeleton and nervous system resembling vegetation. Contemplating the loss of a child before birth, the speaker in the poems sees nature as a solace in time of grief, but emphasises the unique and irreplaceable quality of individual human life: the mother gathers 'tendrils of cold moss' and 'broken birch twigs' much as one would gather flowers, yet in spite of their visual similarities to the once-living tissue of the child's body, these remain only themselves: 'I bore home gladly / these gifts of the wild; / I arrange and arrange them, / but they're not my lost child' (WE).

In adopting such a variety of perspectives on these drawings, Jamie prompts us to think of them not as reflective of clinical processes but each as a product of a unique way of looking at the human body. At various stages in this creative project, the poet dwells on both the experiential reality of embodied life and its metaphorical power. Yet all the poems in this series also draw attention to what is unrepresentable – to the sheer inability of any matter to stand in for another and to replicate its emotional resonance. In this way, though the anatomical drawings speak to universality of experience, Jamie's poems stress its particularity, and remind us of the moral obligation to be attentive to our own lives as well as to the greater materiality of the earth.

WORKS CITED (SEE ALSO BIBLIOGRAPHY)

Barthes, Roland, A Lover's Discourse (London: Penguin Books, 1990).
Bell, John, Engravings of the Bones, Muscles, and Joints, illustrating the first volume of The Anatomy of the Human Body (London: Longman, Hurst, Rees and Orme, 1810).
Bennett, Jane, Vibrant Matter: A Political Ecology of Things (Durham, NC: Duke University Press, 2010).
Caldwell, Janis McLarren, 'The Strange Death of the Animated Cadaver: Changing Conventions in Nineteenth-Century British Anatomical Illustration', Literature and Medicine 25: 2 (Fall, 2006), pp. 325–57.
Gilman, Sander L., Health and Illness: Images of Difference (London: Reaktion Books, 2004).
Greenlaw, Lavinia (ed.), Signs and Humours: The Poetry of Medicine (London: Calouste Gulbenkian Foundation, 2007).
Harvey, Karen, 'Visualising Reproduction: a Cultural History of Early-Modern and Modern Medical Illustrations', Journal of Medical Humanities 31 (2010), pp. 37–51.
Knox, Robert, A Manual of Artistic Anatomy (London: Henry Renshaw, 1852).
Lizars, John, A System of Anatomical Plates; accompanied with descriptions, and physiological, pathological, and surgical observations (Edinburgh: D. Lizars, 1822).

McTavish, Lianne, 'Practices of Looking and the Medical Humanities: Imagining the Unborn in France, 1550–1800', *Journal of Medical Humanities* 31 (2010), pp. 11–26.

Neher, Allister, 'John Knox and the Anatomy of Beauty', *Medical Humanities* 37: 1 (2011), pp. 46–50.

Sawday, Jonathan, *The Body Emblazoned: Dissection and the Human Body in Renaissance Culture* (London: Routledge, 1996).

Scarpa, Antonio, *Engravings of the cardiac nerves, the nerves of the ninth pair, the glosso-pharyngeal, and the pharyngeal branch of the pneomo-gastric*, tr. Robert Knox (Edinburgh: Peter Brown, 1836).

Scarry, Elaine, *The Body in Pain: The Making and Unmaking of the World* (New York: Oxford University Press, 1987).

Stephens, Elizabeth, *Anatomy as Spectacle: Public Exhibitions of the Body from 1700 to the Present* (Liverpool: Liverpool University Press, 2011).

Whittier, Gayle, 'The Ethics of Metaphor and the Infant Body in Pain', *Literature and Medicine* 18: 2 (1999), pp. 210–35.

NOTES

1. The essay was later published in Jamie's 2012 collection of essays, *Sightlines*. Page numbers for this volume are used throughout. Jamie, 'Pathologies', p. 24.
2. Bennett, *Vibrant Matter*, 1590 (e-book).
3. 'Anatomy Acts' (http://www.anatomyacts.co.uk – accessed 24 May 2014), a Scotland and Medicine initiative, is the largest touring exhibition of medical materials in Scotland's history. Jamie was commissioned to write poems in response to some of the objects on display. The poems later appeared as a limited edition titled *This Weird Estate*.
4. Bennett, *Vibrant Matter*, 339 (e-book).
5. Ibid., 324 (e-book).
6. Barthes, *A Lover's Discourse*, p. 81.
7. Fraser interview, 'Kathleen Jamie', p. 16.
8. Greenlaw, *Signs and Humours*, pp. 43–4.
9. Ibid., p. 43.
10. Knox, *A Manual of Artistic Anatomy*, p. 77. For a discussion of Knox's theories see Neher, 'John Knox and the Anatomy of Beauty'.
11. Caldwell, 'Strange Death', p. 334.
12. Bell, *Engravings of the bones*, p. iii.
13. Ibid., p. iv.
14. Stephens, *Anatomy as Spectacle*, p. 3.
15. Sawday, *The Body Emblazoned*, p. 2.
16. Peu's attitudes towards the use of anatomical illustration are discussed by McTavish in 'Practices of Looking and the Medical Humanities', pp. 18–19.
17. Gilman, *Health and Illness*, p. 14. Caldwell also emphasises the important relationship between text and visual image.
18. Hunter quoted in Harvey, 'Visualising Reproduction', p. 45.
19. The text was translated by Robert Knox and its engravings copied by Edward Mitchell from Scarpa's 'Tabulae Neurologicae'. This image (Supplementary Plate VII) is from Felix Vicq d'Azyr (1746–94), a French physician and anatomist. This example offers some support for Bell's assertion that illustrations were copied from earlier publications rather than derived from personal observation.
20. *This Weird Estate* is unpaginated.

21. This comment is made in Jamie's introduction to her reading of the poem on the CD accompanying *This Weird Estate*. In the tale from a medieval verse romance, 'Thomas the Rhymer' was carried off by the Queen of Elfland and endowed with the gift of prophecy. The story was also the basis of a popular ballad, later reworked by Sir Walter Scott.

22. Excerpt from Kathleen Jamie's note to the poem available at http://www.anatomyacts.co.uk/artists/KathleensPoem.htm (last accessed 24 May 2014). This is the only poem of the six in the series available on the exhibition website. It is also the only one of the poems in *This Weird Estate* printed with a title, which is rendered in lower-case type.

23. Lizars, *System of Anatomical Plates* (Plate VIII, 'View of the Fetus in Utero'). Details of the two Lizars texts are transposed in the list of illustrations included in the print version of *This Weird Estate*. This error is corrected in the references here.

24. This poem from *This Weird Estate* is reprinted in its entirety by kind permission of Kathleen Jamie.

25. Preterm infants are especially prone to being described metaphorically; they are often seen as 'organisms' rather than as fully human. See Whittier, 'The Ethics of Metaphor', p. 217. By contrast, Jamie emphasises the foetus as both human and part of nature.

26. Gilman, *Health and Illness*, pp. 12–16.

What the Water Says

Poured water flexes and twists

a body is poured over itself
skin over ribs and muscle

creamy bloom
rising up through the skin
bone-milk

*

My name is water
says the ghost of water

pooling as sweat
in the dent of your shoulder

laying a net of salt on the tongue
that licks your shoulder

Birds barrack in the shade
The grass stems wait in parallel

Someone sitting beside you
casts you half in sun, half out

*

The jug stands on the table – damp-lipped
as if a girl licked her lower lip
Damp makes it look pliant
and deepens its red glaze

Voices in the long evening
The dog sinks with a sigh
outside the door
In a house two fields away a woman laughs
over and over

The kitchen air is speckled by dust
The jug stands on the table just where you put it
Thick glaze, squatness, an inescapable quality of clay

*

The masters painted this over and over: thin arch of eyebrow, elongated forehead. The slant, hieratic eye they outlined with black strokes not, after all, so different from the techniques of icon-painters. Madonna and Child. Virgin and Child with Patron.

Such an expanse of cheek before the high malar, the amused green eye. Magdalena's ivory skin gave nothing away. In a pleasure-boat on a glacial lake, sailing to Albania, I laid my head on her knee and tried to sleep. I tumbled down into darkness, where her voice lapped and lapped like little waves on a lake.

*

The line drifts

like morning mist
where the river runs

below the field
between the trees –

like words
half-realized then lost

as mist dissolves
and morning runs on

the field
brightening above the wood

and tree pollen
making a white mist

*

Running everywhere

in the lime tree
on the tongue of an iris

I am the cross
and the chrism
                I am in the bottom field

where the cattle hooves go *plock plock*
through blue morning mist
                       I run
here and there
about the parish:

the wet world in the eye of the parish

*

Stretching as she comes, the small cat
strolls toward you
through splashes of dark and light

The heat wants you to undress
Black pupil, white bone –
it expects a confession

Come sit in the black and white
under the trees:
the smudge and dazzle of sunlight

Fiona Sampson

12. Into the Centre of Things: Poetic Travel Narratives in the Work of Kathleen Jamie and Nan Shepherd

Eleanor Bell

> Here then may be lived a life of the senses so pure, so untouched by any mode of apprehension but their own, that the body may be said to think. Each sense heightened to its most exquisite awareness, is in itself total experience. (*The Living Mountain* 82)

These reflections on walking in the Cairngorms are from Nan Shepherd's *The Living Mountain*, written in the 1940s. For Shepherd, the 'total experience' offered by the mountains opened up deeper channels of the self, during which, she writes, 'I am not out of myself, but in myself. I am'.[1] Previous critics have picked up on the meditative qualities within Shepherd's work, where the mountains always remain magical and ultimately impenetrable in her Zen-like reflections: 'The journey is itself part of the technique by which the god is sought. It is a journey into Being; for as I penetrate more deeply into the mountain's life, I penetrate also into my own.' (84) While critics such as Robert Macfarlane have recently acknowledged Nan Shepherd's significant contribution to mountain literature, bringing this previously neglected work into prominence, this essay will reflect on some of the possible reasons why *The Living Mountain* lay unpublished for three decades, until it was eventually published by Aberdeen University Press in 1977. In doing so, specific connections will be made between Nan Shepherd and Kathleen Jamie, both explorers and poets whose texts, although produced over half a century apart, are similar in their blurring of the boundaries between travel and nature writing. Yet while open to the spiritual dimensions of travel writing, Jamie has also been realistic and critical of the genre, acknowledging, for example, its often-inherent masculine bias and negative environmental impacts. In comparing Shepherd's *The Living Mountain* with some of Jamie's essays in *Findings* and *Sightlines*, which focus on travel and nature, this essay will examine the social and cultural context of each writer's quest, illuminating in turn some of their own particular 'findings'.

Before discussing *The Living Mountain*, however, it is worth reflecting on the context of Scottish travel writing preceding Shepherd's earlier in the twentieth century. When Edwin Muir set off on his famous *Scottish Journey* in 1934 in a 1921 Standard car gifted from the artist Stanley Cursiter, for example, his intention was to provide 'a record of a journey' and, he continued,

> to give my impressions of contemporary Scotland; not the romantic Scotland of the past, nor the Scotland of the tourist, but the Scotland which presents itself to one who is not looking for anything in particular, and is willing to believe what his eyes and ears tell him.'[2]

Muir's *Scottish Journey* provides an interesting snapshot of Scotland at the time, especially in terms of the binary oppositions it constructs between the rural and the urban (its depictions of Glasgow are particularly haunting), and in terms of its politics of place. Yet Muir's text was not the first of its kind; there were several other important travelogues and investigations of nation prior to Muir's *Scottish Journey* that could be mentioned here: H. V. Morton's *In Search of Scotland* (1929), Harry Batsford and Charles Fry's *The Face of Scotland* (1933), followed by George Blake's *The Heart of Scotland* (1934), which then became the source of documentary films for John Grierson (*The Face of Scotland* (1938) and *The Heart of Scotland* (1961)). Another important text at the time was Hugh MacDiarmid and James Leslie Mitchell's (Lewis Grassic Gibbon's) *Scottish Scene: or The Intelligent Man's Guide to Albyn* (1934), comprising a series of essays, stories and poems written alternately by Mitchell and MacDiarmid, again attempting to take the literary and cultural pulse of the country at the time.

While all of the texts mentioned above share this similar 'intelligent man's' desire to document place, recording aspects of lived experience as a means of capturing elements of Scotland in transition, Shepherd's travelogue is far more modest by comparison. Illuminating an urge for solitary exploration and deep reflection, her text has no ambition to be authoritative or age-defining. Rather, throughout Shepherd's text is the impulse to absolve the self of ego, to give precedence to the power of nature in order to fully experience Being. As critics such as Margery Palmer McCulloch have pointed out, many of the women associated with the Scottish literary revival era were similarly motivated by the search for self-determination at personal rather than national levels.[3] While Shepherd was in correspondence with many writers at the heart of the Scottish Renaissance movement, clearly familiar with its objectives, she nonetheless chose to produce a text in which 'journeying out' is a means of 'journeying in'; the focus is on interiority, the sensory awareness and limitlessness of the self offered in the face of the sublimity of the mountains.

Another crucial reason for the neglect of Shepherd's text relates to its moment of historical production. While the 1930s saw a burgeoning interest in and fascination with travel in the Scottish, and more widely British contexts, by the time Shepherd produced her text towards the end of World War Two the culture had clearly shifted away from such concerns.[4] Shepherd commented that 'the only person who read the manuscript then was Neil Gunn, and that he should like it was not strange, because our minds met in just such experience as I was trying to describe.'[5] Although Gunn was a firm supporter of her work ('he made a couple of suggestions as to publication, but added that in the circumstances of the time a publisher would be hard to find'), she continues:

> I wrote one letter at his instigation and received a courteous and negative reply and the manuscript went into a drawer and has lain there ever since.
>
> Now, an old woman, I begin tidying out my possessions, and, reading it again, I realize that the tale of my traffic with a mountain is as valid today as it was then. That it was a traffic of love is sufficiently clear; but love pursued with fervour is one of the roads to knowledge.[6]

The Living Mountain contains many passages where this 'traffic of love' is evidently clear. In her preface to the 1977 edition Shepherd makes a sharp contrast between 'man' and 'mountain', between the natural landscape and the lived space into which it is transformed:

> Aviemore erupts and goes on erupting.
> Bulldozers *birze* their way into the hill.
> Roads are made, and re-made, where there were never
> roads before.
> Skiers, swift, elate, controlled, miracles of grace and
> Precision, swoop and soar – or flounder – but all with
> exhilaration . . . [7]

The man-made often jars with nature, yet the natural world is of a higher order, where human endeavours can only be understood as transient by comparison. For the attuned observer such as Shepherd, the immensity of the natural world readily usurps the marks made by mankind. Shepherd writes: 'all these are matters that involve man. But behind them is the mountain itself, its substance, its strength, its structure, its weathers. It is fundamental to all that man does to it or on it' (iv). To look upon this juxtaposition of nature and the man-made is all part of a wider need to see beyond the commonplace, to reach for some form of connection with higher being: 'so, simply to look on anything, such as a mountain, with the love that penetrates to its essence, is to widen the domain of being in the vastness of non-being. Man has no other reason for his existence' (79–80).

Commenting on *The Living Mountain* in his own poetic travel narrative, *Beside the Loch of the Green Corrie*, Andrew Greig observes that:

> Hard to believe it was written in the Forties; it anticipates by sixty years aspects of the 'Nature writing' of our time. The product of years of stravaiging around in the Cairngorms, [*The Living Mountain*] understands and conveys better than anyone the absolute physicality, the immanence of the transcendence that abruptly swoops and plucks you in its hooked talons out of the ordinary and carries you not away from this world but into the beating, unsayable heart of it

. . . She was a wonderful noticer, the kind of noticing that opens a crack into the centre of things.[8]

Given Shepherd's anticipation of the concerns of contemporary nature writing, it is not surprising that Robert Macfarlane, a key writer at the heart of this movement, provided the introduction for the reissue of *The Living Mountain* published by Canongate in 2011. Having first read Shepherd's text in 2003, Macfarlane, drawing on connections with Merleau-Ponty's theories of embodiment, goes on to explain the reasons why he continues to be humbled by the radical nature of her text:

> Radical, because Shepherd was a woman writing out of a Highland Scottish culture in which the cherishing of the body was not easily discussed. And radical because, as philosophy, it was cutting-edge. In the same years that Shepherd composed *The Living Mountain*, the French philosopher Maurice Merleau-Ponty developed his influential theory of the body–subject. [. . .] His work, particularly *The Phenomenology of Perception* (1945), was dedicated to enriching the idea of the body, such that it could be said both to perceive and to think. Merleau-Ponty described this embodied experience as 'knowledge in the hands', a phrase that could have come straight from Shepherd. 'The body is not . . . negligible,' she wrote, 'but paramount'.[9]

In many ways Shepherd's text defies simple categorisation. On the surface it is an attempt to explore the Cairngorms, to document the experience of walking in the mountains, but it is more deeply concerned with the sense of transcendence offered to those who are attuned; travel writing, nature writing, philosophical quest – all three are inherently interconnected in *The Living Mountain*. The *raison d'être* of Shepherd's text, it seems, is to articulate the moment of connection between mind, body and environment: her 'traffic of love' in the Cairngorms as a quest for connection with nature in the most authentic possible sense, especially given the fraught ways in which the man-made world continues to impinge on nature.

While for Shepherd 'journeying out' could be described as a spiritual and largely timeless quest (with the exception of a few incidental man-made interruptions), in Jamie's writings, by contrast, the trappings of the twenty-first century are all too present. Tensions between writing, motherhood and the need to juggle many aspects of a busy life are simultaneously set against the need to probe beneath the surface of the everyday in order to illuminate small moments of lived experience and aspects of the natural environment more thoroughly. In doing so, in Jamie's work it is not uncommon for the profound to interconnect with the mundane, for the poetic to be interspersed with the domestic. In this sense Jamie writes from a personal space which sees the value of recording the everyday within a grander order. It is perhaps these very human qualities of her essays on travel and nature, though – seeing the domestic within the wild, and vice versa – which are central to their appeal. Thus it is not unusual for moments of potential transcendence in her work to come down to earth with a realist bump.[10]

In her essay 'Darkness and Light' in *Findings*, for example, where she aspires to experience darkness in its most natural forms ('I'd a notion to sail by night, to enter into the dark for the love of its textures and wild intimacy'), Jamie attempts to visit Maes Howe, the Neolithic burial chamber in Orkney, during the winter solstice (F 3). The irony of finding the authentic in such an oft-visited place is not lost on Jamie: 'In its long, long existence it has been more forgotten about than known, but in our era it is open to the public, with tickets and guides and explanatory booklets' (F 10). Despite Jamie's best attempts to experience Maes Howe in isolation, she ends up being escorted by a Historic Scotland guide, only to be informed that there are also surveyors, with light-emitting equipment, working on site:

> Inside was bright as a tube train, and the effect was brutal. I'd expected not utter darkness, but perhaps a wombish-red. Rob was carrying a torch but this light revealed every crack, every joint and fissure in the ancient stonework. At once a man's voice said, 'Sorry, I'll switch it off,' but the moment was lost and, anyway, I'd been forewarned . . . We entered the tomb and, in that fierce white light, it was like that moment which can occur in midlife, when you look at your mother and realise with a shock that she is old. (F 14)

The sharp contrasts between light and dark in this essay can also be read as juxtapositions between culture and nature, the sense that 'nature' cannot be apprehended in isolation; nature is perhaps most meaningful when mediated through personal experience, and often in Jamie's works this takes a domestic turn. Reflecting on her first, technologically illuminated experience of Maes Howe, and a subsequent return trip, this time with only the Historic Scotland guide, Jamie stops to do some Christmas shopping in Stromness:

> I wandered into a toy shop, all bright and lit for Christmas, and in there picked up a silver plastic tiara. My little daughter [. . .] would love this. Standing there in the bright shop with this ridiculous tiara in my hand, turning it so it sparkled, I was thinking about light. I suppose I'd been hoping for a trick of the light at Maes Howe. No, trick was the wrong word. The tomb-builders had constructed their cairn to admit a single beam of solstice light: it was the bending of a natural phenomenon to a human end, somewhere between technology and art. But not art either: drama. [. . .] A very ancient drama, going right back to the Neolithic. Were they the first people, I wondered, to articulate this metaphor of light and dark, of life and death [. . .]
> Then the shop-keeper said, 'Enjoy it while it lasts.'
> 'I'm sorry?'
> She nodded toward the plastic tiara in my hand.
> 'My little girl used to love these things, all glittery and bright. But she's fourteen now, and wears nothing but black.' (F 22–3)

Here, an ironic association between the Neolithic drama of light and dark, life and death, is to be read alongside a contemporary drama of light and dark: the plastic tiara shimmering in a toy shop, symbolic of childhood innocence set against adolescent darkness. Such contemporary, seemingly superficial comparative backdrops, therefore, allow Jamie access to hidden recesses, deeper levels of comparison. Jamie may feel compelled to incorporate elements of lived family life into her reflections as this is what comes naturally to her, yet as readers we see that often the most perceptive examinations of nature are found in the most unexpected places, that our very understanding of what nature is, is often best mediated through the seemingly trivial or commonplace.

The 2008 *Granta* issue *The New Nature Writing* contains writing by, among others, Kathleen Jamie, Richard Mabey, Jonathan Raban and Robert Macfarlane. In his editorial introduction, Jason Cowley suggests that 'the best new nature writing is also an experiment in forms: the field report, the essay, the memoir, the travelogue', and, he goes on, 'if travel writing can often seem like a debased and exhausted genre, nature writing is its opposite: something urgent, vital and alert to the defining particulars of our times'.[11] Cowley goes on to explain that the writers in this particular edition are all 'on a journey of discovery, as the best travel writers were'; the 'new nature writing' is 'about new ways of seeing'.[12] Often these investigative reflections are at a local level, for, as Tim Dee writes, 'the more a globalised future awaits, the sweeter the local patch seems.'[13]

Both *Findings* (2005) and *Sightlines* (2012) reveal a narrative voice that, while always questioning and open to poetic discovery, is nonetheless confident and assured. Building on *The Golden Peak: Travels in Northern Pakistan* (1993), in which the young poet travels solo in the Northern mountains, Jamie's two most recent collections are simultaneously rooted in Scotland, yet keen to discover it anew through journeys into the self and nature. As with Shepherd's focus on the body as site of mediation for nature, Jamie's investigations are likewise often either mediated through the body or indeed use the body as the source of investigation itself, as is the case in her *Sightlines* essay 'Pathologies' (which also appeared in the 2008 *Granta* 'New Nature Writing' issue). In this essay, Jamie explains that after attending a conference on nature, where she had come home 'grumpy', thinking 'it's not all primroses and otters', she was compelled to get in touch with an acquaintance, a clinical consultant pathologist, at Ninewells Hospital in Dundee, as a means of exploring 'inner nature'. Jamie writes: 'there's our own, intimate, inner natural world, the body's weird shapes and forms, and sometimes they go awry' (S 24). With consent from the pathologist, Jamie observes some of his work, during which one of the examinations is of a section of human colon containing a tumour. The strangest thing that Jamie has to come to terms with is the defamiliarising notion of the pathologist dissecting the tissue ('The pile of sliced colon mounting at the far edge of his board looked like chanterelle mushrooms, the fat squished under his fingers like cottage cheese. It might have been "nature", but there was nothing uplifting about it' (S 28)), and to then square this with the fact that the patient from whom it was removed is recovering in a ward upstairs. On a subsequent trip to the lab, Jamie observes sections of a liver tumour under the microscope: 'I was looking down from a great height upon a pink countryside, a landscape. There was an estuary, with a north bank and a south [. . .] "It's like the Tay!" I said. "At low tide. With the sandbanks."' (S 30). This uncanny flip between the alien, cellular landscape of the fleshy material and the comparison with the homely is again familiar Jamie territory: to make the unknown somehow manageable, comprehensible, to partially domesticate the wild without usurping its innate magic. After observing a post-mortem, clearly her toughest challenge, for example, Jamie concludes the essay by leaving the hospital as visiting hour is commencing, feeling it was 'good to be part of that rough tribe of the mortal' (S 41); the dramatic clash between the bustling hospital and the wildness of the earlier microscopic visions remaining all too apparent for the reader.

The Living Mountain, it seems, was too difficult a text to be assimilated into its age, not purely as a consequence of the economics of publishing, but also due to the impossibility of its very categorisation.[14] Yet it is precisely this fusion of the exploration of the local, combined with philosophical rootedness in the body, and concomitant ontological quest, which have made this text so relevant for contemporary nature writers. While Shepherd's work lay hidden from view in a drawer for thirty years, her observations being too out of step with her contemporary world, for the contemporary 'new nature writers' this blending of the boundaries of travel and nature is de rigueur. While Shepherd is finely attuned to the possibilities of Being in The Living Mountain, Jamie is clearly writing from a more cluttered age, where the search for such purity of thought and solitary experience has inevitably become more challenging and difficult to negotiate. Yet, for Jamie, the mixture of mediating the natural world and the wild through the body, domesticating the wild in small, ordinary ways in order to make it at least partially comprehensible, can be regarded as central to her vision.

WORKS CITED (SEE ALSO BIBLIOGRAPHY)

Greig, Andrew, At the Loch of the Green Corrie (London: Quercus, 2010).
Macfarlane, Robert, 'I walk therefore I am', The Guardian (30 Aug 2008), http://www.theguardian.com/books/2008/aug/30/scienceandnature.travel (last accessed 24 May 2014).
McCulloch, Margery Palmer, Scottish Modernism and its Contexts 1918–1959: Literature, National Identity and Cultural Exchange (Edinburgh: Edinburgh University Press, 2009).
Muir, Edwin, Scottish Journey: A Modern Classic (Edinburgh: Mainstream Publishing, 1996).
Shepherd, Nan, The Press and Journal (27 Oct 1977), NLS MS.27443.
Shepherd, Nan, 'The Living Mountain', The Grampian Quartet (Edinburgh: Canongate, 1996).
Shepherd, Nan, The Living Mountain: a celebration of the Cairngorm Mountains of Scotland, introduced by Robert Macfarlane (Edinburgh: Canongate, 2011).

NOTES

1. Nan Shepherd, The Living Mountain, p. 84 (1996 edition). Subsequent page references are to this edition.
2. Muir, Scottish Journey: A Modern Classic, p. 101.
3. 'This divergence in priorities is true in the Scottish context as elsewhere. While the interwar cultural and political revival initiated by MacDiarmid was dominated by the aim to escape from a provincial North British identity and to achieve self-determination – politically in the longer term and more immediately through the rediscovery and renewal of distinctly

Scottish forms of literary and artistic expression – for the women, especially as manifested in their writing, the search for self-determination in a gender sense came first. This does not mean that they were insensitive to or completely uninvolved in the national project.' McCulloch, *Scottish Modernism*, p. 70.

4. In the wider British context, for example, the mid-thirties saw the production of a series of travel books including Evelyn Waugh's *Ninety-Two Days*, Graham Greene's *Journey without Maps* and Orwell's *The Road to Wigan Pier*, as well as J. B. Priestley's *English Journey*. Priestley's book was published the year before Edwin Muir's – these were companion books, commissioned by Heinemann and Gollancz.
5. Shepherd, *The Press and Journal* (1977).
6. Ibid.
7. Ibid., iii.
8. Greig, *At the Loch of the Green Corrie*, p. 94.
9. Macfarlane, 'I walk therefore I am'.
10. Deborah Lilley also suggests that nature and the domestic are firmly entwined in Jamie's work: 'both the laundry and the birds are resolutely of the same world'. Lilley, 'Kathleen Jamie: Rethinking the Externality and Idealisation of Nature', in *Green Letters*, p. 22.
11. Cowley, 'Editor's Letter: The New Nature Writing', p. 10.
12. Ibid., pp. 10–11.
13. Dee, 'Nature Writing', p. 24.
14. As Robert Macfarlane writes in his introduction to Shepherd's text: 'The Living Mountain is a formidably difficult book to describe. A celebratory prose-poem? A geo-poetic quest? A place-paean? A philosophical enquiry into the nature of knowledge? A metaphysical mash-up of Presbyterianism and the Tao? None of these descriptions quite fits the whole, though it is all of these things in part.' (Shepherd, *Living Mountain* (2011), p. xiv)

13. 'Connective Leaps': *Sightlines* and *The Overhaul*

Louisa Gairn

When asked to define the genre of her 2005 essay collection, *Findings*, Kathleen Jamie encountered a challenge: 'There didn't really seem to be a word for it', she notes;[1] 'It's not nature writing, but it is; it's not autobiography, but it is; it's not travel writing, but it is'.[2] Matt McGuire notes that her work 'disrupts the demarcation lines within recent Scottish criticism', operating 'in the gaps, in the places where other discourses fail to reach'.[3] Similar border-crossings take place in Jamie's latest book of essays, *Sightlines* (2012), which, together with her latest poetry collection, *The Overhaul* (2012), continues her focus on ecological interrelationship. In a 2009 interview, she distanced herself from the issues of national identity and gender which had characterised her earlier works, instead stating her main interest as 'the world which is more-than-human, which is beyond the human'.[4] In engaging with this broader question, Jamie asserts that 'the role of the poet is not to be political but shamanic [. . .] mediating between various worlds and bringing messages back and forth between them'.[5] *Sightlines* appears to have this idea of mediation or negotiation at its core, suggested by the subtitle to the American 2013 edition: 'a conversation with the natural world'.[6] For Jamie, attempting this 'conversation' invites us to contemplate our place within a wider ecology, recognising ourselves as 'animal bodies', part of nature as much as culture (S 5). In this way, her work aligns with contemporary ecocritical views such as that of her former colleague, John Burnside, who proposes that poetry and ecology may work together as 'a science of belonging', and that 'for an ecologically mindful poet, the task is one of reconnecting, of rediscovering, as it were, one's own nature through connection with a wider reality, with the more-than-human'.[7]

The shifting and sometimes uneasy ideas of home, belonging and identity, considered in the broader context of ecological thought, thus remain important themes within Jamie's work. Ecologically-minded interpretations of home are often influenced by Heidegger's notion of 'dwelling', which 'implies the long-term imbrication of humans in a landscape of memory, ancestry and death, of ritual, life and work'.[8] This is the idea expressed by Seamus Heaney in his essay 'The Sense of Place' (1977), that 'We are dwellers, we are namers, we are lovers, we make homes and we search for our histories'.[9] Similarly, Jonathan Bate's 'ecopoetics' concerns poetry 'which effect[s] an imaginative reunification of mind and nature, [. . .] a *poiesis* (Greek "making") of the *oikos* (Greek "home" or "dwelling-place")'.[10] Jamie's idea of reconciliation with the natural world involves recognising the evidence of dwelling, rejecting the notion of certain landscapes as untouched wildernesses and acknowledging ourselves, in Burnside's words, as 'participants in a natural history'.[11] In drawing attention to the 'relics of a lost intelligence, the long-forsaken fields' in *Sightlines* (195), and noting the evidence of cultivation 'raked / down the threadbare hillsides' in *The Overhaul*'s 'Highland Sketch' (O 17), Jamie adopts what might be considered a 'dwelling perspective',[12] as defined by the ecological theorist and anthropologist Tim Ingold, where 'to perceive the landscape is [. . .] to carry out an act of remembrance [. . .] engaging perceptually with an environment that is itself pregnant with the past'.[13] As Peter Mackay argues in the present volume, Jamie does not conform to theories of 'dwelling' in the sense of rootedness or stability, particularly given her own impulses to 'stravaig' or escape from domestic life. However, like Burnside and other 'ecologically mindful' writers, Jamie is concerned with the challenge of being at home in the world. She accepts this is an activity which has practical as well as philosophical implications:

> We're conscious, intelligent and organic, so how are we to live? How are we to conduct ourselves? Why does the world meet us with beauty and wonder? Why is there evil? What is our right response to stupidity and greed, especially our own? Will a poem about a flower suffice?[14]

For Jamie, discovering or maintaining a sense of belonging is not a given. As Ingold notes, 'while we may acknowledge that dwelling is a way of being at home in the world, home is not necessarily a comfortable or pleasant place to be, nor are we alone there'.[15] Similar to Burnside's assertion that our homes are 'provisional and constantly negotiated',[16] Jamie's depictions of dwelling places often evoke a sense of transience or tenuousness, contemplating the 'cold empty doors' of St Kilda's abandoned cottages in *Sightlines* (161), or the comfortless shelter of 'The Long House' in *The Overhaul* (O 12–13). Perhaps as antidote to such unhomeliness, Jamie's poetry offers conceptual dwelling places, liminal zones like 'The Tree House' of her 2004 collection, a space which Jamie suggests is 'a sort of negotiated settlement, part reverie, part domestic, part wild'.[17] In her most recent poetry, Jamie imagines further reconciliations with or escapes into the 'other' of nature, as in 'Glamourie', where woodland that is 'just some auld fairmer's / shelter belt' nevertheless generates a sense of wild enchantment or acceptance of the human visitor by 'hosts, who appeared / as diffuse golden light, / as tiny spiders' (O 42–3). These versions of 'dwelling' are necessarily fleeting and unstable reveries in which the sense of belonging flickers between comfort and unease. In *Sightlines*, this duality of belonging is also explored on an intimate, physical level, signalling our own ambivalent status as embodied beings often struggling against 'nature' in the form of mortality, or simply inhospitable terrain. In 'Aurora', the opening essay of the collection, Jamie describes her experience of visiting the Arctic, with its mysterious landscape of icebergs and aurora borealis, but notes the difficulty of truly immersing oneself in such 'sublime' experiences: 'the flickering and pulsing of our own minds, our own mutability, tell us that's enough' (S 15), while 'It's cold, our animal bodies say; best keep moving. Keep warm, keep hunting' (S 5). Here, reverie cannot be maintained for long, yet in the face of the alienating 'mineral silence' of ice and rock, Jamie discovers a sense of belonging in her own subjective and physical reaction, recognising that 'we are animals' (S 5). As she comments in a recent interview, 'We are mortal, biological creatures; that is the nature of our being in the world, and worth acknowledging.'[18]

In emphasising our identity as 'creatures', Jamie's approach to landscapes, wildlife and human artefacts in Sightlines seems to draw on a phenomenological point of view, where the apparent divide between mind and body, or self and world, is rejected in favour of holistic lived experience, the world encountered through the senses. As Merleau-Ponty suggests, 'we are in the world through our body', thus physical experience is perhaps more compelling or more meaningful than ideal aesthetic categories designed to appeal to disembodied intellects. It is only by 'reawaken[ing] our experience of the world as it appears [. . .] to our body', by 'remaking contact with the body and with the world, [that] we shall also rediscover ourselves'.[19] This embodied perspective takes a darker turn in the Sightlines essay 'Pathologies', focusing on the interpolation of the natural world and the body in the context of disease. Recalling a conference she attended on environmental change, despite 'reverent talk of far-off polar bears and "transforming experiences"' (S 25), Jamie writes that she was left with a sense of frustration, doubting the truthfulness or usefulness of this 'foreshortened definition of "nature"' (S 23). Instead, as Deborah Lilley notes, the view of 'nature' Jamie develops by looking through the pathologist's microscope is more inclusive as well as more disturbing, drawing on an awareness of mortality, and challenging 'conceptions of nature as external or stable; reminding us of the transience and temporality of its forms'.[20] This, Lilley argues, is an example of Jamie's rejection of nature as an idealised 'other', instead seeing it as coterminous with human identity, history and bodily experiences, including death – something which Jamie senses at her mother's hospital bedside as an almost tangible 'animal presence' (S 23). Indeed, elsewhere Jamie contends that the 'wildness' of nature is 'a force requiring [. . .] lifelong negotiation', in which the boundary between the human self and the natural world is frequently blurred or breached: 'to give birth is to be in a wild place, so is to struggle with pneumonia'.[21] This duality, the need to control or resist the disruptive force of nature while recognising it as an innate part of human life, perhaps speaks to Jamie's sense of truth as multiple or unstable – 'tricksterish', or a 'shape-shifter', as she suggests in a 2000 essay.[22] As such, in Sightlines, Jamie argues that negotiating the 'other' of nature is central to human experience: 'We need disease to dance us on our way; we need to halt it if we're to live morally. Twin truths, like boxing hares' (S 37).

Sightlines and The Overhaul thus build on the exploratory ecopoetics of Jamie's previous collections, driven by the need to seek out 'truths' about the nature of belonging, however provisional or shape-shifting these may ultimately be. This includes an ongoing examination of preconceptions about landscape and community, particularly within a Scottish context. Accordingly, while Jamie admits to the romantic attraction of places such as 'Wild, remote, famous, oft-imagined St Kilda', she comes to recognise that this is illusory: these were 'Places with such long human histories, I soon came to distrust any starry-eyed notions of "wild" or "remote". Remote from what? London? But what was London?' (*S* 142–3) In *The Overhaul*, depicting a group of Western Isles shepherds in 'The Gather', Jamie undercuts pastoral stereotypes: the men retain their cultural distinctiveness, yet converse in English rather than Gaelic, make jokes about urban popular culture, and drink Coca-Cola while commenting on economic challenges of sheep farming. The poem closes with a striking image of vitality, as the shepherds leave in their boat, at first slowly, appearing 'old-fashioned, / like a scene in a documentary', but then 'roar[ing] off at top speed, / throwing us a grand wave' (*O* 28–9) – recalling the confident 'waving citizens' (*QS* 51) of Jamie's 1994 poem, 'The Republic of Fife', de-marginalising the local or provincial, and instead asserting the relevance of rural communities as part of an interconnected, globalised world. This calls to mind similar approaches in the work of earlier Scottish writers, such as Iain Crichton Smith's resistance to the dismissal of rural or island communities as 'unreal, off the edge of things' in his essay 'Real People in a Real Place' (1982), or the assertion of distinctive cultural and environmental identity by George Mackay Brown, the Orkney poet admired by Jamie for writing which 'enacts the ecology it describes, the soundscape of an interconnected, secure community'.[23] While there is an element of identity politics at work here, Jamie's dissatisfaction with the facile use of terms like 'wild' or 'remote' also reflects a long-standing aversion to what she describes in *Among Muslims* (2002) as the 'words we reach for out of habit', suggesting we should instead think carefully and critically about the language we use to represent the world (*Among Muslims* 239). Seeking to avoid the perpetuation of what she has termed 'fantasies and false distinctions' about nature and landscape, Jamie echoes contemporary ecocritics who assert that the concept of the pristine wilderness is itself artificial.[24] As William Cronon argues, modern environmentalism's idea of wilderness derives from the Romantic sublime, generating unhelpful divisions between supposedly 'pure' landscapes in contrast to places marked by human activity: 'if it doesn't permit us the illusion that we are alone on the planet, then it really isn't natural. It's too small, too plain, or too crowded to be authentically wild'.[25] Jamie seeks to dispel such misconceptions, as she makes clear in a 2012 interview: 'There is nothing untouched. To hanker after the truly wild is a fantasy. We have to accept what we have and deal with it'.[26]

In *Sightlines*, hard-won knowledge wins out over idealism. Knowing the scientific or objective facts, however, does not preclude a sense of mystery or respect. In the essay 'Storm Petrel' Jamie contemplates the vast distances covered by a migratory bird, whose individual history is known to us only because of human intervention. The petrel carries a metal ring on its leg, part of a long-term international program which tags and tracks migrating wild birds. Jamie comments that a 'purist' who 'carried a torch for "the wild" and believe[d] in a pristine natural world over and beyond us' might consider such tagging an 'intrusion' or even a violation (*S* 215). Yet such knowledge only enhances the 'otherness' of the bird:

this one ringed bird had extended my imagination. The ring showed only that it was wedded to the sea and, if anything, the scale of its journeyings made it seem even wilder than before. (S 216)

Jamie's approbation of scientific knowledge might seem to run counter to some ecocritical discourses, where science and technology are viewed as part of the problem, a way of looking at the non-human world as merely a resource, of 'enframing' nature. This is the critique of technology stemming from Heidegger's condemnation of science for 'dissolv[ing] nature into the orbit of the mathematical order of world-commerce, industrialization, and in a particular sense, machine technology'.[27] Jamie, significantly, often embraces knowledge gained through scientific enquiry or the affordances of modern technology as a means of deepening our understanding of the world – although she also critiques the damage inflicted by technological society, as in the essays 'The Hvalsalen' and 'Voyager, Chief', which explore the history and consequences of industrial whaling. Her approach seems related to Burnside's concept of 'knowing the *how*, and celebrating the *that*', where ecologically-minded writing is conceived as 'a form of *scientia*, a technique for reclaiming the authentic, a method for reinstating the real'.[28] Jamie's engagement with scientific knowledge also connects with older 'ecopoetic' traditions in Scottish writing, such as Hugh MacDiarmid's linking of poetry and science, and Nan Shepherd's *The Living Mountain*, a book Jamie discovered while working on *Sightlines*.[29]

If the title of *Findings* called up associations of scientific research 'findings' as well as chance discoveries, *Sightlines* might suggest clarity, precision, the scope of the visual field, as well as the lines of connection that can be drawn between observations. In a 2009 interview, Jamie explicitly relates the craft of writing to the practice of scientific observation, '[taking] notes almost like a naturalist'.[30] She finds inspiration for this in the work of other writers, such as the American poet Elizabeth Bishop's depictions of animals; however, 'learning to take patient notes' also emerges as something of an apprenticeship served with the various scientists and specialists described in *Sightlines* – an experience which Jamie says 'taught me to change my focus' (S 158). Jamie's take on seeing and understanding is, as Lilley suggests, 'not just a process of noticing, but of actually looking differently', often guided by scientific specialists.[31] Indeed, when asked to comment on her approach in *Findings*, Jamie reflects that the 'best "seers" I have ever met are naturalists and scientists' – a choice of words which cannily denotes shamanic as much as scientific insight.[32] *Sightlines* as a whole recounts an ongoing education of perception and understanding, moving from 'float[ing] on the surface of knowledge' in 'Aurora', or from romanticising St Kilda, by learning to observe and interpret, whether looking through a microscope or surveying an abandoned landscape:

This careful recording was a wholly different way of looking at St Kilda to what I'd have done alone. Alone, I'd have rushed around, thrilled but hampered by a kind of illiteracy, unable to read the land. I wouldn't have studied the cats'-paw pattern of lichen on a lintel-stone, so similar to the patterns made by the wind on the surface of the sea below. I wouldn't have noticed a clump of tiny violets quivering on a cleit roof. (S 156)

Here, rather than limiting experience, expert knowledge enhances perception: 'The outer world also had flown open like a door, and I wondered [. . .] what is it that we're *just not seeing*?' (S 37, italics in original) Working on the essays collected in *Findings*, Jamie described an evolving ethic which combined paying heed with hard work, 'the quality of attention we can bring to a task', whether making a poem or analysing a blood sample in the lab.[33] *Sightlines* seems to evoke an ever deeper sense of kinship between the writer and the scientist in terms of observational ability; the capacity for attention, precision and insight.

However, Jamie also applies poetic craft to her encounters with the medical specialists, museum curators and naturalists of *Sightlines*, making intuitive bridges between different scientific perspectives, as well as 'translating' their expertise into a more readily accessible form. In 'Pathologies', she reads the cross-sections of cells displayed through the microscope as a richly coloured landscape, a topography or aerial archaeology, like 'our local river, as seen by a hawk' (S 30), while in 'On Rona', the sound of the killer whales is 'regular and industrial, like a Victorian machine' (S 197). For Jamie, as for Burnside and Shepherd, scientific enquiry may help to open up the world for discovery; however, 'the wherewithal of the scientific gaze' cannot access the whole 'truth' (S 148). Metaphor, pathetic fallacy, and simile, conceived as tools of the intellect, are deployed in *Sightlines* as imaginative links between human and non-human – perhaps also fulfilling the notion of writing's capacity for 'shamanic' negotiation. The poet's ability to articulate such lines of connection is, Jamie suggests, intrinsically human:

> our ability, born perhaps of thousands of years of watching the transforming play of firelight – to think in simile, in metaphor. We can say look, that shadow is like an antler, this line suggests an ibex horn, that girl is a deer, this problem is like that; therefore, that solution might just do the trick. The connective leaps, the careful taxonomies, how our minds work. (S 171)

From an ecopoetic point of view, such imaginative connections may also help to dissolve the conventional barrier between subject and object, following Gaston Bachelard's idea that poetic imagination or reverie unites self and world, human and non-human: 'The I no longer opposes itself to the world. In reverie, there is no more non-I'.[34]

In *The Overhaul*, Jamie explores such 'connective leaps' by linking together the non-human world with the intimate emotional and embodied world of the family and the self. In her poem 'The Galilean Moons', Jamie relates Jupiter's moons to her own children, soon to be grown up: 'a short time to watch, / eye to the eyepiece, / how a truth unfolds', before the children leave home, transposed into 'mere bright voice-motes' calling home across the distance (O 34–5). In 'Highland Sketch', an anecdote about a visit to the Scottish Highlands turns into a contemplation of shared personal history and relationship, the land like the speaker's own body, bearing the physical marks to show 'where a crop was raised' (O 17). In *Sightlines*, Jamie at times appears self-conscious about adopting such poetic tools, concerned with truthfulness and precision. In the essay 'Eclipse', although she admits to employing 'a fine example of the pathetic fallacy', and although the moon is 'only a rock', her reaction to the lunar eclipse is something like the sympathy experienced when 'a friend goes into labour, or a crisis, or has to undergo some kind of procedure'. Jamie links together the moon's conventional feminine associations with the optical transformation it undergoes during an eclipse, 'becoming less barren', and taking on 'mammalian colours, the shades of an incarnation, colours liable to pain' (S 125–6). Other stony worlds are similarly transfigured. Just as, in *Findings*, Maes Howe in Orkney reminded Jamie of 'a cranium' (F 12), the interior of the cave in *Sightlines* is also experienced anatomically, first 'like the inside of a cranium, a mind-space, as though the cave were thinking us' (S 166), and later as a 'cave-uterus' (S 169). Jamie's contemplation of such archaeological sites in *Sightlines* evokes a sense of liminality or phenomenological reverie where 'the membranes between body and stone [. . .] are dissolved', and where the scale of time itself is rendered unstable (S 45). This sense of simultaneous closeness and distance, 'feel[ing] unhooked from time', is evoked in the essay 'The Woman in the Field', describing Jamie's experience as a teenage volunteer on an archaeological dig, helping to unearth a woman interred at the centre of a Neolithic henge (S 58). Working on the excavation was profoundly liberating: it was 'a turning place, a henge, a hinge indeed' (S 65) which spurred her to embark on her career as a poet, sensing that 'The Stone Age was closer to me than secretarial college ever would be' (S 50). Implying endurance and renewal, the re-emergence of the buried woman resonates symbolically throughout Jamie's work, inspiring one of her earliest poems, 'Inhumation', and likely also the resurrected female poet of 'Meadowsweet' in *Jizzen*, suggesting, as McGuire notes, both a personal or physical 'heightened sense of identification' (J 65) with nature, and an assertion that poetry's place is 'amid the grime and physicality of everyday life'.[35]

For Jamie, however, the science of archaeology also provides an illuminating parallel for poetic craft. In *Sightlines*, Jamie notes that the archaeological process effectively destroys the evidence it seeks to reveal, stripping away layers of earth and time, displacing objects from their environment for cataloguing and analysis, and eventual storage or display in a museum archive. The process, she observes, is 'ruthless . . . even as the mystery is revealed, it's dismantled and destroyed' (S 59); the archaeologists' 'ritualised undoing' (S 67) of the historical site parallels its original creation. However, without this careful destruction and reconstruction, the truth cannot emerge. Similarly, poetry cannot provide an immediate access to the truth of the world, but may enact a process of revelation:

> The opening of the cist under that thunderclap was thrilling, transgressive. So, in its quiet way, was writing poems. The weight and heft of a word, the play of sounds, the sense of carefully revealing something authentic, an artefact which didn't always display 'meaning', but which was a true expression of – what? – a self, a consciousness. This was thrilling too. (S 66)

This concept of careful revelation aligns with the idea of poetry as craft or *poiesis*, defined by Heidegger as 'an instance of *techne*', 'an active bringing-forth, a process of unconcealment'.[36] The process of archaeology has been used in a similar way by other modern poets to contemplate poetry's role, such as Heaney's 'Digging' in *Death of a Naturalist* (1966), where physical labour on the land corresponds to a search for truth.[37] However, here the idea of poetry as *techne* or craft also correlates with Jamie's description of the 'weight and heft' of poetic language, the sense of words as material artefacts or perhaps tools which, as Ingold suggests, help us to understand the world through a 'coupling of perception and action'.[38] This concern with language and craft, linked to a sense of archaeological time, is also explored in *The Overhaul*. In the sonnet 'Excavation and Recovery', Jamie juxtaposes modernity with the guessed-at past, where specialists in 'hi-viz jackets' inspect a Bronze Age logboat embedded in mud of the Tay estuary, an 'axe-hewn hollowed-out oak' (O 8). The shift into alliteration recalls the cadences of Old English verse, a gesture of connection across time, telescoping the present day into the ancestral past, and calling attention to the different linguistic registers in which the River Tay has been addressed over the centuries. The poem sounds out the right words to describe the river; using the potentially reductive language of science, '*an estuary with a discharge of 160 cubic metres of water per second*', or attempting to invoke a more ancient and ambiguous identity:

> *or Tay/Toy/Taum* – a goddess;
> the Flowing (?), the Silent One (?)

The question marks are significant. The possibility for language to reconcile us with the natural world is an open-ended question which recurs throughout Jamie's poetry and prose – the difficulty of interpreting 'A word niver spoken or read' (MMS 159). The question surfaces elsewhere in *The Overhaul*, for example in 'An Avowal', where Jamie contemplates a wildflower's 'nodding assent' to multiple interpretations (O 32).

Poetic language nevertheless facilitates encounters, even conversations, with the 'more-than-human' world – even if, as Mackay contends, these remain unavoidably attenuated or fragmentary, a 'stunted communication' (see Mackay's essay in this volume). In *The Overhaul*, 'The Spider' adopts the animal's perspective, opening a conversation about a wider reality we tend to dismiss or overlook: 'had you never considered / how the world sustains? / The ants by day / clearing, clearing / the spiders mending endlessly –' (O 20). As McGuire suggests, Jamie's ability to leap from the apparently insignificant and mundane to consider grand moral and existential questions is a 'cross-contextualisation [which] recalls the nature of the environmental crisis, where our everyday behaviour has potentially catastrophic consequences for life on the planet'.[39] This might be considered as a modern take on Scottish poetry's rich tradition of animal encounters – one might think here of Robert Burns's 'To a Louse' or 'To a Mouse', where conversational directness enhances the sense of human and animal as 'fellow mortal[s]',[40] or the animal poems of Norman MacCaig, a poet Jamie encountered early on in her career at an Edinburgh writers' workshop.[41]

However, the 'animal encounter' motif is also, as Burnside notes, central to much contemporary ecopoetry, providing an opportunity to explore the borderline between self and other, human and animal identities – what Burnside describes as a 'fleeting entry into the otherworld'.[42] Quoting the American ecologist Paul Shepard, Burnside suggests that we are 'coarsened' by the loss of animals in our daily lives, which is why such poetic representations are now 'more urgent than ever', forcing us to confront the knowledge that 'we are tamed and we have almost lost the common stamp of creatureliness'[43] – a view which Jamie seems to share, remarking that although 'we share the closest kinship with animals [. . .] the daily immediacy of wild animals is lost'.[44] This is indeed a key feature of Burnside's own poetry, where such encounters elicit a 'sense of our presence as creatures / about to be touched'.[45] Similarly, in the poem 'Fragment 1', Jamie evokes an encounter with a deer during a woodland walk. Separated into brief two-line stanzas, this poem maintains a sparse rhythm which perhaps mimics the bounding of the deer, or the sense of disorientation at being lost in the woods. As in Burnside's 'animal encounter' poems, identity begins to dissolve; the deer's startled reaction may provide evidence of human presence, but the poem is threaded with an atmosphere of doubt: 'What form I take / I scarcely know myself' (O 10). This liminality also reflects our own human subjectivity, our provisional and limited knowledge of the natural world which may equally lead to belonging or alienation. Looking at ancient cave paintings of animals in the essay 'La Cueva', Jamie observes that 'no animal is complete; all are partial, half-disclosed, which is much how we encounter them alive' (S 169).

Sightlines maintains this awareness of 'creatureliness' throughout, repeating the idea of the 'animal body' as a unifying theme. In 'Aurora', the term emphasises our susceptibility to biological imperatives, the need to be moving and getting on with life, while 'Pathologies' considers our embodied vulnerability: 'if we are to be alive and available for joy and discovery, then it's as an animal body, available for cancer and infection and pain' (S 40). However, animal physicality may also lead to an enhanced sense of belonging, as in 'On Rona', where Jamie's excitement in encountering a group of killer whales leads to a realisation of kinship even in the midst of difference: 'suddenly I was reminded mine was an animal body, all muscle and nerve – and so were they, the killer whales, surging animal bodies, in their black and whites, outclassing us utterly' (S 199). Such encounters rely on the poetics of phenomenology, on physical empathy as well as an imaginative 'connective leap'. Developing this kind of ecological empathy might also have broader implications, as defined by Timothy Morton:

> The ecological thought doesn't just 'occur in the mind'. It's a practice and a process of becoming fully aware of how human beings are connected with other beings – animal, vegetable, or mineral. Ultimately, this includes thinking about democracy. What would a truly democratic encounter between truly equal beings look like, what would it be – can we even imagine it?[46]

This seems particularly relevant to Jamie's work – she has argued in the past that since 'poetry is a method of approaching truths . . . [it] is inherently democratic', 'a moral and democratic place where language concerns itself with truth'.[47] In Jamie's writing, the meeting and merging of human and non-human might be read as part of this 'democratic' ideal, describing the urge to connect with the world 'in a complicit / homage of equals' (*J* 13), and affirming our need 'to reach out for the natural' (*S* 236), even while admitting that this impulse may reflect mixed motives of 'wonder or shame or excitement or greed' (*S* 236). This sense of equality and potential reconciliation is heightened by the insights gained from science, 'discovering that we'd all travelled together, separating and overlapping, out of a deep, shared evolutionary origin' (*S* 171). As a complement to the 'paring down' and 'preference for the shorter lyric' which McGuire observes in Jamie's recent poetry, the narrative mix of autobiography, travel and nature writing in *Sightlines* makes more explicit 'connective leaps' between science and *poiesis*, self and other, which acknowledge our identity as well as our responsibility as part of the more-than-human world.[48]

WORKS CITED (SEE ALSO BIBLIOGRAPHY)

Bachelard, Gaston, *Poetics of Reverie: Childhood, Language and the Cosmos* (Boston, MA: Beacon Press, 1971).

Brandes, Rand, 'Seamus Heaney's Working Titles', in Bernard O'Donoghue (ed.), *The Cambridge Companion to Seamus Heaney* (Cambridge: Cambridge University Press, 2008), pp. 19–36.

Burns, Robert, *Poems and Songs*, ed. James Kinsley (London: Oxford University Press, 1969).

Burnside, John, *The Myth of the Twin* (London: Cape, 1994).

Burnside, John, 'Travelling into the Quotidian: Some notes on Allison Funk's "Heartland" poems', *Poetry Review*, 95: 2 (Summer 2005), pp. 59–70.

Burnside, John, 'Celebrating the animal encounter in poetry', *The New Statesman*, 15 August 2012, http://www.newstatesman.com/2012/08/call-wild (last accessed 25 May 2014).

Burnside, John, 'A Science of Belonging: Poetry as Ecology', in Robert Crawford (ed.), *Contemporary Poetry and Contemporary Science* (Oxford: Oxford University Press, 2006), pp. 91–106.

Crichton Smith, Ian, 'Real People in a Real Place', *Towards the Human: Selected Essays* (Midlothian: Macdonald Publishers, 1986), pp. 13–70.

Cronon, William, 'The Trouble with Wilderness, or, Getting Back to the Wrong Nature', in J. Baird Callicott and Michael P. Nelson (eds), *The Great New Wilderness Debate* (Athens, GA: The University of Georgia Press, 1998), pp. 471–99.

Heaney, Seamus, 'The Sense of Place', *Preoccupations: Selected Prose, 1968–1978* (London: Faber, 1980), pp. 131–49.

Ingold, Tim, 'The Temporality of the Landscape', *World Archaeology*, 25: 2 (October 1993), pp. 152–74.

Ingold, Tim, *The Perception of the Environment: Essays on Livelihood, Dwelling and Skill* (London: Routledge, 2000).

Ingold, Tim, 'Epilogue: Towards a Politics of Dwelling', *Conservation and Society*, 3:2 (2005), pp. 501–8.

Ingold, Tim, *Being Alive: Essays on Movement, Knowledge and Description* (London: Routledge, 2011).

McCulloch, Andrew, 'Introduction to "Field Mice" by John Burnside', *Times Literary Supplement*, 29 Nov 2011, www.the-tls.co.uk/tls/public/article832513.ece (last accessed 25 May 2014).

Merleau-Ponty, Maurice, *The Phenomenology of Perception*, tr. Colin Smith (London: Routledge, 2002).

O'Donoghue, Heather, 'The Poetry of Recovery and Memory', in Peter Robinson (ed.), *The Oxford Handbook of Contemporary British and Irish Poetry* (Oxford: Oxford University Press, 2013), pp. 341–58.

Pattison, George, *The Later Heidegger* (London: Routledge, 2000).

Shepherd, Nan, 'The Living Mountain', *The Grampian Quartet* (Edinburgh: Canongate, 1996).

NOTES

1. Crown interview, 'A life in writing: Kathleen Jamie'.
2. Scott interview, 'In the nature of things'.
3. McGuire, 'Kathleen Jamie', pp. 142–3.
4. Dósa interview, 'Kathleen Jamie: More than Human', p. 142.
5. Ibid., p. 142.
6. The subtitle picks up on Richard Mabey's description of *Findings*, http://www.sortof.co.uk/authors/kathleen-jamie (last accessed 25 May 2014).
7. Burnside, 'A Science of Belonging', pp. 92, 99.
8. Garrard, *Ecocriticism*, p. 108.
9. Heaney, 'The Sense of Place', pp. 148–9.
10. Bate, *The Song of the Earth*, p. 245.
11. See Gairn, 'Clearing Space', p. 243; O'Donoghue, 'The Poetry of Recovery and Memory', pp. 347–9; Lilley, 'Kathleen Jamie: rethinking the externality and idealisation of nature', pp. 19–24; Burnside, 'A Science of Belonging', p. 92.
12. Ingold, *The Perception of the Environment*, p. 5.
13. Ingold, 'The Temporality of the Landscape', pp. 152–3.
14. Jamie, 'Author's note', 'The Glass-hulled Boat' and *The Tree House*, Scottish Poetry Library.
15. Ingold, 'Epilogue: Towards a Politics of Dwelling', p. 503.
16. Burnside, quoted in Andrew McCulloch, 'Introduction to "Field Mice" by John Burnside'.
17. Jamie, 'Author's note'.
18. Ramaswamy, 'Interview: Kathleen Jamie' (2012).
19. Merleau-Ponty, *The Phenomenology of Perception*, p. 239.
20. Lilley, 'Kathleen Jamie: rethinking the externality', p. 21.
21. Jamie, 'A Lone Enraptured Male' (2008), pp. 25–7.
22. Jamie, 'Holding Fast' (2000), p. 280.
23. Smith, 'Real People in a Real Place', p. 14; Jamie, 'Primal Seam' (2005).
24. Ramaswamy, 'Interview: Kathleen Jamie'. Jamie's critique of 'wildness' is also examined in Lilley, 'Kathleen Jamie: rethinking the externality', pp. 17–20.
25. Cronon, 'The Trouble with Wilderness', p. 492.
26. Ramaswamy, 'Interview: Kathleen Jamie'.
27. Heidegger, quoted in Bate, p. 257.
28. Burnside, 'A Science of Belonging', pp. 94–5.
29. Goring interview, 'Kathleen Jamie: The SRB Interview' (2012).
30. Dósa, 'Kathleen Jamie: More than Human', p. 137.
31. Lilley, 'Kathleen Jamie: rethinking the externality', p. 23.
32. Anon., 'Interview with Kathleen Jamie', *Books from Scotland*.
33. Jamie, 'Counting the Cobwebs', pp. 38–9. See also Gairn, 'Clearing Space', p. 240, and Gairn, *Ecology and Modern Scottish Literature*, p. 10.
34. Bachelard, *Poetics of Reverie: Childhood, Language and the Cosmos*, p. 144.
35. McGuire, 'Kathleen Jamie', p. 145.

36. Heidegger, quoted in Pattison, *The Later Heidegger*, p. 51. See also Bate, *Song of the Earth*, p. 253. The idea of 'unconcealment' in Jamie's poetry is also discussed in Gairn, *Ecology and Modern Scottish Literature*, pp. 158–9.
37. See Brandes, 'Seamus Heaney's Working Titles', p. 21.
38. Ingold, *Being Alive: Essays on Movement, Knowledge and Description*, p. 17.
39. McGuire, 'Kathleen Jamie', p. 149.
40. Burns, *Poems and Songs*, p. 102.
41. Jamie remarks on her acquaintance with MacCaig in Goring, 'Kathleen Jamie: The SRB Interview' (2012).
42. Burnside, 'Travelling into the Quotidian', p. 65.
43. Burnside, 'Celebrating the animal encounter in poetry'.
44. Jamie, 'Ice age carvings: strange yet familiar'.
45. Burnside, *The Myth of the Twin*, p. 38.
46. Morton, *The Ecological Thought*, p. 7.
47. Jamie, 'Holding Fast: Truth and Change in Poetry' (2000), p. 281.
48. McGuire, 'Kathleen Jamie', p. 153.

To KJ, in her attic

Gifts, elegies and regrets
unscroll in mid-life:
the view out the window
and the light inside.

The games, the twice-locked code,
the hall of facing mirrors –
leave that to the kids.
They'll make a better fist of it.

For us remains still life,
the bowl of earthly fruit, slightly gone . . .

You sit to bash out praise
above the brackish estuary
where river turns to sea,
still lost, and found, and unafraid.

Andrew Greig

14. Life Lines, Sight Lines: Collaborative Works

Eleanor Spencer

Lines written by a young Spitfire pilot to his sweetheart, tentative at first, but growing increasingly desperate, progressively more honest. A black and white photograph of an austerely beautiful Tibetan plain, delicately, almost imperceptibly marked with a neat line of irregular white stones. The livid line of a recent mastectomy scar, surgically inscribed on the changed and changing body of a breast cancer survivor.

Kathleen Jamie's collaborative projects to date have, at first glance, little in common. In 1986, Jamie collaborated with Andrew Greig on *A Flame in Your Heart*, an epistolary poem charting the all too brief romance of a pilot and a nurse played out as the Battle of Britain roars overhead. *The Autonomous Region: Poems and Photographs from Tibet*, published in 1993, is a collaborative volume produced with photographer Sean Mayne Smith, comprising poetic and photographic reflections on a trek to Amdo and Tibet at the time of the Tiananmen Square Massacre in 1989. More recently, Jamie has collaborated with artist and illustrator Brigid Collins on an exhibition and a volume of words and images, *Frissure*. Published in 2013, the prose poems and images chart the poet's physical and psychological recovery from breast cancer and a resultant mastectomy. What, if anything, links these three diverse texts is a preoccupation with the 'line'; either a visible line marked on paper, earth or skin, or an altogether more intangible line, a sustaining connection that exists between the geographically or temporally estranged.

Jamie's travels have long been her *materia poetica*. *The Way We Live* (1987) included 'Karakoram Highway', a series of poems written in Northern Pakistan, and the poetic travelogue *The Golden Peak* (first published in 1992, and reissued as *Among Muslims* in 2002), came about when Jamie 'fell in with some mountaineers who were all for going to the Himalayas.'[1] Douglas Dunn suggests that Jamie possesses 'what I call an innocent eye, which I find very beguiling. What was it William Blake said? As a man sees, so a man is. Well, as a woman sees, so a woman is.'[2] Is this 'innocent eye' a chance gift, or must the poet consciously nurture, preserve, or protect it? Jamie's travels have taken her to places where she cannot help but look with an innocent eye. This Scottish traveller discovers a 'loch' called Quinghai, and increasingly lapses into a familiar Scots tongue that grows broader the further she journeys from home, for example in 'For Paola' and 'Sang o the blin beggar'. When the traveller returns home to Scotland, too, familiar spaces and places are seen as if for the first time. Paradoxically, it seems that what Jamie discovers in the remote Tibetan foothills is a renewed 'at homeness' with her own cultural and linguistic heritage. In a 2005 interview, however, Jamie insinuated that in future she might have ethical questions about travelling: 'I'm getting seriously, seriously concerned about flying for environmental reasons [. . .] Just jump on a plane and go here for the weekend, never mind about the tonnes of carbon you're dumping.'[3]

Jamie's poems and Sean Mayne Smith's photographs reveal a sparsely peopled landscape nevertheless richly inscribed by what Jamie describes as 'ghosts, lines of energy and wanderings, criss-crossed routes of travel' (AR 6). In 'Landscape with mani stone near Mount Kailash, West Tibet', lines of stones demarcate a route taken by traders and pilgrims, and the six syllabled mantra of Avalokiteshvara (Om mani padme hum) is carved on the mani stones in the foreground (AR 12). In her introduction, Jamie explains that on this journey she 'met' two historical characters, Fa-hsien, a fourth-century Chinese Buddhist monk and fellow 'travel writer' (his Record of Buddhist Countries, written in AD 414, is today known as the Travels of Fa-Hsien), and Princess Wen Cheng, who in AD 640 travelled to Tibet to marry the then king. Jamie performs a complex act of ventriloquism here, and both Fa-hsien and Wen Cheng seem to travel not only across space but also through time, and in many of the poems it is unclear who is speaking, and through whose eyes we are seeing. At one point, Wen Cheng is transposed to the present day, recast as a hedonistic, reckless adventuress:

> Wen Cheng's
> 　　　　Acting up, yes
> She's wilding in the dining-car
> I hear the
> 　　　　Smash of crockery, the waiter
> Swirling like a matador and fair enough
> It's 2 a.m. (Beijing) (AR 34)

It is this desire to tell untold tales that inspires A Flame in Your Heart, Jamie's only collaboration with a fellow 'makar' to date. Whilst we have, at the behest of critics such as Harold Bloom, Michel Foucault and Martha Woodmansee, stopped thinking of any poet as an impregnable 'autonomous ego', genuine collaboration between established poets is still a relatively novel occurrence.[4] Though we recognise that 'every poet is a being caught up in a dialectical relationship (transference, repetition, error, communication) with another poet or poets', a deliberate and sustained collaborative process and product challenges the still-powerful Romantic model of the isolated poet–prophet.[5] Still unduly influenced by Romantic concepts of genius and inspiration, we tend to regard the writing of poetry (or at least 'real' poetry) as a necessarily solitary activity.

A shortened version of A Flame in Your Heart was broadcast by BBC Radio 4 in

1985 under the title *Rumours of Guns*, and the poems lend themselves to radio dram-atisation in their creation of the two idiosyncratic and believable voices of Katie and Len. Whereas some of the poems are explicitly presented as letters or journal entries, others read more as barely mediated streams of consciousness. Though these poems are untitled (save for the penultimate poem, 'War Widow'), a footnote on each page tells the reader from whom the poem originates. The unobtrusive rhymes and chimes lend a faint but insistent musicality to the poems, like a half-remembered tune heard distantly on the evening air. The occasional full rhymes serve to jar the reader or listener, and to draw attention subtly to those poignantly prescient moments in the first poems in the volume. Early on in their courtship, Len writes:

> Let it come!
> I'm seeing her Thursday. No worries no fear.
> Alive till we die, that much is clear.
> It's going to be a scorcher, you can tell. (*FYH* 17)

This sudden reversion to end-stopped lines after seven stanzas of enjambed lines, coupled with the vigorous full rhyme of 'fear' and 'clear', creates a sense of forced joviality, a studied but strained performance of nonchalance.

The final line of this poem is an ominous foreshadowing of the violent death that awaits this young pilot; the final poem of section V leaves us with the isolated line, '*Len entering the fire he became.*' (*FYH* 70) This is one of the unattributed poems, dif-ferentiated by their use of italics, that intersperse Len and Katie's 'lines'. The speaker is seemingly omnipresent, an eyewitness of both Len's final moments thousands of feet above the earth, yet also able to observe Katie, who in that moment '*stumbled and steadied herself / between one bed and the next / one hand grabbing a bedrail / the other over her belly.*' (*FYH* 70) It is with these unattributed poems that the volume begins and ends. The opening poem imagines or anticipates the spectral return of the dead pilots to their now derelict airfield. In traditional elegies we are aware of a gradual upwards movement of the dead, a dynamic transcendence of earthly encumbrances. In accordance with elegiac convention, then, these heroes take to the skies once more:

> *They share cigarettes, and talk*
> *For an hour by the Dispersal Hut,*
> *Then one by one take off and climb*
> *Above the clouds, where it is always blue,*
> *Burning and burning at that summer's end.* (*FYH* 10)

Though the repetition of 'burning' serves as an uncomfortable reminder of the violent nature of these young men's untimely deaths, we see them received into a paradise of sorts, 'where it is always blue' and the last heady, halcyon days of summer are eternal.

The final poem in the volume, though, does not offer such easy consolation, and even threatens to reverse that traditional upwards movement of the dead: 'another stumbles dead-drunk in the hall, his tan boots sunk a foot below the floor' (*FYH* 74). Again, these spectral lads linger on in their familiar haunts, though they find themselves now out of time and out of place, 'in an airless living-room in the new estate, / grouped around the feature fireplace' (*FYH* 74). The final lines of this poem perhaps give us some clue as to the identity of this seemingly omniscient speaker:

> Above my bed the Airfix kits,
> The Hurricane, Spitfire, Messerschmitt,
> Spun on their threads in the draught. (*FYH* 74)

Several of Katie's poems tacitly suggest that she is pregnant ('You ought to know: I'm very late') (*FYH* 47). Is this speaker, gazing up at a collection of painstakingly crafted Airfix planes, the son of Katie and Len? The grainy illustration on page 75, of a child held aloft by a young woman, would suggest that this is the case.

One point of contact between this, Jamie's earliest collaborative work and *Frissure*, her most recent, is a shared realisation of how a brush with death quickens our appreciation of the world around us. After a near miss, Len muses, more to himself than to his lover, how:

> When you give yourself away
> And get life back again, unexpectedly,
> Walking in the evening you will see
> Houses, trees, faces, all sharpened in intense relief. (*FYH* 25)

In 2011, in what she describes as 'a case of life imitating art', Jamie was diagnosed with breast cancer (*F* v). In the introduction to *Frissure*, the volume of poems and images charting her recovery from a subsequent mastectomy, Jamie recalls a sense of the tables having been turned as the observer becomes the observed: 'Then, suddenly, it was my turn: my own body was the subject of this attention, my biopsies were sent to the very lab I had visited' (*F* v). Jamie refers here to the several years she spent 'in medical museums, gazing at body-parts preserved in oil' as research for her 2007 volume, *This Weird Estate* (*F* v). Like *Frissure*, *This Weird Estate* might also be considered a collaborative work of sorts, in that the poems take inspiration from, and respond to, the nineteenth-century anatomical atlases and X-rays held in the Royal College of Surgeons of Edinburgh and St Andrews University. The volume includes full-colour reproductions of these images alongside the poems. Furthermore, Jamie makes 'found poetry' out of surgeon's notes and medical records discovered in the collections – for example, in 'Janet', where the dispassionate observations of the surgeon John Lizar, given in italics, are reclaimed by the poet as she ventriloquises in (or through) the voice of the unfortunate Janet.[6] The poems in this volume are humane but never sentimental as they explore the relationship between the anatomical specimen and the living, and, crucially, *loving*, human body. In *Findings* (2005), Jamie writes,

Unless you have a professional interest, it's possible that the only bodies you've been intimate with, have scrutinised, have been the bodies of lovers, of children. The act of unhurried, unmediated examination has hitherto been an act of love. Perhaps as a consequence, or perhaps because given the opportunity we do indeed feel for all of suffering humanity, a stranger's arm with his corroding carcinoma, a diseased breast, a kidney taken from a man gassed on the Western Front, all call forth the same plain tenderness. (F 131)

Necessarily, perhaps, when a surgeon or an anatomist scrutinises a body, 'tenderness' must be expunged, or at least temporarily set aside; all patients become 'strangers' under the surgeon's scalpel. Bodies are dissected, either literally or metaphorically, reduced to a 'corroding carcinoma, a diseased breast'. The anatomical illustrations and X-rays dramatically defamiliarise the human body, revealing our most intimate home to be an unnervingly 'weird estate'. If the surgeon is like the Renaissance poet who visually dissects his beloved into a blazon of discrete body parts, then Jamie is, ironically, the doctor who must piece these patients back together and restore them to wholeness, reinvesting them with identity and autonomy.

Plate III, taken from John Lizars's 1825 text *Observations on extraction of diseased ovaria*, is a series of nine illustrations which appear at first glance to chart the development of a foetus in the womb. However, the Plate's title makes clear that it is the womb alone which is of scientific interest rather than the burgeoning human life within it; the pregnancy is merely incidental to the disease. Jamie's accompanying sonnet, however, deliberately inverts the surgeon's pathological focus, making no mention of the abnormality of the womb in question. Though the metaphorical description of the foetus as 'a nut tucked in its shell, seed in a pod' (*WE*), may seem to deny or overlook its humanity and subject-hood, that the poem is a direct address to this 'Little man' reveals that the speaker's interest is maternal, rather than medical; indeed, Jamie uses the more intimate 'wee man'[7] on the accompanying recording. The line 'So it must have been for each of us', reveals that for Jamie the quotidian miracle of childbirth is of greater interest than the 'weird' singularity of the diseased womb.

Similarly, Jamie's writing in *Frissure* is concerned not so much with illness or disease as with her re-emergence or rebirth back into the world. Jamie's introduction reveals an acute sense of being 'looked at', of being 'examined': 'the radiologist and pathologist looked with their eyes, the surgeon with his fingertips' (F v). However, determined to retain and maintain that familiar sense of herself as an observer, Jamie recounts that 'throughout, I tried to keep looking' (F v). Of being shown her own mammogram images, she recalls:

I sat beside the radiologist in front of her computer screen, as she pointed with her pencil. The image was rather beautiful, a grey-glowing circle, like the full moon seen through binoculars. (F v)

Jamie's figuring of the breast as a full moon recurs in the final of Collins's images in the volume; 'In September' has the line 'I lost the moon but gained the river' almost invisibly inlaid on one side of the paper (*Fr* 33). In this moment Jamie is both a looking subject and a looked-at object. Looking at herself even as she is being looked at by others allows her to retain a sense of imaginative ownership of her own body (parts). Of the first plate in *Weird Estate*, Jamie writes 'this image of the brain reminded me of a landscape'. This tendency to 'see' images of the human body as landscapes is something we find again and again in *Frissure*. In the introduction, she writes of her mastectomy scar, 'As I turned this way and that, I thought it looked like the low shores of an island, seen from afar. Or a river, seen from above. A bird's eye view of a river. Or a map', and later, 'It looked like a landscape' (*Fr* vi). On one hand, this could be interpreted as a desire for dissociation from the scar, as the poet imagines her scar to be a distant geographical feature ('seen from afar'), or more distant still, 'the full moon' viewed through binoculars, rather than a permanent mark on, or part of, her own body. Jamie recalls, 'I said [to Brigid] I wanted it off my body and onto paper, so we could both have a proper look at it.' (*Fr* vii) This desire to see the scar 'off' her body, though, came not from revulsion but from curiosity; indeed, Jamie describes her scar as 'this curious line of mine' (*Fr* vii).

Whilst Jamie does not suggest that her medical treatment was unduly invasive or distressing, she clearly anticipated, before work on *Frissure* began, that being subject to an artist's gaze would be a kind of antidote or corrective to being subject to 'a lot of medical gaze' (*Fr* vii). In many ways, this proved to be the case; it became 'proto-col' that sittings would begin with conversations 'about life and work, family, births, death, personal histories, flowers or birds we'd seen . . . the pressures of the modern world and the place of the artist, especially if she's a woman.' (*Fr* vii) Sharing the minute facets of personal experience and identity, of little or no consequence to the surgeon, became an integral aspect of these sittings. Whereas A. K. Maxwell's images, included in Jamie's introduction, depict not even a body but merely a dis-figured breast, Collins's pieces depict not only a body but an *embodied* experience.

Several of Collins's images in *Frissure* call to the mind the Japanese art variously known as *kintsugi* ('to patch with gold') or *kintsukuroi* ('to repair with gold'), whereby broken ceramics are repaired with a lacquer resin sprinkled with powdered gold.[8] The image titled 'North Sky', for example, described by Collins as 'a semi-abstract landscape', looks strikingly like a vein of gold 'patching' or fusing together a rent in the canvas. Collins has integrated lines from one of Jamie's fragments ('Healings 2') into the piece, though the words are indistinct, almost illegible, as if buffeted and eroded by the 'strange sea' Collins describes in her notes. Ceramics repaired by *kintsugi* are considered more precious and more desirable than pristine vessels as they are the embodiment of the aesthetic of *wabi-sabi*, the central tenet of which is the acceptance, even celebration, of transience and imperfection. In their preface to the volume, Jane Macnaughton and Corinne Saunders suggest that when looked upon by the artist, 'the surgical scar becomes a fissure bathed in light illuminating the path to a new way of seeing' (*Fr* iii). The very title of the volume represents this deliberate re-presenting of something negative or painful as something positive and even pleasurable. Jamie explains: 'We're calling it "Frissure"; a word coined by Brigid quite by accident, which falls between "frisson" and "fissure".'

The woman's battle with breast cancer has since the 1970s become a powerful cultural narrative in which the woman is cast as a survivor or a 'warrior', as in Deena Metzger's well-known *Tree Poster* (also known as *The Warrior*).[9] Metzger stands with arms flung wide, and an intricate tattoo representing the tree of life deliberately draws the eye to her mastectomy site like a *kintsugi* repair. Metzger writes of the poster,

> The photograph taken of me by Hella Hammid has become known as *The Warrior*. Our intention in turning it into a poster was to invite the world to look at a one-breasted woman and exult in the health and vitality she had not carried so powerfully before cancer. The illness I suffered was the means of profound spiritual transformation.[10]

Whilst Jamie characteristically refrains from such explicit proselytising, it appears that for her, too, surviving breast cancer has been a quietly transformative experience. She is less concerned with casting herself as a kind of warrior as with locating herself within a community or continuity of fellow sufferers. In 'Heredity 2' Jamie offers a nod of recognition to 'Isabella Telford, Margaret Hewit, Isabella Thomson, Margaret Stirling, / Isabella Parker', explaining 'Though we span two centuries, / we could all sit around the same table' (*Fr* 25). Like Janet in *This Weird Estate*, these women are perhaps some of 'the many, many unsung heroines of medical advances.'[11] In 'Gift 2', the disquieting medical illustrations she has become so familiar with remind her of what she has been delivered from. 'We can gaze at these,' she writes, 'then walk out into the day again, changed, saved, haunted a while' (*Fr* 21). It is indeed the case, as Wallace Stevens suggested, that 'death is the mother of beauty', as in the aftermath of her surgery, Jamie experiences a new kind of affecting imminence with the natural landscape, an agreeable hyper-sensitivity to the beauty around her, 'notic[ing] flowers, especially roses in the park, as never before' (*Fr* vi). Similarly, in 'Gift 1' the sound of the waves is an 'ever-present solace', and in 'Healings 2' she reveals that waking in the pre-dawn hours, 'at 2 or 4 or 6am, you breathe light into your body' (*Fr* 7).

Though *Frissure* is as surely about a journey as is *The Autonomous Region*, both the text and the images in *Frissure* quietly resist in their abstractness any attempt to coerce them into a satisfying linear narrative of recovery. Jamie recalls: 'At first I tried to write 'poems' but the tone was all wrong. Too smart, too concluded. A looser weave was required, something thready, gauzy, that could be unpicked' (*Fr* xi). Jamie's words suggest a privileging of ongoing poetic process over concluded poetic product. In keeping with *wabi-sabi*, Jamie's lines foreground their own provisionality, their own transience. These are not sustained or purposeful meditations but rather fleeting thoughts or sudden epiphanies, rather like the 'birds [that] arrived in the rowan tree, a density in their branches, then flew off again' (*Fr* vi). In Collins's images, these 'fragments? prose-poems?' are 'unpicked' yet further, as the artist selects 'fugitive' words and phrases in the same way as she might choose colours from a palette (*Fr* xiii). Just as Collins deconstructs Jamie's fragments, so too does she deconstruct her own creations, and this deconstruction becomes part of the creative process. In 'At the Edge of Sense', typewritten words are partially revealed as Collins sands back through the many layers of pigmented gesso and shellac that she has previously painstakingly applied. Frayed edges, loose threads and exposed bindings are accentuated, picked out in gold leaf, rather than concealed (*Fr* 5).

There is, however, a subtle evolution of sorts in Collins's images throughout the volume, whereby the images begin to trace less and less closely the 'line' of Jamie's scar and begin instead to look outward, to the landscape and seascape. The first of Collins's images in the volume, entitled 'Wild Music', was created by the artist scoring deep lines in the paper and creating rents which were bound with thin strips of surgical tape. The addition of delicate rose petals and gold leaf cannot, nor is it intended to, conceal the trauma that has been inflicted here. Though described as an imaginative response to Jamie's experience rather than a mimetic representation of the scar itself, this image looks very like a recently closed wound, with the uncomfortable puckering of the closed edges, and the splotches of brown-red pigment and wax disquietingly reminiscent of dried blood (*Fr* xiii). Similarly, Collins's second image, 'For the First Time', though, conceived of as 'hypothetical pathway, or river', assiduously traces Jamie's 'scar line' with two lines of minute sutures in turquoise surgical thread (*Fr* x). The predominant colours in this image are those of a hypertrophic scar or a fading bruise. In the later images, though, bodily contours give way to geological formations, as in the triptych of images entitled 'What is a line?', where the demarcation between land and sea becomes increasingly indistinct. 'Jagged edges become smoothed and soothed,' Collins explains, 'until they almost disappear' (*Fr* 19). Somewhere along the way, Jamie's scar has faded, if not from her body, then from her mind. It no longer preoccupies her imagination in the way it once did. If this scar is, as Jamie suggests, 'a map', then it leads her to a place far beyond itself.

WORKS CITED (SEE ALSO BIBLIOGRAPHY)

Bloom, Harold, *A Map of Misreading* (New York: Oxford University Press, 1975).
Hammid, Hella, Deena Metzger, and Sheila Levrant de Bretteville, '"I Am No Longer Afraid of Mirrors" (Tree Poster)' (Los Angeles: Peace Press, 1981).
Iten, Charly, 'Ceramics Mended with Lacquer – Fundamental Aesthetic Principles, Techniques and Artistic Concepts', in *Flickwerk: The Aesthetics of Mended Japanese Ceramics* (Ithaca, NY, and Münster, Germany: Herbert F. Johnson Museum of Art, Cornell University, and Museum für Lackkunst, 2008), pp. 18–25.
Metzger, Deena. *Tree: Essays and Pieces* (Berkeley: NorthAtlantic, 1997).

NOTES

1. Crown interview, 'Kathleen Jamie: a life in writing'.
2. Ibid., p. 12.
3. Scott interview, 'In the nature of things'.
4. Bloom, *A Map of Misreading*, p. 91.
5. Ibid., p. 91.
6. See Jamie, 'Janet', Anatomy Acts Object Guide No.172.

7. Jamie narr., *This Weird Estate*, track 3.
8. Iten, 'Ceramics Mended with Lacquer', p. 18.
9. Hammid et al., '"I Am No Longer Afraid of Mirrors" (Tree Poster)'.
10. Metzger, *Tree: Essays and Pieces*, p. 268.
11. Jamie, 'Janet'.

15. Midlife Music: *The Overhaul* and *Frissure*

Rachel Falconer

At the end of her poem 'The Cave of the Fish', Kathleen Jamie writes, 'Today I sit at the cave's / cool mouth, halfway / through my life' (*TH* 11). This tercet recalls the famous opening line of Dante's *Commedia*: 'In the middle of the journey of our life / I found myself . . .'. It must be partly because of Dante's cultural legacy that this narrative pattern seems so familiar, even to twenty-first-century secular readers: the pattern of a life shaped into two halves, hinged by a critical turning point.[1] For Dante's pilgrim, the midlife turn leads to the discovery of the *via diritta*, the one path that leads to Beatrice and the eternal rose. Readers of Dante today may hear echoes of a critical turn in their own lives – a turn perhaps prompted by the experience of a serious illness, a separation, or the death of someone close. In any case, what marks the arrival at such a midlife threshold is finding yourself lost. This paradoxical condition initiates the woodland adventure in Jamie's 'Glamourie': 'When I found I'd lost you' (*O* 42). The found–lost soul in Dante's *Commedia* is taken on a very circuitous route to reach his desire, but at least by the time he takes up with Virgil, he has a direction and a purpose; he's a lost soul found. The farther side of the midlife threshold is marked by a shift toward certainty, toward a concentration and clarification of aims. One model for Dante's hinged life-narrative is Virgil's *Aeneid*, where the midway turning point of the epic journey happens in the descent to the underworld. Aeneas emerges from that descent as a newly forged imperial hero, focused on his Roman destiny. In contemporary narratives, the midlife threshold can assume a similar shape and function; the experience of crisis or loss leads to a narrowing of focus, a commitment to a cause, or less programmatically, to a way of being (where you resolve to be 'true to yourself', as the saying goes).[2] Salman Rushdie once described this critical turn as the moment when you discover who your enemy is, since that is the first step to 'discovering what you are *for*.'[3]

I'd like to suggest that Jamie's conception of being at the midlife 'hinge' is a very different kind of experience: rather than leading on to a singular trajectory, the midlife threshold opens out onto a resonant, mobile sense of subjectivity. Quite the opposite of affirming one's sense of personal identity (whether or not in relation to a quest, a cause or an adversary), the midlife turn discloses a more diffuse sense of being. In Jamie's poetry, being midlife is like a spider's web, a haunted cave, an oblong of moonlight, a hawk and its shadow, a drum of skin stretched over an interior landscape. In 'The Cave of the Fish', the speaker halfway through her life is entranced by a shore road used by both fishermen and shepherds. It is not a singular *via diritta* because 'the path below led home / for both, neither / more true nor more right.' The speaker, meanwhile, doesn't follow the path at all; she sits at the cave-mouth, thinking about it. A similar rejection of a narrowing trajectory appears in a review by Kathleen Jamie of Edwin Morgan's collection *A Book of Lives* (2007), published three years before Morgan's death. Jamie relishes how, rather than developing a consciously controlled, disenchanted 'late style' of the kind noted by Edward Said, Morgan's late poetry remains open, daring and joyful. This is poetry that can 'show us how to live, and keep on living'.[4]

Jamie's sense of truth being transitive, liminal, edgy – as we have seen in previous work – is pushed further and intensified in her two 'midlife' collections, *The Overhaul* (2012) and *Frissure* (2013), since here, the poetry and fragmentary 'prose-poems' unfold at a temporal threshold of maximal resonance, with past and future gathered into a temporary equilibrium. Following on from Faith Lawrence's notion of Jamie's 'poetics of listening', discussed earlier in this volume, I'll posit here that Jamie's 'midlife' poetry constitutes a performance closely analogous to Jean-Luc Nancy's conception of music as an art that sets in motion 'the infinite vanishing point of return to self, of folding-over or folding-back in which the "self" consists'.[5]

If we recognise in Jamie's work that listening is an ethical practice, even perhaps a form of prayer, it is a step further to describe her poetry as musical. When I refer to the music of, or in, Jamie's poetry, to begin with I mean its rhythmic organisation of sound, the patterns of repetition and fracture, and also the sonority of these patterns, the way they amplify in the recurrence, as we saw in Lynn Davidson's essay. I mean as well the pace of the poems and the way pace relates to movement in the poems' content. Although she is justly known for her creation of superbly clear, striking images, I see these images as musically composed, in the sense that they are continually released into movement. While this could be said of all her poetry,[6] the poems and fragments of *The Overhaul* and *Frissure* in particular are concerned with breath, storms, seasonal light-changes, river flow and bird flight, and all these elements have an 'airt', a liveliness expressed as decisive motion. If *The Tree House* depicted Jamie's native landscape, *The Overhaul* performs its weather. And in *Frissure*, the weather performs itself on a human, female body which is also a landscape.[7] So in a broader sense, when I say *The Overhaul* and *Frissure* are 'musical' I mean they articulate a sense of midlife being which arrives, stutters, flowers, folds and disappears in a double-facing time–space of grief and hope, fracture and healing.

For Nancy, 'presence' in music is always emergent or fading away, in part because of the nature of sound waves which travel more slowly than light, and so more noticeably arrive and disappear. And music is always a relational, singular–plural performance: an instrument is struck, strummed, blown or plucked, producing an attack or cry (*envoi*) against a chamber of some kind which produces a resonance or referral of sound (*renvoi*). Thus for him, the self-reflexive direction 'ascoltando' ('play while listening') is in fact a condition of all musical performance, since in striking any instrument (including the voice, of course), a musician simultaneously listens out for the noise being made.[8] To play is *se sentir*, to listen out for an exchange of *envoi* and *renvoi*. This disposition of sound (always straining toward, anticipating, a response) provides Nancy with a model of being in relation to meaning which is open and unfinalised; in music, the self tensely anticipates 'meaning in its nascent state', 'completely ahead of signification'.[9] This is the relation of being to meaning, I'll suggest, that *The Overhaul* and *Frissure* listen for, and perform, at the midlife caesura.

In bringing together these texts, I also wish to challenge two (in my view) mis-interpretations of *The Overhaul*: first that the 2012 volume is essentially a repeat performance of the achievements of the 2004 volume *The Tree House*; and second that Jamie's 'current trajectory is . . . a focusing inward' which 'strains for the universal in what is actually only personal'.[10] *The Overhaul* does indeed share many of the preoccupations of *The Tree House*, and certain key words, images and patterns recur. The 'tilt' and 'unchanciness' of being, discussed by Peter MacKay, recur in the later volume, as do the intimate invocations to other-than-human species. But *The Overhaul* also has its distinctive *timbre* – tone, mood, and colour – which arises from, or is thinking its way into, a sense of being 'in the middest'. This becomes more audible when it is read beside *Frissure*, which, appearing less than a year later, is *The Overhaul*'s most immediate *à venir*. Reading these two recent volumes side by side should dispel the notion that *The Overhaul* either over-personalises or strains to universalise.

In philosophical terms, also, I see these two works moving beyond Heideggerian ecopoetics, such as is applied to Romantic poetry in Jonathan Bate's *Song of the Earth*, as well as the Levinasian concept of the Other's *face* as the site of his or her unique interiority, which as MacKay's essay suggests, are central to Jamie's negotiations in *The Tree House*. While Jamie's work remains suffused with a sense of ethical responsibility toward otherness – both particular others, and the environmental world in general, the Levinasian encounter with the Other's face underlines the distinctness of individual subjectivity, whereas I see Jamie's later work exploring the porous edges and interpenetration of being. Most of Levinas's writing about the expressive face of the Other concerns the *human* face exclusively, whereas Jamie's poetry has habitually engaged with the non-human other. In Jamie's midlife writing, the face-to-face encounter is contagious rather than differentiating. That is to say, what Jamie's work explores here is the sense of an openness of being that overrides or dissolves distinctions between self and other. If Levinas's thinking about human finitude leads to the notion of the 'horror of being', in Jamie's midlife writing an awareness of mortal finitude becomes the condition, the resonant chamber, in which we can produce the brightest, liveliest sound. These ideas are most clearly expressed in *The Overhaul* and *Frissure*, I believe, because both collections are centrally concerned with the experience of temporality. If, as Nancy writes, 'music's openness is a function of its temporality',[11] Jamie's two recent collections musically perform a radical opening out of being toward meaning at midlife.

'Sometimes I almost hear a sweet wild music a kind of fairy music at the edge of sense.' This line begins the first fragment, or prose-poem, of *Frissure*, and introduces

Jamie's speaker in a characteristic, listening stance; it also immediately makes clear that the music she hears is not limited to human composition. What is not immediately obvious is how this listening is also a performance of musical presence: the line evokes a sonic edge of meaning which has already escaped the intentionality of an individual 'I'. In the introduction to *Frissure*, Jamie explains that in the month she turned 49 she was diagnosed with breast cancer, which eventually left her with a scar from a mastectomy operation (*Fr* v). The idea of a collaboration with artist Brigid Collins grew out of a desire to 'get the scar off my body and onto paper, so we could both have a proper look at it.' Any poet applying the stethoscope (literally or figuratively) to her own body might well be accused of over-personalisation, and indeed, Jamie admits to initial misgivings in her introduction: 'I felt suddenly protective of it [the scar] . . . I considered calling the whole thing off. The project was . . . vain, narcissistic and weird' (*Fr* xi). On the other hand, though, Jamie sees in the scar 'referents to the natural world, to change, to the things beyond itself: maps, rivers, roses, fruit' (*Fr* vii). In the work of both artists, the scar becomes a line (of a poem or a drawing) leading 'from fear and loss back into the beautiful world' (*Fr* xiii), as Eleanor Spencer's essay explores. We find here, then, something of Dante's midlife caesura, where the soul lost is found, but here the turn is not to transcendent grace, but rather a heightened sense of finitude, or timeliness: 'To be healed is not to be saved from mortality but rather, released back into it: we are returned to the wild, into possibilities for ageing and change' (*Fr* 7). The line of this scar is in one sense, then, an *envoi* (cry, attack of sound) which strains toward meaning, in a *renvoi* or chamber that we might describe as an awareness of mortality, the outer edge of selfhood. It's the cry striking at this outer edge of being that produces the resonance, the sense of a timely, 'musical' presence in *Frissure*.

The first gesture toward this midlife, musical presence – timely, diffuse, expansive, fractured and healing – is in the physical shape of the book. It is bound in a muted, sea-green cloth cover, textured like an artist's canvas; and it conspicuously lacks the name of an author. It bears no visual image besides the single word of the title, *Frissure*, which is set into an oblong of black ink and fractured or fissured down the middle. The fracture is more like a stutter than a violent tear, and it is offset by the regular open weave of the cloth: either the cloth is torn by the word, or the word mended by the woven cloth; we're on a threshold that holds both those truths in balance. Then, opening up the book, it's difficult to say where it actually begins, where the dividing line is between prefatory matter and the 'text' proper. We come first to the endpapers – a print of a collage work made from plant matter by Brigid Collins – then to the preface by the artists' two medical collaborators, a 'word' from Collins, and an introductory essay by Jamie. All these prose passages are headed with photos of their authors, so from having no author, *Frissure* passes very quickly into having several. Jamie's introduction is also accompanied by a medical drawing of a mastectomy scar (not hers) and mixed-media visual works by Brigid Collins which incorporate the titles or subject matter of the prose-poems by Jamie that are still to come. So by the time we get to the 'sweet wild music' that signals the start of Jamie's 'own' writing, it is already in the air, adrift from the 'I' who hears and performs it.

It is a richly collaborative work, with Jamie's fragmentary prose-poems balanced by Brigid Collins's artwork, and by Collins's explanations of the process of composition. Brigid Collins's work probes and loosens distinctions between human and plant life, between human body and land, sea and sky. Her thorny stems of wild rose – such as the one on the cover of this volume – are minutely realistic representations but they are also interpretations of Jamie's scar, as well as Jamie's lines of verse and, behind hers, a line of Robert Burns. The visual images seem to free up Jamie to play more loosely with words. The verbal fragments auscultate, play while listening for, a diffuse, echoistic sense of being: 'It's audible in the spaces between the rowan leaves . . . in the sound of the distant traffic whose destination is nothing to do with me. / The sound of a handing over, the best surrender . . . the sound of the benign indifference of the world.' (Fr 3) With Nancy, we could add that in auscultating this sound of 'a handing over', Jamie is evoking a notion of presence as a 'movement of an infinite referral [renvoi].'[12]

Nancy argues that music evokes, rather than manifests, presence: 'it anticipates its arrival and remembers its departure, itself remaining suspended and straining between the two.'[13] Stretched between the 'now' which opens the first poem, and 'gone' which closes the last, The Overhaul sets resonating the sense of being on a temporal threshold between arrival at a certain stage of maturity, and departure into an openness that senses its limit. Published in Kathleen Jamie's fiftieth year, the volume is also fifty pages long. The sequence of poems unfolds over roughly three seasons of a year, beginning in February and closing with the approach of the following winter. The opening poem, 'The Beach', begins on an edge of both time and land, with the speaker combing the bay for driftwood, in a company of 'brave souls' – 'all hankering for a changed life' (O 3). In this respect it bears some resemblance to the opening of Dante's Purgatorio, which also begins on the shore, with Dante having emerged from the darkness of Hell, soon finding himself amongst a dazed but expectant crowd of souls. The difference is that for Dante and the other souls, change comes from a directive above and outside time, whereas in 'The Beach' it comes from the storm itself, or rather, the materials (some of them human-made) 'thrown back at us' from the sea. That suggestive phrase, 'thrown back', also highlights how 'The Beach' performs its arrival musically, in Nancy's sense, by anticipating rather than manifesting the entry on the threshold. The speaker proposes the journey in a direct address to us ('let's drive to the storm beach') and then anticipates what we will find: 'A few brave souls / will be there already'. The body of the poem, then, describes an à venir that will come to presence after a negotiation of sorts with a listener. A poem like this materialises in the space created by the tacit agreement of speaker and addressee or, in Nancy's terms, the resonant chamber of voice and ear.

'The Beach' also 'remembers its departure' in the sense that it anticipates, and is echoed by, the volume's closing poem, 'Materials', which again depicts the speaker on the shore, in companionable proximity to an addressee. In this poem, a colony of gannets, raucously scraping together nests on the cliff face, provides an analogy for sociable human creativity. Here again, writing is an act of negotiating something into presence: 'd'you ever imagine chasing just one strand, letting it lead you / to an unsung cleft in a rock. . . ?' (O 50). The beachcombing of the opening poem continues here, as the start of composition for artists and birds alike: 'look at us! Out all day and damn all to show for it. / Bird-bones, rope-scraps, a cursory sketch –' (3). If 'The Beach' sounds a note of expectancy ('hoping for the marvellous'), 'Materials' encompasses the whole arc of the creative act, beginning here with its closure: 'See when it all unravels – the entire project' (O 50). From that anticipation of disintegration, the poem knits together its analogy between human and avian creativity. This happens also very minutely in the knitting together of sound – for example, the repeated vowel that hooks up 'nest' to 'next', which in turn is 'swagged' to 'left' and then 'vest', a final tug of which we hear in 'sketch'. With its long irregular lines, the ragged form of 'Materials' is matched by a light-hearted *timbre* ('that space confirmed / – don't laugh – by your own work'). And the closing line masterfully folds the moment of arrival (of the poem, and of the work) into departure: 'a bit o' bruck's / all we need to get us started, all we'll leave behind us when we're gone.'

Between these two edges, the *envoi* of 'The Beach' and *renvoi* of 'Materials', Jamie sets in motion the distinctive midlife music of *The Overhaul*. Spring arrives with a violence of storms, searing light, and flooding water, in the opening section. 'The Beach' and 'The Dash', the five 'Tay Sonnets', and the couplet poems, 'Fragment 1' and 'Fragment 2', all unleash the weather on waiting souls which, whether human, animal or mineral, are broken, battered, and unhoused by these storms, and newly receptive to change, to 'the marvellous' ('The Beach'). This is even or especially true of the River Tay in the sonnet 'Springs' where, driven back on its course by the 'Full March moon and gale-force easters', it bursts through dykes, spilling into the town and revealing 'Evidence of an inner life, secrets / of your estuarine soul hawked halfway // up Shore Street' (O 6).

These opening poems convey the movement of souls lost, arriving at a breaking point of being. In 'Fragment 1', the speaker glimpses a deer fleeing her presence, and the thought of how she is seen, or not seen, by the deer triggers an existential doubt in her own self: 'how can you tell / what form I take? // What form I take / I scarcely know myself' (O 10). The repeated line links the deer's uncertainty to the speaker's, as well as the speaker's existential doubt to her uncertainty about poetic form. These swift, precise leaps to the line end, and to the stanza break between couplets, convey the animal's movement, as well as the speaker's 'found–lost' condition: 'adrift in a wood', 'for a while now / this is how it's been' (O 10). Like several poems in *The Overhaul*, 'Fragment 1' ends unpunctuated. One effect of this is to heighten the sense of the words resonating into silence and the possibility of a response. In Nancy's terms, we incline toward 'the opening of meaning' that is in part 'a reserve that is anterior and posterior to any signifying punctuation'.[14] *The Overhaul* does not, then, concern itself simply with the recovery of a lost self, or individual poetic form, but rather shapes a self, and sense of poetic form, out of two reciprocal and contrasting movements: the one approaching, the other bounding away.

Along with the weather, it is often the cry of a bird that commands a listening ear into sonorous presence: the 'terse screams' of swifts, the gull's 'torn-throated cries' (O 41), rooks' 'iterated "kaah . . ."' (44), and penultimately, the raven's 'old crocked voice' (49). All of these cries rupture silence and tense the listening ear toward meaning 'in its nascent state', toward forms of being we don't yet know. The wind and the cry of birds also seem to tear open old or fresh wounds, memories of loss that snag the surface of these poems. For example, the sight of two women (a mother and daughter, seemingly) bundled against a northern gale causes the speaker and her companion to flee in horror from their dwelling place, an old house with 'a roof / low and broken like a cry' (13). The moon is another disturbing maternal presence, sometimes distant, sometimes commiserating, and though silent, commanding a vocal response, tempting inanimate objects into 'unexpected life' and intimate confessionals (39). But if the moon is *The Overhaul*'s Beatrice, she is a heavenly body that exists within time, as the speaker reminds her (*'we're both scarred now'* (40)). The moon's repeated appearances, however transformative, also break open painful memories of loss (*'You are not my mother; / with my mother, I waited unto death.'* (40)). Finally, a blackbird's repetitive song in 'May' captures the double-facing, painful–joyful sense of arrival at midlife. Spring is not a birth, but a rebirth; thus the poem begins 'Again' the blossom is 'powering down at dusk', and again 'a blackbird, telling us / what he thinks to it, telling us / what he thinks . . . ' (7). Here the point is not so much that the blackbird's views on springtime can't be conveyed to the reader (as in 'The Dipper'), but that his iterative song means 'in a nascent state' – tending and intending into the silence of the blank half-line that follows his second 'telling'. In the very openness and insistence of the blackbird's song, the listener is compelled into a response, however incomplete: 'How can we bear it?' and 'what can we say . . . ?' 'What we can say' is also left open, though by an associative leap, we could see a human response suggested in the final image/sound of glasshouse windows at sunset which 'crimson, then go mute' (O 7).

All these cries into the spring and summer night are joyful, lively, or painful, but they would not be musical if they were performed into a dead space. What makes the cry sonorous is the edge or womb or cave or listening ear against which it echoes and amplifies. As in *Frissure* so in *The Overhaul*, this rebound of sound is closely associated with the visual metaphor of weaving. Thus in 'The Spider', a human shriek which 'tore the night' is caught up and re-woven by the poem's speaker, a personified spider who pictures her species 'mending endlessly'. (O 20) In 'Fragment 2' a human speaker invites an addressee to imagine mending the sound of fracture: 'splintering of wood, a bird's / cry over still water' (11). But the human speaker who mends what's torn most effectively in *The Overhaul* is described in a long poem called 'The Gather' positioned at the centre of the collection (and gathering up its two halves): here we meet the old tenant sheep-farmer 'whose every sentence / was a slow sea-wave / raking unhurriedly back' (21). As if he has internalised the rook's cry and is sending it back, the long 'aa's of his 'backwash voice' intimate a receptive ear, patient manner and timely livelihood. The boat which conveys him gladly to and from the island where his flock grazes is, in a sense, the doubled image of the boat in the title poem, an elegant 14-footer, hauled up above the tideline, patiently waiting to fulfill the promise of its name, 'Lively'. The farmer's boat might also be compared to the boat which greets Dante's dazzled eyes at the beginning of *Purgatorio*, moving toward him so swiftly with its load of souls that it makes no depression in the surface of the water (*Purg.* 2.41–2). As we know from Jamie's 'The Blue Boat' as well as Nancy's *The Fall of Sleep*, the boat at sea is an image of the soul mid-voyage, but it is also the shell of an ear receptive to a musical cry.[15]

In *The Overhaul*, as previously in Jamie's writing, the cry is often an invitation to be elsewhere, to be journeying. In earlier poems such as 'Rooms' (*QS* 58), she has brilliantly conveyed the opposing tugs of home and away, and in *The Overhaul* the idea of taking flight, being off somewhere, is an important, recurring motif. But here the imagined elsewhere is more often temporal than spatial. Firstly, we are in a turning, becoming world, where spring yields to high summer and to winter, where 'halflings' are on the cusp of becoming eagles, and children, their 'bodies / aglow, grown' becoming 'mere bright voice-motes / calling from the opposite / side of the world' (*O* 35). And secondly, there is a constant reminder of an outer, temporal edge: 'then they're flown', 'when we're gone', 'when winter's wi us' 'the children will be gone'. But there is another sense of an edge between the time of the actual, material world and that of a contiguous world of the marvellous. References to Celtic fairy-lore have always had a place in Jamie's poetry, but they come to the fore in this collection and in *Frissure*, providing a sonorous edge to the sense of human finitude. A number of poems articulate the lure of fairyland. Sometimes the speaker succumbs (as in 'Glamourie'), sometimes she stays just this side of what might have proved to be a fatal enchantment (as in 'The Wood' and 'Whales'). But in all these poems, the very thought of being gone, *disparu*, off and away, adds a shimmering intensity to being here in the material present. For example, in 'Doing Away', one of the five 'Tay Sonnets', the speaker is at first happily grounded in the here and now: 'Nowhere to go, nowhere I'd rather be/ than here' (*O* 9). But the temptation of else-where is already latent in her present satisfaction: 'Why would one want to absent oneself?' Her eye is then drawn to the river at low tide, exposed 'like a lover's bed', already suggestive of desire, and then in the setting light, 'shining / like an Elfland'. The visual image compels her like a voice, reversing the nature of her desire, from 'nowhere I'd rather be' to the enchanted *I'd rather be nowhere*. She imagines being gone ('Someday I'll . . . leave the car'), and the poem closes with the car, empty of her presence: 'when they find it / engine thrumming quietly'. What remains after the speaker's imagined 'doing away' is not emptiness, but a ghostly presence which 'thrums' like the empty car, resonant with anticipation of new presences (the 'they' she imagines finding the car), and the memory of her having been there (and after all, she *is* there, as the narrator of her own disappearance).

Toward the end of the volume, 'The Wood' and 'Glamourie' enact contrast-ing *timbres* or moods of enchantment. In the former, the pull of the other world is sudden and malevolent: 'She comes to me as a jay's shriek.' The poem doesn't specify who 'she' is, but she seems to sum up the whole volume's ambivalence toward maternal presence, both authentic and false: she 'calls me "babe", / coaxing me to fall / once more for her / scarlet-berry promises' (*O* 45). As with many sounds and images in *The Overhaul*, enchantment has a double face, two contrasting tones of voice. The 'fairmer's shelter belt' of 'Glamourie' is the enchanted wood in its golden aspect. Finding herself separated from her companion, the poem's speaker strolls on through a benevolent shady maze, hosted by 'diffuse golden light' and 'tiny spiders / examining my hair' (43). The thought of being netted by the spiders, tangled in the wood, doesn't alarm the lost soul here, but fills her with gratitude: '*I might be gone for ages, / maybe seven years!*' Seven years is a fairy-tale number, and this disappearance is not so much an intimation of death as the promise of a reversal of time. The thought of being abducted fills the speaker with 'sudden joie de vivre', as if she'd slipped into childhood, and she leaps over a ditch, 'blithe as a girl'. Ironically, by jumping over ditchwater, she breaks the spell and – the regret is audible in the 'ach, I jumped' – returns to material adult presence.

In her manifestation as 'jay's shriek', the witchy temptress of 'The Wood' is also a reminder of the original form of siren, not (as in Homer's *Ulysses*) woman–fish, but woman–bird, as Lacoue-Labarthe reminds us in *Le Chant des Muses* (44). The danger this 'she' presents, then, is partly the threat of species hybridisation, dilution or dissolution. At the end of *The Tree House*, Jamie resisted the Romantic poets' identification with songbirds by insisting that the dipper's 'supple, undammable song' 'isn't mine to give' (49). She was careful to express her admiration without symbolically appropriating its amphibious knowledge of 'the depth of the river'. But we are a step beyond that gesture here, where the speaker allows the jay's shriek to lure and transform her into an other-than-human mode of being. If 'the visual is on the side of an imaginary capture,' according to Nancy, 'the sonorous . . . [has] to do with participation, sharing, or contagion'.[16] Participation, sharing, and contagion characterise nearly every human–animal encounter in *The Overhaul*, even when the dominant metaphor is visual rather than sonorous. In 'Stags', for example, the speaker and her companion are on the hunt for a sighting of a herd of stags in a glen. But the accented first syllable of the poem, 'This', functions as a musical attack of sound that announces an arrival, an opening out toward presence. It's as if the 'this' draws back the curtain on a sacerdotal scene: 'This is the multitude, the beasts' (O 16).[17] What unfolds is a visual scene, but the movement of the verse is peculiarly slow and stately, the *timbre* of the language, measured and Biblical: 'Below us . . . is the grave / calm brotherhood, . . . kneeling / like the signatories of a covenant' (O 16). The two human watchers are in turn gazed upon by the beasts, but the gaze into the other's face is discomfortingly asymmetric:

We lie close together, and though the wind
whips away our man-and-woman smell, every
stag-face seems to look toward us, toward,
but not to us: we're held, and hold them,
in civil regard.

Being looked 'toward' (rather than 'at') locks the human watchers in place, as they try to avoid causing alarm in the herd. As each face looks toward each, there's a suggestion of political, ontological equity, with its echo of the Levinasian encounter. But here the *entente* is based on contiguity (the nearness, almost a touch, that holds them still) rather than insight into the other's interiority. Though gazed upon, this herd is *heard*, and actively listens. As if there has been a contagion across species, the human watchers begin to behave and move like stags – lying close together, aware of their species smell, then 'moving quietly away', one following the other. When the speaker says to her companion, 'I suspect you'd / hoped to . . . lead me deeper / into what you know', she addresses him as a stag-like creature, and it is not certain who is leading whom deeper into the wood.[18] 'The Stags' enacts a compassionate exchange between species, if we follow Nancy in understanding that 'com-passion is the contagion, the contact of being with one another in this (the world's) turmoil. Compassion is not altruism, nor is it identification; it is the disturbance of violent relatedness.'[19]

Species-contagion occurs again and again in *The Overhaul*, but perhaps nowhere more disturbingly than in 'The Widden Burd', a Scots poem that appears in the volume's closing section. In a demonic reversal of 'May', with its insistently vocal blackbird, this poem describes a living soul trapped in the body of a silent 'blackie' made of wood, wire and feathers. Reversing the movement of the other enchantments in *The Overhaul*, this soul seems to have been sent back from the afterlife as a punishment for speculating on 'whit tends tae us aa / ayont the dyke', what becomes of us when we're gone. Addressed in the second person, the *timbre* of the poem is swift, informal and lively – flowing ballad quatrains, two beats to a line, and brisk consonantal variations ('back', 'blackie', 'bark'). But the very liveliness of the speaker's voice throws into relief the horrifying plight of the addressee: immured alive, with a throat 'that cannae wheep' (O 47). The poem's dedication, '*i.m. ITJ*', points toward a real but private grief, one that remains secret and locked away, but for the final lines which burst out of the end-stopped ballad metre with the cry to a 'you' that definitely isn't the general reader: 'Och / how could ye no' / hae gone quaitely?' In itself, and beyond its folkloric logic (loquaciousness punished with muteness), the poem constitutes a bleakly ironic performance of what it means to be unmusical: a 'burnt' or lively eye with no instrument to sound; an intention with no resonant chamber that would shape it into (or toward) meaning.

In this closing section of *The Overhaul* especially, Jamie's writing emphasises the need for a sense of limit, because without this resonant edge the voice becomes inarticulate, strangles or suffocates. In her Scots translation of Hölderlin, 'Tae the Fates', the speaker asks the gods for 'jist ane simmer mair' in which to write, for the soul that leaves mortal life unfulfilled, 'wil waunner Orcus disjaiskit' ('wander discontented in the underworld') (O 38). Unlike Orpheus, this speaker is ready to leave her lyre behind and give up singing when her time comes, because having written 'ane perfect poem', 'Ah'd hae lived, / aince, lik the gods; and aince is eneuch.' Perhaps there's an ironic suggestion here that a writer's soul is doomed to be 'disjaiskit' because it's impossible to write a perfect poem. But the repetition in the final line casts the emphasis, I think, on the value of living '*aince*' ('once'): with that sense of a resonating outer edge to our work and experience. In the last poems of *The Overhaul*, the farther side of the midlife caesura comes to look something like this: every creative act promises a disappearance; the act resonates into and *because* of the silence that follows. The penultimate poem, 'Even the Raven', performs this idea brilliantly with its vanishing structure, from three triplets, to two couplets, to a final, hanging line, where the raven's voice 'asks you what you're waiting for' (O 49). If, as the speaker has said of the surrounding sea and hills, 'it's here, everything / you wanted', then what happens next? If the poem is a countdown, then what follows in the open space after the unpunctuated question/injunction? The silence after 'for' resonates in (at least) two directions simultaneously: 3, 2, 1, go! and 3, 2, 1, zero. In this silence (unlike the private sound, the sound of privation, in 'The Widden Burd'), perhaps every reader can, to paraphrase Nancy, hear their own body resonate, their own breath, their 'heart and all its resounding cave'.[20]

The Overhaul closes with a dash toward action – not heroically concentrated on a goal, but gladly instinctual and liberating. This is akin to the closing movement of a Gigue in a Bach Suite, which gathers up (amongst other things) the sombre, death-facing Sarabande, and sets it spinning in a rough-and-ready peasant's dance.[21] It's even more closely akin to migratory birds, as Jamie describes the sand martins and house martins preparing themselves for flight in September, 'sensing in the shortening days a door they must dash through before it shuts' (*Fr* 31).

WORKS CITED (SEE ALSO BIBLIOGRAPHY)

Bach, Johann Sebastian, *Sechs Suiten: Violoncello solo BWV 1007–1012*, ed. Egon Voss (Munich: G. Henle Verlag, 2007).
Baker, J. A., *The Peregrine*, ed. John Fanshawe (London: HarperCollins, 2011).
Calarco, Matthew, 'Facing Beyond Anthropocentrism', in Brigitte Maire and Lazare Benaroyo (eds), *Le Visage: expressions de l'identité* (forthcoming, 2014).
Cavarero, Adriana, *Relating Narratives: Storytelling and Selfhood*, tr. Paul Kottman (London: Routledge, 2000).
Cavarero, Adriana, *For More than One Voice: toward a philosophy of vocal expression*, tr. Paul Kottman (Stanford: Stanford University Press, 2005).
Dante Alighieri, *The Divine Comedy*, six vols, tr. Charles Singleton (Princeton: Princeton University Press, 1982).
Deleuze, Gilles, and Félix Guattari, *A Thousand Plateaus*, tr. Brian Massumi (London: Continuum, 2004).
Falconer, Rachel, *Hell in Contemporary Literature: Western Descent Narratives since 1945* (Edinburgh: Edinburgh University Press, 2005).
Grosz, Elizabeth, *The Nick of Time: Politics, Evolution and the Untimely* (Durham: Duke University Press, 2004).
Hughes, Ted, *Collected Poems* (London: Farrar, Straus and Giroux, 2005).
Lacoue-Labarthe, Philippe, *Le Chant des Muses* (Lonrai: Normandie Roto Impression, 2005).
Levinas, Emmanuel, *Totality and Infinity: an Essay on Exteriority*, tr. Alfonso Lingis (Pittsburgh: Duquesne University Press, 1969).
Levinas, Emmanuel, *Ethics and Infinity*, tr. Alfonso Lingis (Pittsburgh: Duquesne University Press, 1985).
Nancy, Jean-Luc, *Being Singular Plural*, tr. Robert Richardson and Anne O'Byrne (Stanford: Stanford University Press, 2000). Originally published as *Être singulier pluriel* (Paris: Galilée, 1996).
Nancy, Jean-Luc, *À l'écoute* (Paris: Galilée, 2002).
Nancy, Jean-Luc, *Listening*, tr. Charlotte Mandell (New York: Fordham University Press, 2007).
Nancy, Jean-Luc, *The Fall of Sleep*, tr. Charlotte Mandell (New York: Fordham University Press, 2009). Originally published as *Tombe de Sommeil* (Paris: Galilée, 2007).
Nancy, Jean-Luc, 'Foreword', in Peter Szendy, *Listen: A History of Our Ears*, tr. Charlotte Mandell (New York: Fordham University Press, 2008).
Rushdie, Salman, *The Ground Beneath Her Feet* (London: Jonathan Cape, 1999).

NOTES

1. Jamie refers to this life-narrative pattern in a 2006 review of a biography of George Mackay Brown: 'if life is a game of two halves . . . '. Jamie, 'Orcadian Rhythms'.
2. See Falconer, *Hell in Contemporary Literature*.
3. Rushdie, *The Ground Beneath Her Feet*, p. 223.
4. Jamie, 'The lifeline of love'.
5. Nancy, 'Foreword' to Szendy's *Listen: A History of Our Ears*, p. xii.
6. 'Two things have been constant over the years: a rigour, and a concern for musicality.' Jamie, 'Author Statement', British Council website.
7. 'And now I had a line, quite a line! inscribed on my body. It looked like a landscape. Because it was changing colour as it healed, it seemed to me as if it had its own weather.' (*Frissure*, p. vi)
8. Nancy, 'Foreword', p. ix.
9. Nancy, *Listening*, p. 27; 'en amont de la signification, sens à l'état naissant' (À *l'écoute*, p. 52).
10. The first was a remark made (though partly retracted) by a distinguished poet, in September 2013. The second appears in Clare Pollard's review of *The Overhaul*, 'The Scale of Things', *Poetry Review* 103:1 (Spring 2013).
11. Nancy, *Listening*, p. 66.
12. Nancy, *Listening*, p. 9. Or, in the original: 'Accès au soi . . . c'est-à-dire à la forme, à la structure et au movement d'un renvoi infini' (À *l'écoute*, p. 25). Nancy's writing on the echo of a subject has evolved in conversation with Philippe Lacoue-Labarthe, as is clear from his essay, 'Philippe' in Jacob Rogozinski, ed., *Philippe Lacoue-Labarthe: la césure et l'impossible* (Paris: Lignes, 2010). I am grateful to Nidesh Lawtoo for this reference.
13. Nancy, *Listening*, p. 20. 'Elle anticipe sa venue et reticent son depart, restant elle-même suspendue et tendue entre les deux' (À *l'écoute*, p. 42).
14. Nancy, *Listening*, p. 27: 'une reserve antérieure et postérieure à toute punctuation signifiante' (À *l'écoute*, p. 52).
15. The soul is 'like a signal, like a lantern, like a lookout on the top of a tall mast' (Nancy, *The Fall of Sleep*, p. 36). Cf. Jamie, 'The Blue Boat' (*The Tree House*, p. 41) and Dante *passim*, but most notably the opening lines of the *Purgatorio*: 'To course over better waters the little bark of my genius [*ingegno*] now hoists her sails' (*Purg.*1.1–2, tr Singleton).
16. Nancy, *Listening*, p. 10: 'le sonore [est] . . . dans l'ordre de la participation, du partage ou de la contagion' (À *l'écoute*, p. 27).
17. Compare the opening middle C of the Prelude of Bach's *Cello Suite* no. 3, *Sechs Suiten*, p. 12. Thanks to Lausanne cellist Pascal Desarzens for conversations about the Suites.
18. Thanks to Matthew Campbell for his thoughts about this poem.
19. Nancy, *Being Singular Plural*, p. xii. This idea of contagion accords with pre-Freudian ideas about a mimetic unconscious, which affectively responds to the other. See Nidesh Lawtoo, *The Phantom of the Ego: Modernism and the Mimetic Unconscious* (East Lansing, MI: Michigan State University Press, 2013), pp. 13–19.
20. Nancy, *Listening*, p. 21: 'dans une condition de silence parfait on entend résonner son propre corps, son souffle, son cœur et toute sa caverne retentissante' (À *l'écoute*, p. 44).
21. J. S. Bach, *Sech Suiten*, pp. 6–7. Thanks to Sebastian Knowles for discussion of the Sarabandes.

16. 'We Do Language Like Spiders Do Webs': Kathleen Jamie and Michael Longley in Conversation

Maria Johnston

'I love Donald Hall's definition of poetic tradition as "conversations with the dead great ones and with the living young". Poetry, even the most intensely lyrical, is unlikely to be a solo flight.'

Michael Longley[1]

Introducing Kathleen Jamie and Douglas Dunn at a poetry reading titled 'The Friendship of Poets' – part of the symposium *Comparisons and Relations between Irish and Scottish Poetry Since 1890* at Queen's University Belfast in 2006 – the Northern Irish poet Michael Longley paid fitting tribute to Jamie as a poet of magnitude and metamorphosis, whose 'generous, transfiguring imagination [. . .] takes in the world'.[2] 'She has perfect pitch, a natural sense of cadence and verbal melody that helps to give her work the feel of organic inevitability', Longley continued, making clear his profound appreciation for, and attentiveness to, Jamie's sonorous, shaping art as it harmonises with his own sense of poetry's instinctive musical vitality. 'Her poetry is full of sky and hills, rock pools, glimmerings, plum trees, holly, birds and birds' nests, lochs and rushy shores,' Longley spotlighted the elusive fixtures of Jamie's brimming poetic imagination, but, as any reader of contemporary poetry will recognise, he could just as well have been cataloguing the contents of his own vast, intricately detailed poetic universe. Going on then to repeat Richard Mabey's apt description of Jamie's *Findings* as 'a conversation with the natural world',[3] Longley flew close to the heart of his own work, revealing, in the process, their shared aesthetic practice, central to which are the sustaining forces of translation and conversation; the concept of the poetic act as, to use Jamie's own words, a mediating 'art of listening [that involves] bringing the quality of attention to the world.'[4] These poets share not only common themes and concerns but, more significantly, an uncommon sensitivity to poetic form as living and dynamic process with the only constants being, as Jamie has professed, 'a rigour, and a concern for musicality'.[5] Tracing lines of connection between the aesthetic processes of these kindred poets illuminates a number of important aspects of Jamie's developing work that risk being overlooked in critical accounts that focus predominately on the politics of gender and national identity. In this way, it makes available a fuller understanding of Jamie's complex, searching formal artistry, of what Longley in his glowing introduction astutely termed its 'inner radiance', as well as its 'surface-shimmer'.

As the title of the 2006 symposium indicates, the question of mutual influence between Scottish and Irish poets has been generating an increasing amount of critical interest in recent years, with the collection of essays *Modern Irish and Scottish Poetry* (2011) comprising 'the first sustained comparison of modern Irish and Scottish poetry'.[6] A long-time visitor to Scotland's most remote reaches, Longley has been keen to point out the 'rich interchange' that animates Scottish and Northern Irish poetry as well as, more personally, his reverence for Hugh MacDiarmid's lyrics in Scots and the 'subtle influence' of Ian Hamilton Finlay on his work.[7] Ever since his vertiginous overture 'The Hebrides' (*No Continuing City*, 1969) reorchestrated the various formative influences of Hart Crane, George Herbert and Robert Lowell into a startlingly atonal Scottish symphony far from the home key, the outermost terrain of the Scottish islands and highlands has been part of his own extended landscape, akin to the west of Ireland that so famously become his poetic 'home from home' during the years of the Troubles in the north of Ireland. Arguing for the poem as 'central to his *oeuvre* as a whole', Fran Brearton has noted the 'schizophrenic' mindset that 'The Hebrides' puts forward as 'a marker at the outset of what Longley is trying to do [. . .] that his aesthetic will always be one of a deliberate uncertainty, and that definitions – of home, tradition, lineage – will always be resistant to single interpretations.'[8] In the same collection, 'For Bessie Smith' has the blues-struck poet transported to three sites on his poetic compass that he must keep returning to: Inisheer off the west of Ireland; Tra na Rossan in Donegal; and, looking to Scotland's Outer Hebrides, 'Harris, drenched by horizontal rain', all of whose liquid place names evoke their fluidity through returning sound waves.[9]

Tracking Longley's Scottish movements across his career brings to light how many of these mark significant points of development in his poetic technique, opening up trade routes of exploratory and improvisatory possibility for the poetic self and its art. Occupying a central place in 1973's *An Exploded View*, 'Skara Brae' was one of a number of poems that came as a breakthrough into more relaxed rhythms after a time of artistic impasse for Longley in the early 1970s.[10] More recently, the example of other Scottish makars inspires Longley's formal adventures in *The Weather in Japan* (2000). In 'An Elegy', in memory of George Mackay Brown, the 13-syllable lines of the poem reproduce the long, sweeping strokes of the poet's emblematic scythe while, in 'Paper Boats', a homage to Ian Hamilton Finlay, the unanchored poetic lines make for a 'ship-shape' feat of hydrodynamic compactness (CP 273). It seems from this that Longley's sojourns in that country's peripheral zones allow him, as a familiar outsider, a freedom and release where both poetic form and poetic self are concerned; the poet 'losing his way', as he puts it in 'The Hebrides', only to discover new soul-spaces to inhabit. Indeed, when Edna Longley contrasts the poetry from Northern Ireland ('quite formalist') with that from Scotland, which has been 'more successfully interested in avant-garde forms',[11] it must be deduced that it is precisely this 'avant-garde' possibility that has for so long drawn the poet Longley to the shifting home-ground of modern Scottish poets. This may then be seen to continue into his most recent collection, *A Hundred Doors* (2011), where each poem is amplified by the white spaces between words, lines and stanzas, to become, like the swans' nest in 'Lullaby', its own 'experimental nest'.[12] Indeed, that Ulster Scots has long been a valuable linguistic resource for Longley – full of 'fresh sounds and suggestions' – in travelling the 'long way home' from Ulster to Homer provides a suggestive linguistic linkage between dialects for this most dialectical of poets.[13] 'It's a good place to go', Jamie has written of Skara Brae, 'it re-calibrates your sense of time' (F 11). In Longley's work, and, as we shall see, in Jamie's more recent work also, this unflinching mode of being in liminal landscapes, far from the comforts or consolations of a coherent self or unchanging home-place, makes movingly possible living poetic forms that are themselves lasting recalibrations of time and space, re-tunings of both words and world.

'Now I want to go back to the places of the imagination', Jamie declared in 1994.[14] Having produced her 'Scottish book', *The Queen of Sheba*, the need to expand her poetics towards the expansive 'energy of the land' beyond the narrower avenues of 'Scottishness' and 'woman-ness' was intensifying.[15] For both Longley and Jamie, questions of national identity and the responsibilities that come with being from a particular time and place have been pressing and inescapable. Jamie has on more than one occasion divulged how she 'wanted to be a nature poet' but 'every-thing else got in the way – issues of identity and gender and politics'.[16] Frustrated by the fact that such limiting categorisations continue to be applied to her work, she now looks to a more enlightened future in which: 'It may seem that there was a school of poets of similar interest, whose "northerness" or "marginalness" – rather than "Scottishness" – was important.'[17] Also situating himself 'on the fringes of Europe, next to the Atlantic', Longley could be counted among this 'eccentric' (to recall his Scottish escape poem 'Ghost Town') grouping of like-minded poets that are, as Jamie phrases it, 'thinking along similar lines', out on the edge of things, the cold places of human existence, and not bound by any one style, voice, national or cultural identity. In one of the most helpful accounts of Irish and Scottish poetic relations to date, Alan Gillis examines the significance of place names in the work of a number of poets that includes Jamie and Longley. After correctly noting the 'absence of tribal or nationalistic concern' in Jamie's 'Bairnsang' (*Jizzen*, 1999), Gillis ends by signalling the importance of Longley's poetic model for a new century in which 'the political context of vernacular poetry will surely mutate to become more ecological than tribal or nationalistic'.[18] In this, Gillis recognises the constant call that has long been making itself felt in the work of Longley, and now, more recently, Jamie; that is, an urgent, necessary call for the ecological to be brought into proper focus.

When Jamie, in a piece on Friedrich Hölderlin, expresses her attraction to the 'anxious earth-love'[19] that suffuses his ecopoetry, she simultaneously comes up with the perfect encapsulation of not only her own ecopoetry, but Longley's also. His is a poetry of a drifting consciousness, with the indeterminate self always between states in a world that is similarly in constant flux. Longley's 'anxious earth-love' is felt most of all when he writes from Carrigskeewaun, his soul-scape of choice. That it is 'precarious, isolated and vulnerable' and 'haunted by [. . .] the ghosts of [. . .] the famine' matters deeply to Longley as elegist and love poet. This is emphatically not a 'cosy community', for, ultimately, as Longley has written: 'the bones of the landscape make me feel in my own bones how provisional dwelling and home are'.[20] Despite the truth of this as it registers in the forms of the poetry, Longley himself has had to contend with these poems 'about landscapes, flowers and animals' being 'dismissed as escapist' (quoting Ciaran Carson's pejorative description of his 'wee poems about swans and primroses' to prove the point).[21] 'It's interesting that the Greek word for home provides the root for ecological because the world is our home,'[22] Longley has had to point out in a bid to cast light on the larger reality. Thus, to ascribe the role of 'nature poet' to Longley in some consoling, pastoral sense is not to understand the ambivalence and tensions that enliven his poetic forms. Far from bestowing a stable sense of place or single identity, as Peter McDonald has perceptively noted, 'Longley's west of Ireland [. . .] continues to challenge, rather than confirm, the poet's sense of his own place in things.'[23]

Jamie's outlook is similarly informed by the reality of threat and extinction that is always in the foreground. 'The wind and sea. Everything else is provisional. A wing's beat and it's gone', Jamie's *Sightlines* knowingly concludes. As Longley noted in his introduction to Jamie, again recognising his own preoccupations in her work: 'Her central concern becomes even clearer; how do we share the globe with the plants and the other creatures?' And it chimes with his own pressing concerns:

> The most urgent political problems are ecological: how we share the planet with the plants and the other animals. My nature writing is my most political. [. . .] Describing the world in a meticulous way is a consecration and a stay against damaging dogmatism.[24]

For Jamie, as she opined in a public conversation with Jonathan Bate, nature poetry is 'not a safe haven, but a place for quite radical thought'.[25] There is nothing then homely or sentimental about either poet's anxious, earth-shaped poetics. 'There's no such place as home. And we live there, you and me,' Jamie has quoted approvingly Philip Hoare's existential conundrum.[26] If home is, for Longley, a 'hollow between the waves', then his spirit must feel recharged in Scotland's watery, eccentric spaces, in what Jamie describes as 'the sculptural, wind-honed archipelago' (F 7) that is the Orkney islands. The fact of violent change, of obsolescence, is everywhere. As Jamie reminds us in her review of Tim Dee's *Four Fields*: 'Nowadays in "nature" or "the environment" we are far from consoled. It's in nature we find the most frightening changes.'[27] As both Longley and Jamie know, questions of habitation, of 'home', are never straightforward or stable, and both share a deep sense of poetry as an unending exploratory form of ecological inquiry and existential negotiation. Their concerns are global, never narrowly confined to only one co-ordinate or compass point.

'I'm interested in the world which is more-than-human, which is beyond the human',[28] Jamie has stated, and her move into a necessarily deeper ecological atten-tiveness brings her ever closer to Longley, not merely in terms of theme but, more essentially, technique. Longley's poems as sustained Homeric odysseys attest to the whole of life and art as a constant journeying, and in this it cannot be insignificant that Jamie chose as epigraph to her 1999 collection *Jizzen* the closing line of Longley's poem 'Tree-House' (*Gorse Fires*, 1991), in which Odysseus's boundless skill as craftsman and builder is reconstructed in the long-lined musculature of the poem itself. Clearly drawn to the idea of the tree-house as 'a place where nature and culture meet, a sort of negotiated settlement, part reverie, part domestic, part wild,'[29] Jamie would then go on to use this as the title of her subsequent collection *The Tree House* in 2004, wherein her engagement with the world beyond the human becomes even deeper. This move testified to Jamie's new-found belief in language itself as home and the poet's love-work as one of deliberate, careful crafting. As Brearton observes of Longley's 'Tree-House', 'Recognition is about trust, about believing "at last" in the Odysseus who is "love poet, carpenter".'[30] The poet necessarily 'oscillates between craft and vision', Longley reminds us.[31] By invoking Longley's 'Tree-House' Jamie is herself placing trust in poetry as a groundless process of making and remaking, and in poetic structures themselves as temporary stays or dwelling places, fashioned by a provisional self that, moment to moment, is always in transit. Thus, musing on the process of writing poetry, Jamie compares it to 'very slowly falling out of a tree' with the writerly self in free-fall:

> You reach out tentatively for the next thing, the next idea, but all that happens is that you dislodge yourself and begin falling again. [. . .]. There is no limit to this falling, and no thump when you hit ground, because there is no ground.[32]

Because the tree-house that Jamie inhabits is one from which she is constantly falling, the compulsion to pay attention, to listen, requires a similarly attuned attention to poetic forms that can accommodate ambivalence and uncertainty as they unfold. Longley very early on in his career signalled his own 'preoccupation with form [. . .] pushing a shape as far as it will go, exploring its capacities to control, and its tendencies to disintegrate.'[33] For him, as his poem 'Form' casts the slippery artistic predicament, the form of the poem is a 'make-shift shelter': 'form' being both the term for the hare's grassy nest and, of course, the hold-space of the poem itself (*CP* 197). In the same sensitive and sentient spirit, Jamie's tree-house is also a make-shift shelter that occupies a *zona media* between states just as her interceding 'wishing-tree' stands 'neither in the wilderness / nor fairyland' (*TH* 3). Given this, it is the form of the poem that becomes the light-filled space for the writerly self and soul to inhabit for a time and pass through, and forms of life both in art and in the world, human and beyond, are to the fore in the poetry of both. In Jamie's 'Pipistrelles' the titular bats in clear, vessel-like formation comprise 'a single / edgy intelligence, testing their idea / for a new form / which unfolded and cohered // before our eyes' only to then vanish 'suddenly, / before we'd understood' (*TH* 30–1). The idea of the form of the poem itself as what remains of something that has passed is pivotal in the work of both Longley and Jamie. As Angela Leighton in her consideration of Yeats's formal legacy has perceptively defined it: form may be regarded as 'something left over when the creature has gone', for, as Leighton concludes, 'form is simply the rhythm of what came and went, and was saved in the various forms of language itself, as well as in the sound of all those wandering, beating, escaping feet.'[34] Readers of the poetry of both Jamie and Longley must tune in to the far-reaching frequencies of these poetic forms on the air that, ghosted with traces of the disappeared and disappearing, embody both presence and absence, their lines vibrating across boundaries of time, space and self.

'My poetry would be a dead thing if it couldn't retain its liquidity, couldn't change shape or direction', Jamie has declared.[35] Similarly, Longley's professed aim is 'a linguistic energy which is like pushing water through a dynamo, the principles of hydroelectricity'.[36] Just as nature has formed us, it also returns to us forms in which to think, live and write. Thus, in *Frissure*, Jamie's scrutiny of the scar-line on her skin after cancer treatment prompts her to muse associatively on the poetic line itself as it 'opens up possibilities within the language, and brings forth voices out of silence' (*Fr* vi). In 'Line', the relation of the poetic line to geological, mapping lines illuminates the deep connection in Jamie's work between forms in nature and forms in art: 'What is a line but landscape?' (*Fr* 17) Reviewing George Mackay Brown's *Collected Poems* in 2005, Jamie provided a master-class on reading attentively and listening out across the lines, to show how 'Brown's music enacts the ecology it describes'. 'What is revealed', Jamie perceptively hears, 'is a dense web wherein no sound is left alone and unsupported, unless for good reason'.[37] In the work of both Jamie and Longley, as we shall now examine, the poem's unique landscape is never a mere diorama but a pulsating web of music and meaning, a contrapuntal, modulating soundscape that must be closely attended to and journeyed through.

Listening closely then to the ongoing conversation between these two kindred poets, we find ourselves in the liminal territory of Jamie's 'Poem', dedicated to Longley and included in the festschrift *Love Poet, Carpenter* (2009). This meta-poetic event starts out in the internal, private space of the poetic mind as it engages in the tentative act of composition:

I walk at the land's edge,
turning in my mind
a private predicament.[38]

Turning over their enjambed edges, the opening three lines convey the speaker's internal crisis, or turning point, the syntax underlining the 'edgy intelligence' of the writer as she moves on the cusp, between states, and out on her own. Colour then floods into the viewfinder as the observing consciousness focuses on its surroundings ('Today the sea is indigo') and, as the walker moves along the edge and the mind moves too in its own unfathomable processes, the poem enacts its own coming into being, step by step, line by line, seeping, like the sea, into its own territory as it creates its own form out of the surrounding silence. 'But every time the sea / appears differently', the speaker notes, in answer to which the form of the poem itself opens up, with propulsive dashes and a colon becoming the only punctuation markings from this point onwards, as the sea spills into the line of vision and processes of continuous change hold sway. The self is held to account, then relinquished, in the same way that Jamie has described writing itself as a process of self-weaving and unweaving, as 'an exchange between an *ad hoc* self and its world'.[39] As she recognises it, every poetic act of discovery entails the slow fashioning of a new self that is 'not fixed, but provisional [. . .] we are a series of selves, one for every book, like a string of paper dolls'.

Still in bottomless free-fall, the second stanza continues the poem's progression as a single sentence that never finishes, never 'resolve[s]', but remains open-ended, still going on: 'Nothing resolved, / I tread back over the moor', the ambulatory poet in progress reports, her provisional self's unravelling matched by the 'tufts of bog-cotton' that 'unbutton themselves in the wind' in this unmarked, desolate landscape. 'Let me make room for bog cotton, a desert flower –', Longley's 'Bog Cotton' from *The Echo Gate* opens (CP 136), and, as Neil Corcoran notes, this wildflower flourishes in Longley's lyrics as 'an emblem of endurance in place and in function, even if this is an endurance at the very edge of capacity, "hanging on by a thread"'.[40] By allowing Longley's emblematic bog-cotton to fertilise her own poetics, Jamie articulates a similar instinct for poetic forms as precarious, spinning structures. With both self and form 'hanging on', the poem disperses itself over the lines, out onto the open road that is at once 'wearily familiar' and strange, full of unknown possibility: 'the old shining road / that leads everywhere', at which point the words of the poem end. Jamie's flowing poetic lines are mimetic of the mind's own turnings, the ley lines of the mind leading where they will to create a poem that itself turns, resisting resolution or closure (the absence of a final full stop at poem's end) as the white space becomes 'everywhere'. Everything 'appears differently'; that this phrase is repeated – along with the key words 'today', 'moor', 'road', 'sea' and 'same' – lends the poem an inner musical memory, enforcing the fact that nothing, even if repeated, is ever the *same*. Living in language, in metaphor – the sea a 'tumultuous dream' – the writer grants the poem its own agency as 'Poem' enacts its own coming into being and one isolated writer's voice reaches out across the sea's wordless spaces to another.

We find ourselves in the same intermediary zone in Longley's poem for Jamie, 'Inlet', published for the first time at the beginning of this volume. Here again, on this unnamed inlet in the Scottish highlands, geographical origins must make way for word origins as the only details that matter. That 'inlet', as the *OED* informs us, means 'a way of admission; an entrance. A narrow opening by which the water penetrates into the land' will be obvious to all, but that it can also mean, in adjectival form, 'ornamented with lace, etc., let in or inserted as in needlework' adds another layer of meaning to the poem as a woven text: the threads are many and various in this textual weave. Moreover, the fact that 'sound' is a synonym for 'inlet' seems deeply relevant to this as a poem celebrating a shared poetics of eye- and ear-music. The poem is the 'inlet'; a sound-filled entrance into a world where every detail is seen as for the first time. Thus, Longley addresses Jamie in this hymn to craft and vision:

I have seen your face
Among the pebbles
In a Highland pool.

Other echoes and reverberations are audible. The opening line seems to rehearse a favourite quotation of Longley's, from Elizabeth Bowen's *The Heat of the Day*: 'To have turned away from everything to one face is to find oneself face to face with everything',[41] while, in the second stanza, the 'bladderwrack' left by 'the sea at spring tide' brings to mind another of his poems of friendship, 'Petalwort', addressed to the naturalist Michael Viney, whose ashes will one day 'swirl' amongst 'crab shells / Bladderwrack, phosphorescence at spring tide –' (*CP* 290). As a wreath, Longley offers Viney, 'a flower so small / Even you haven't spotted'. That Viney has failed to 'spot' the flower is significant: Jamie, on the other hand, supremely attentive, 'will have noticed' in the third and following stanzas here, as her efforts of attention towards all that is precarious and fragile and rare ability to reveal the cosmic in the tiny particulars are paid tribute to in Longley's meticulously itemising lines: 'You will have noticed / A planetary rose-hip / Hanging from the sky'. As in a Jamie poem, each word here is perfectly placed, with so much depending on that participle 'hanging' as one line turns into another. The entire poem as it moves not only invokes Jamie's spirit but tunes with exquisite sensitivity into the music of her poetic mind in motion, ending, fittingly, with her arrival to their shared source of inspiration: 'you reach the pool'. Thus, Jamie becomes his spirit-guide as he, like her, is drawn again and again to the same soul-locations, the same remote spaces, where questions of survival and endurance are paramount.

In his most recent collection, *A Hundred Doors* (2011), we encounter the poet Longley walking, and thinking, through the same poetic terrain that Jamie has become so adept at exploring in both her poetry and prose as a way of forging deeper his relation to both the human world and the non-human. Given that Longley's own daughter, the artist Sarah Longley, resides in the north-west Highlands of Scotland, and that his own most recent poetry has been 'inspired by visits to the places captured in his daughter's paintings',[42] it seems wholly fitting to see Longley now in late career not only as father to his daughter the artist, but also, by extension, father-poet to Jamie, who shares his daughter's acute, painterly eye for the minute details made luminous in poems 'reflecting what light remains'.[43] 'The morning you were born I wrote a poem / About the Shetlands', Longley writes to his new-born granddaughter in 'A Garland' (*AHD* 9). As he positions himself as father- and grand-father-poet on these remote islands, far out of the reach of the usual signals, he retraces Jamie's sound-prints, repeating the same place names that had been sonorously summoned in Jamie's lullaby for her newborn son 'Bairnsang' from the sequence 'Ultrasound' in *Jizzen* (1999):

> but ye cannae yet daunce
> sae maun courie in my erms
> and sleep, saftly sleep, Unst and Yell (*J* 16)

'We wait at Toft for the Yell ferry', Longley's poet–speaker in transit puts it in 'On the Shetlands', while 'Shetland Mouse-Ear' opens 'we got as far as Unst, / no nearer' (*AHD* 12–13). What seems to link Jamie and Longley is, again, that word 'sound'; it is not too fanciful to hear in Jamie's title 'Ultrasound' the place name 'Uyeasound' as one sound-image modulates and metamorphoses into another. Not only poems but the landscapes themselves are full of ghosts: 'On the Shetlands' moves to Gallow Hill, Scalloway, a seventeenth-century place of execution where witches were burned. Death pervades these landscapes, for Longley as for Jamie. As before in the poem for Viney, the art of attention is vital, as once again here the poet's companion fails to notice the fleeting signs of life all around: 'Too deep in conversation and sad news / to notice an otter's kelp-flashes.' (*AHD* 12).

Following Jamie's inspirational footprints, Longley's sonnet 'Prelude' recalls her earlier 'The Well at the Broch of Gurness' wherein, even as the broch is now 'rubble / Her homestead's lintels tilt / through mown turf', today's visitors follow the ghost of a one-time inhabitant to 'seek / the same replenishing water, / invisible till reached for, / when reached for, touched' (*J* 44). Poetry restores us to the world in its immediacy and infinity, as the invisible is made visible, made tangible by the act of touch, of tending and attending. What Longley's similarly displaced speaker hears is the opening praeludium from J. S. Bach's *The Well-Tempered Clavier*, a work, like Jamie's, of 'perfect-pitch':

> I heard in my inner ear
> At the Broch of Gurness
> Bach – that childlike first prelude (*AHD* 14)

The poet is led by sound here, as 'Broch' summons 'Bach', then 'rock', and 'barnacles', just as Bach's Prelude itself progresses from one arpeggiated chord to another, building its cascade of harmonies out of repetitions, advances and returns. But suffering and indecision are always part of the music, as: 'Whoever was playing sat / Painfully on his stone chair'. The 'stone' here hauls us back over the years to the 'hard beds, / The table made of stone' of Longley's earlier 'Skara Brae' (*CP* 71). Reflecting on her visit to the Neolithic village of Skara Brae, Jamie has noted of its inhabitants: 'you can feel both their presence [. . .] and their utter absence' (*F* 11). Such sites of ruin and threshold places inspire poetic forms that are similarly shaped out of earth and air, sounds and silence, absence and presence.

'I think that to become the writer I am now took a lot of overcoming and ground-clearing,' Jamie has stated.[44] Central to this, as she goes on to state, was the example and encouragement of a network of poetic friendships. In a similar way, looking back on the poetic friendships that began and were cultivated during the years of the Troubles in the north of Ireland, Longley has recognised how this 'sodality of the imagination' was deeply 'important': 'we provided each other with some kind of shelter.'[45] Moreover, the ability of such poetic friendships to privilege 'poetic not national identities' has been noted by Fran Brearton in an essay on the formative friendships of Longley, Dunn and Derek Mahon in the 1960s.[46] Beyond Ireland, Longley's engagement with Japanese aesthetics and that culture's 'people of like mind' strengthened his belief in his own artistic practice at a critical time: to feel 'on the same wavelength' with sympathetic others is vital for Longley, as it is for many poets.[47] As Wallace Stevens put it in a letter to Marianne Moore, 'The web of friendship between poets is the most delicate thing in the world – and the most precious.'[48] Literary friendships make possible a stretching out and enlarging of self and song, and Jamie's growing belief in poetry's exploratory formal possibility comes across nowhere more compellingly than in her most recent collection, *The Overhaul* (2012), in which the poems are as floating devices plotting their own independent courses. The expert weaving and unravelling of lines form the activity as the collection's final poem self-reflexively describes how the birds 'mediate between sea and shore, that space confirmed/ – don't laugh – by your own work', in lines that scrutinise and celebrate the processes of life and art, of art as life's work (O 50).

Extending the limits of the lyric, the core of the work of both boundary-crossing poets continues to be fuelled by the energies of music, movement and mediation. Both are poets of the singing line and both are searching, sea-faring poets crossing sound- and sight- lines in their endless probings of words and worlds. Both also are, to use a phrase borrowed from Jamie, 'friends of silence', drawn to the edge of the known world, the unknown, and of knowledge itself.[49] Both poets see into the life of poetry as a vibrant and various art of conversion, of conservation, and of conversation, reminding us that 'when song, cast / from such frail enclaves / meets the forest's edge, / it returns in waves' (TH 17).

WORKS CITED (SEE ALSO BIBLIOGRAPHY)

Brearton, Fran, *Reading Michael Longley* (Tarset: Bloodaxe, 2004).

Brearton, Fran, Edna Longley, and Peter Mackay (eds), *Modern Irish and Scottish Poetry* (Cambridge: Cambridge University Press, 2011).

Corcoran, Neil, *Poets of Modern Ireland: Text, Context, Intertext* (Cardiff: University of Wales Press, 1999).

Gillis, Alan, 'Names for Nameless Things: Poetics of Place Names', in Fran Brearton, Edna Longley, and Peter Mackay (eds), *Modern Irish and Scottish Poetry* (Cambridge: Cambridge University Press, 2011), pp. 204–21.

Johnston, Dillon, 'Q & A: Michael Longley', *Irish Literary Supplement* (Fall 1986), pp. 20–22.

Leighton, Angela, *On Form: Poetry, Aestheticism and the Legacy of a Word* (Oxford: Oxford University Press, 2007).

Longley, Edna, 'Irish and Scottish Island Poems', in Robert McColl Millar (ed.), *Northern Lights, Northern Words: Selected Papers from the FRLSU Conference, Kirkwall 2009* (Publications of the Forum for Research on the Languages of Scotland and Ulster, 2010); www.abdn.ac.uk/pfrlsu/volumes/vol2/ (last accessed 25 May 2014).

Longley, Michael, *Secret Marriages* (Manchester: Phoenix Pamphlet Poets Press, 1968).

Longley, Michael, *The Lake without a Name* (Belfast: Blackstaff, 2005).

Longley, Michael, *Collected Poems* (London: Jonathan Cape, 2006).

Longley, Michael, 'Musarum Sacerdos', *Poetry Review* (Winter 2006).

Longley, Michael, 'Perfect River', *Irish Pages*, 4:1 (2007), pp. 71–75.

Longley, Michael, 'A Boat on the River (1960–1969)', reprinted in Pat Boran (ed.), *Flowing Still: Irish Poets on Irish Poetry* (Dublin: Dedalus Press, 2009), pp. 50–56.

Longley, Michael, interview, *Civic Voices: An International Democracy Memory Bank Project*, 18 April 2010; www.civicvoices.org/UserFiles/Michael%20Longley%20formatted1.pdf (last accessed 25 May 2014).

Longley, Michael, *A Hundred Doors* (London: Cape, 2011).

Longley, Sarah, and Michael Longley, *Passing Places: New Work from the Highlands* (Dublin: Peppercanister Gallery, 2013).

McDonald, Peter, 'Faiths and Fidelities: Heaney and Longley in Mid-Career', in Fran Brearton and Eamonn Hughes (eds), *Last Before America: Irish and American Writing* (Belfast: Blackstaff Press, 2001), pp. 3–15.

Patterson, Glenn, interview with Michael Longley, 'Art and Conflict', The Arts Council Conference, 2012.

Randolph, Jody Allen, 'Michael Longley in Conversation with Jody Allen Randolph', *Poetry Ireland Review* 79 (May 2004), pp. 78–89.

Robertson, Robert (ed.), *Love Poet, Carpenter: Michael Longley at Seventy* (London: Enitharmon, 2009).

Stevens, Holly (ed.), *The Letters of Wallace Stevens* (New York: Knopf, 1981).

Waters, Colin, 'Edna and Michael Longley: The *SRB* Interview', *Scottish Review of Books* 4:3 (2008), pp. 6–8.

NOTES

1. Longley, 'Musarum Sacerdos', p. 63.
2. See Longley, 'Perfect River'.
3. Richard Mabey, review of *Findings*, quoted on the author page of Sort Of Books website: http://www.sortof.co.uk/authors/kathleen-jamie (last accessed 25 May 2014).
4. Scott interview, 'In the nature of things', p. 20.
5. Jamie, 'Author Statement', British Council website.
6. Brearton, et al., *Modern Irish and Scottish Poetry*, jacket cover.
7. Michael Longley in Waters, 'Edna and Michael Longley: The *SRB* Interview', p.7.
8. Brearton, *Reading Michael Longley*, pp. 27, 30.
9. Longley, *Collected Poems*, p. 29. All further quotations from this volume will be given with page references in text preceded by the abbreviation *CP*.
10. Brearton reads it as not just an 'elegy for home' but 'pertinent to an understanding of form', as 'the loosening of rhythms and the move away from the complex rhyme schemes of the first volume "explode" Longley's form in the 1970s' (Brearton, *Reading Michael Longley*, pp. 66–7). In the same architecturally-designed volume, the alienated territory of its companion poem, 'Ghost Town', conflates two history-haunted places, both on the Orkney island of Hoy, as Edna Longley has indicated: 'Rackwick (abandoned by crofters) with Lyness (once a Second World War hub).' See Edna Longley, 'Irish and Scottish Island Poems'.
11. Edna Longley in Colin Waters, 'Edna and Michael Longley: The *SRB* Interview', p. 6.
12. Longley, *A Hundred Doors* (London: Cape, 2011), p. 8. All further quotations from this volume will be given with page references in text preceded by the abbreviation *AHD*.
13. Longley, in Clare Brown and Don Paterson (eds), *Don't Ask Me What I Mean: Poets in their Own Words* (London: Picador, 2004), p. 153.
14. Jamie, in Brown and Paterson, *Don't Ask Me What I Mean*, p. 126.
15. Ibid., pp. 125–6.
16. Jamie, introduction to 'Pipistrelles', *Poetry Archive*, www.poetryarchive.org/poetryarchive/singlePoem.do?poemId=195 (last accessed 25 May 2014).
17. Dósa interview, 'Kathleen Jamie: More than Human', p. 142.
18. Gillis, 'Names for Nameless Things', p. 218.
19. Jamie, 'Hölderlin into Scots. Two Poems', p. 57.
20. Longley, preface to *The Lake without a Name*, np.
21. Michael Longley in Brown and Paterson, *Don't Ask Me What I Mean*, p. 153.

22. Longley, *Civic Voices: An International Democracy Memory Bank Project*.
23. McDonald, 'Faiths and Fidelities', p. 13.
24. Randolph, 'Michael Longley in Conversation', pp. 85–6.
25. Jamie, quoted in 'Book Festival Review', *The Scotsman*, 25 August 2010, p. 5.
26. Jamie, 'The Exploding Harpoon', p. 40.
27. Jamie, '*Four Fields* by Tim Dee – review'.
28. Jamie, quoted in Dósa, p. 142.
29. Kathleen Jamie, 'Author's note', 'The Glass-hulled Boat' and *The Tree House*, Scottish Poetry Library.
30. Brearton, *Reading Michael Longley*, p. 170.
31. Longley, in Brown and Paterson, *Don't Ask Me What I Mean*, p. 154.
32. Jamie, 'Author, author: Kathleen Jamie on writing a book'.
33. Longley, introduction to *Secret Marriages*, p. 2.
34. Leighton, *On Form: Poetry, Aestheticism and the Legacy of a Word*, p. 169.
35. Jamie, 'Author Statement'.
36. Michael Longley in Dillon Johnston, 'Q & A: Michael Longley', p. 22.
37. Jamie, 'Primal Seam'.
38. Kathleen Jamie, 'Poem', in Robertson, *Love Poet, Carpenter* (London: Enitharmon, 2009), p. 68.
39. Jamie, 'Author, author'.
40. Neil Corcoran, 'To Stop the Bleeding: The Poetry of Botany in Michael Longley', in Corcoran, *Poets of Modern Ireland*, p. 169.
41. Longley, in Brown and Paterson, *Don't Ask Me What I Mean*, p. 151.
42. See Longley and Longley, *Passing Places*.
43. Michael Longley, 'For Amelia', in Longley and Longley, *Passing Places*, p. 16.
44. Jamie, 'Crossing Borders: New Writing from Africa', British Council website.
45. Michael Longley in Patterson interview, Art and Conflict: The Arts Council Conference, 2012. For a full account of this, see Longley, 'A Boat on the River (1960–1969)', p. 56.
46. Fran Brearton, 'On "The Friendship of Young Poets": Douglas Dunn, Michael Longley, and Derek Mahon', in Brearton et al., *Modern Irish and Scottish Poetry*, p. 277.
47. Longley, in Brown and Paterson, *Don't Ask Me What I Mean*, p. 152.
48. Wallace Stevens, letter to Marianne Moore, 27 March 1953, in Stevens, *The Letters of Wallace Stevens*, p. 771.
49. Jamie, 'Noises Off'.

Notes on Contributors

Timothy L. Baker is Lecturer in Scottish Literature at the University of Aberdeen, and author of *George Mackay Brown and the Philosophy of Community* (2009) and *Contemporary Scottish Gothic* (2015). He is currently preparing two further monographs, provisionally titled *Being Many, Seeming One: Religion and Community in Scottish Fiction, 1808–1878*, and *Postjustabouteverything: The Ends of Contemporary Fiction*.

Amanda Bell is a doctoral candidate in the School of English, Drama and Film, University College Dublin. She is working on an ecocritical study of Kathleen Jamie, Celia de Fréine and Meg Bateman. Her work has appeared in *POST: A Review of Poetry Studies*. Her poetry has been published in *The Stinging Fly*, *Crannóg 35* and *Burning Bush* 2 (6), and has been long-listed for the Mslexia Women's Poetry Competition 2013.

Eleanor Bell is Senior Lecturer at the University of Strathclyde. She is author of *Questioning Scotland: Literature, Nationalism, Postmodernism* (2004), and co-editor of *Scotland in Theory: Reflections on Culture and Literature* (2004). Her recent work focuses on Scottish literary culture of the 1960s, on which she has two co-edited collections: *International Writers' Conference Revisited: Edinburgh, 1962* (2012), and *The Scottish Sixties: Reading, Rebellion, Revolution?* (2013).

Lucy Collins is a Lecturer in English Literature at University College Dublin. She has published widely on contemporary poetry and is currently completing a monograph on Irish women poets. Recent publications include *Poetry by Women in Ireland: A Critical Anthology 1870–1970* (Liverpool University Press), and a co-edited collection of essays, *Aberration in Modern Poetry* (McFarland, 2011). *The Irish Poet and the Natural World: An Anthology of Verse in English from the Tudors to the Romantics*, co-edited with Andrew Carpenter, is due for publication in 2014.

Robert Crawford is Professor of English at the University of St Andrews. He is author of several poetry collections, including 'Full Volume' (2008), which was shortlisted for the T. S. Eliot Prize. Amongst his academic publications are

The Bard: Robert Burns, a Biography (Pimlico, 2010), *On Glasgow and Edinburgh* (Harvard University Press, 2013), and *Bannockburns: Scottish Independence and the Literary Imagination, 1314–2014* (Edinburgh University Press, 2014).

Lynn Davidson has published poetry, fiction and essays. *Common Land* (Victoria University Press, 2012) combines poetry and essays. Her novella, *The Desert Road*, was published in 2014. Her poems have appeared in *The Best of Best New Zealand Poems, Essential New Zealand Poems*, and *PN Review*. She is currently working on a PhD in Creative Writing at Massey University, Wellington. In 2013 she was Writing Fellow at Hawthornden Castle in Scotland.

Rachel Falconer is Professor of Modern English Literature at the University of Lausanne. She has published articles on classical, early modern and contemporary poetry, and is author of *Orpheus (Dis)remembered*, a study of Milton's Orpheus (1996), *Hell in Contemporary Literature* (2005), and *The Crossover Novel* (2009). Recent co-editions include *Re-reading / La relecture* (2012), and *Medieval and Early Modern Literature, Science and Medicine* (2013). Her present research interests are in contemporary poetry, birds and music.

Leontia Flynn is Research Fellow at the Seamus Heaney Centre for Poetry, Belfast. She is the author of *These Days* (2004), *Drives* (2008) and *Profit and Loss* (2011), and has received the Forward Prize for first collection, the Rooney Prize for Irish Literature, and the Lawrence O'Shaughnessy Prize for Irish Poetry. *Profit and Loss* was shortlisted for the T. S. Eliot Prize. She has also written a critical study of Medbh McGuckian (2013).

Louisa Gairn is Lecturer at Aalto University, Finland. She is author of *Ecology and Modern Scottish Literature* (2008), which was shortlisted for the Robin Jenkins Literary Award. Her essays also appear in *The Edinburgh Companion to Contemporary Scottish Literature* (2007) and *The Edinburgh Companion to Hugh MacDiarmid* (2011).

Andrew Greig is a full-time Scottish writer, author of twenty books of poetry, nonfiction and novels. Latest in each genre: *Found At Sea* (2013); *At the Loch of the Green Corrie* (2010); *Fair Helen* (2013). With his wife, novelist Lesley Glaister, he lives in Edinburgh and Orkney.

Maria Johnston has lectured in poetry at Trinity College Dublin, Mater Dei Institute (DCU) and Oxford University, and is a regular reviewer of contemporary poetry for *The Guardian, Edinburgh Review, Poetry Ireland Review* and Oxford's *Tower Poetry Review*. She is the co-editor (with Philip Coleman) of *Reading Pearse Hutchinson: 'From Findrum to Fisterra'* (Irish Academic Press, 2011).

Faith Lawrence produces arts and factual programmes for BBC Radio. She has been producing Radio 3's *The Verb* since 2012, and recent documentaries for Radio 4 include *The Haunted Apparatus* – an exploration of the 'uncanny' side of telephone conversations. She is also a Creative Writing PhD candidate at the University of St Andrews, and her own poems have been published in journals including *Poetry Review*.

Michael Longley is a central figure in contemporary Irish poetry. He is a Fellow of the Royal Society of Literature and a recipient of the Queen's Gold Medal for Poetry. He has won the Whitbread Prize, the T.S. Eliot Prize, and was made a CBE in the Queen's Birthday honours 2010.

Peter Mackay is Lecturer in Literature at the University of St Andrews. He is the author of *Sorley MacLean* (2010) and the co-editor of *Modern Irish and Scottish Poetry* (2011). He has written on Scottish Gaelic and contemporary poetry, and is currently working on a study of Seamus Heaney and William Wordsworth. A collection of his own poetry will be published in 2014; he also works occasionally as a journalist, news producer and reviewer for the BBC.

Jamie McKendrick has published six books of poetry, most recently *Out There*, which won the Hawthornden Prize, as well as a volume of selected poems, *Sky Nails: Poems 1978–1997*, and various translations including *The Embrace*, a selection of Valerio Magrelli's poems. *Archipelago*, his translation of the poems of Antonella Anedda, is due to be published later this year.

Michael O'Neill is Professor of English at Durham University. He has published widely on Percy Bysshe Shelley, and on poetry from the Romantics to the present day. Publications include two collections of poems and, as editor, *The Cambridge History of English Poetry* (2010). He is also the co-editor (with Madeleine Callaghan) of *Twentieth-Century British and Irish Poetry: Hardy to Mahon* (2011) and the co-author (with Michael D. Hurley) of *Poetic Form: An Introduction* (2012).

Alan Riach is the Professor of Scottish Literature at Glasgow University and past-President of the Association for Scottish Literary Studies. He is general editor of the *Collected Works of Hugh MacDiarmid*, the author of *Representing Scotland in Literature, Popular Culture and Iconography* and co-author with Alexander Moffat of *Arts of Resistance: Poets, Portraits and Landscapes of Modern Scotland*. He is author of five volumes of poetry, including *Homecoming* (2009).

Fiona Sampson is Professor of Poetry at the University of Roehampton, and Fellow of the Royal Society of the Arts. From 2005–12 the first woman Editor of *Poetry Review* since Muriel Spark, she is now Editor of *Poem: International Quarterly Review*. Her publications include twenty-five volumes of poetry, criticism and philosophy of language. *Night Fugue*, the US edition of her *Selected Poems*, appeared in 2013.

Juliet Simpson is Professor of Art History and Visual Culture at Buckinghamshire New University. She is a scholar of European art, art writing and cultural identity of the long nineteenth century. Her publications include books on Symbolism in art; articles on Zola, Mallarmé, Huysmans, Gauguin, the Goncourts and Fromentin. She has also published on poetry and the visual arts, cultural identity and cosmopolitanism.

Eleanor Spencer teaches in the Department of English Studies at the University of Durham, where she is also the Assistant Senior Tutor at Hatfield College. She is the editor of *American Poetry since 1945* (2015), and has published articles on the dramatic monologue and on Anne Stevenson. In 2011–12 she was a Frank Knox Fellow in English at Harvard University.

Roderick Watson is Professor Emeritus at the University of Stirling. He has published on the poetry of Hugh MacDiarmid, modern Scottish literature, language and identity. His publications include a history, *The Literature of Scotland* (1984; 2007) and a sister anthology, *The Poetry of Scotland* (1995). He currently co-edits the *Journal of Stevenson Studies*. He has published two collections of his own poetry, *True History on the Walls* (1977) and *Into the Blue Wavelengths* (2004).

David Wheatley is Senior Lecturer at the University of Aberdeen. He is the author of four collections of poetry with Gallery Press: *Thirst* (1997), *Misery Hill* (2000), *Mocker* (2006) and *A Nest on the Waves* (2010), and has edited the work of James Clarence Mangan, and Samuel Beckett's *Selected Poems 1930–1989*. His *Reader's Guide to Essential Criticism of Contemporary British Poetry* is published by Palgrave in 2014. His articles and reviews have appeared in journals including *London Review of Books*, *Times Literary Supplement*, *The Guardian* and *Dublin Review*.

Bibliography

COLLECTED WORKS

Black Spiders (Edinburgh: The Salamander Press, 1982).
A Flame in Your Heart, with Andrew Greig (Newcastle upon Tyne: Bloodaxe, 1986).
The Way We Live (Newcastle upon Tyne: Bloodaxe, 1987).
A Matter of Weeks, radio drama (BBC Radio, 1990).
The Golden Peak: Travels in North Pakistan (London: Virago Press, 1992; reissued as *Among Muslims*, 2002).
The Autonomous Region: poems and photographs from Tibet, with Sean Mayne Smith (Newcastle upon Tyne: Bloodaxe, 1993).
The Queen of Sheba (Newcastle upon Tyne: Bloodaxe, 1994).
Full Strength Angels: New Writing Scotland, Vol 14, editor with James McGonigal (Aberdeen: Association for Scottish Literary Studies, 1996).
Penguin Modern Poets 9, contributor with John Burnside and Robert Crawford (Harmondsworth: Penguin, 1996).
Some Sort of Embrace: New Writing Scotland, Vol 15, editor with Donny O'Rourke and Rody Gormin (Aberdeen: Association for Scottish Literary Studies, 1997.
The Glory Signs: New Writing Scotland, Vol 16, editor with Donny O'Rourke (Aberdeen: Association for Scottish Literary Studies, 1998).
Poetry Quartets 1, audio cassette (The British Council/Bloodaxe Books, 1998).
Jizzen (London: Picador, 1999).
Mr and Mrs Scotland Are Dead: poems 1980–1994, ed. Lilias Fraser (Newcastle upon Tyne: Bloodaxe, 2002).
Among Muslims: Meetings at the Frontiers of Pakistan (London: Sort Of Books, 2002). A reissue of *The Golden Peak*, with additional Preface and Epilogue.
The Tree House (London: Picador, 2004).
Findings (London: Sort Of Books, 2005). Published in the USA by Graywolf Press (2007), with the added subtitle *Essays on the Natural and Unnatural World*.
Waterlight: Selected Poems (Minnesota: Graywolf Press, 2007).
This Weird Estate (Edinburgh: Scotland and Medicine, 2007).
The Overhaul (London: Picador, 2012).
Sightlines (London: Sort Of Books, 2012). Published in the USA by The Experiment, LLC (2013), with the added subtitle *A Conversation with the Natural World*.
Frissure (Edinburgh: Polygon, 2013).

REVIEWS, UNCOLLECTED POEMS AND OCCASIONAL WRITING

'Author Statement', British Council website (undated), http://literature.britishcouncil.org/
kathleen-jamie (last accessed 25 May 2014).
'Author Statement – Crossing Borders: New Writing from Africa', British Council website
(undated), http://www.transculturalwriting.com/radiophonics/contents/writersonwriting/
kathleenjamie/ (last accessed 25 May 2014).
'Author's note: 'The Glass-hulled Boat' and *The Tree House*', Scottish Poetry Library
(undated), http://www.scottishpoetrylibrary.org.uk/poetry/poems/glass-hulled-boat (last accessed
25 May 2014).
Note on 'The Autonomous Region', in W. N. Herbert and Richard Price (eds), *The
McAvantgarde: Edwin Morgan, Frank Kuppner, Tom Leonard, Kathleen Jamie, the unpublished
MacDiarmid* (Dundee: Gairfish, 1992).
'Interregnum', *London Review of Books* 20:1 (1 January 1998), p. 20.
'Holding Fast: Truth and Change in Poetry', in W. N. Herbert and Matthew Hollis (eds), *Strong
Words: Modern Poets on Modern Poetry* (Tarset, Northumberland: Bloodaxe Books, 2000), pp.
152–7.
'For a New Scottish Parliament', in *Without Day: Proposals for a New Scottish Parliament*
(Edinburgh: Polygon, 2001), p. 9.
'At Robert Fergusson's Grave', *London Review of Books* 23:6 (22 March 2001), p. 12.
'Whale Watching', *London Review of Books* 23:23 (29 November 2001), pp. 36–7.
'Counting the Cobwebs: The Crush of Hope', *London Review of Books* 24:11 (6 June 2002), pp.
38–9.
'Into the Dark: A Winter Solstice', *London Review of Books* 25:24 (18 December 2003), pp.
29–33.
'Primal Seam', review of George Mackay Brown: *Collected Poems*, ed. Archie Bevan and Brian
Murray, *The Scotsman*, 30 July 2005, http://www.scotsman.com/lifestyle/books/primal-
seam-1-726603 (last accessed 25 May 2014).
'Hölderlin into Scots. Two Poems', in *Modern Poetry in Translation: Metamorphoses*, ed. David
Constantine, Issue 3:3 (London, 2005).
'"Janet" by Kathleen Jamie', Anatomy Acts Object Guide No.172 (2006), http://www.
anatomyacts.co.uk/artists/KathleensPoem.htm (last accessed 25 May 2014).
'Orcadian rhythms', review of Maggie Ferguson, *George Mackay Brown: The Life*, *The Guardian*,
6 May 2006, http://www.theguardian.com/books/2006/may/06/featuresreviews.guardianreview8
(last accessed 25 May 2014).
'High and Dry', *London Review of Books* 28:15 (3 August 2006), pp. 38–9.
'Island at the edge of the world', *The Guardian*, 26 August 2006, http://www.theguardian.com/
books/2006/aug/26/featuresreviews.guardianreview4 (last accessed 25 May 2014).
'The lifeline of love', review of Edwin Morgan, *A Book of Lives*, *The Guardian*, 3 March 2007,
http://www.theguardian.com/books/2007/mar/03/featuresreviews.guardianreview27 (last
accessed 25 May 2014).
'Growing pains', review of Richard Mabey, *Beechcombings: The Narratives of Trees*, *The Guardian*,
6 October 2007, http://www.theguardian.com/books/2007/oct/06/featuresreviews.
guardianreview6 (last accessed 25 May 2014).
'Kathleen Jamie: Judge's Report', *Poetry London*, 61 (Autumn 2008), http://www.poetrylondon.
co.uk/magazines/61/poem/judge-s-report (last accessed 25 May 2014).
'A Lone Enraptured Male: The Cult of the Wild', review of Robert Macfarlane, *The Wild Places*,
London Review of Books 30:5 (6 March 2008), pp. 25–7.
'Noises Off', review of Sara Maitland, *A Book of Silence*, *The Guardian*, 15 November 2008, http://
www.theguardian.com/books/2008/nov/15/book-silence-sara-maitland-review (last accessed 25
May 2014).

'The weather woman', review of Roni Horn installation, 'Library of Water', in Stykkishólmur, Iceland, *The Guardian*, 14 March 2009, http://www.theguardian.com/artanddesign/2009/mar/14/roni-horn-tate-modern-exhibition (last accessed 25 May 2014).

'Is the daddy-longlegs doomed?' Shortcuts blog, *The Guardian*, 8 June 2009, http://www.theguardian.com/environment/2009/jun/08/daddylonglegs-climate-change (last accessed 25 May 2014).

'Into the Deep', *The Guardian*, 10 June 2009, http://www.theguardian.com/travel/2009/jun/10/walking-guide-loch-ness (last accessed 25 May 2014).

'*The Magnetic North* by Sara Wheeler', review, *The Guardian*, 24 October 2009, http://www.theguardian.com/books/2009/oct/24/magnetic-north-sara-wheeler-review (last accessed 25 May 2014).

'*Hemispheres* by Stephen Baker', review, *The Guardian*, 11 September 2010, http://www.theguardian.com/books/2010/sep/11/hemispheres-stephen-baker-review (last accessed 25 May 2014).

'In the West Highlands', *London Review of Books* 33:14 (14 July 2011), pp. 38–9.

'*On Extinction* by Melanie Challenger – review', *The Guardian*, 28 September 2011, http://www.theguardian.com/books/2011/sep/28/on-extinction-melanie-challenger-review (last accessed 25 May 2014).

'Bergen's Whale Hall: graveyard of giants', *The Observer*, 8 April 2012, http://www.theguardian.com/environment/2012/apr/08/bergen-whales-museum-kathleen-jamie (last accessed 25 May 2014).

'Author, author: Kathleen Jamie on writing a book', *The Guardian*, 17 August 2012, http://www.theguardian.com/books/2012/aug/17/kathleen-jamie-writing-book-self (last accessed 25 May 2014).

'*Names for the Sea: Strangers in Iceland* by Sarah Moss – review', *The Guardian*, 2 November 2012, http://www.theguardian.com/books/2012/nov/02/sea-iceland-sarah-moss-review (last accessed 25 May 2014).

'The Spirit of Bannockburn', *New Statesman*, 7 February 2013.

'Ice age carvings: strange yet familiar', *The Guardian*, 16 February 2013, http://www.theguardian.com/artanddesign/2013/feb/16/ice-age-carvings-british-museum (last accessed 25 May 2014).

'*All the Birds, Singing* by Evie Wyld – review', *The Guardian*, 27 June 2013, http://www.theguardian.com/books/2013/jun/27/all-birds-singing-wyld-review (last accessed 25 May 2014).

'The Exploding Harpoon', review of Philip Hoare, *The Sea Inside*, *London Review of Books* 35:1 (8 August 2013), p. 40.

'*Four Fields* by Tim Dee – review', *The Guardian*, 24 August 2013, http://www.theguardian.com/books/2013/aug/24/four-fields-tim-dee-review (last accessed 25 May 2014).

RADIO

Night Waves. Jamie reads from *The Tree House*. BBC Radio 4, 8 October 2004.

Poetry Please. Features 'Perfect Day'. BBC Radio 4, 26 December 2004.

Night Waves. Kathleen Jamie on Scottish landscape. BBC Radio 3, 24 June 2005.

Woman's Hour. BBC Radio 4, 11 January 2006.

The Essay. New Nature Writing – Four Talks for Spring. Kathleen Jamie on black grouse lek. BBC Radio 3, 11 April 2007.

Poetry Please. Jamie reads 'Jocky in the Wilderness'. BBC Radio 4, 22 April 2007.

Words and Music: Ballad of the Northern Lights. Reading of prose and poetry on theme of the North, inc. Kathleen Jamie. BBC Radio 3, 3 August 2008.

The Essay: The Elephant in the Poetry Reading. BBC Radio 3, 22 January 2009.

BBC Learning. Jamie discusses 'Cetacean Disco'. BBC Radio 4, 16 April 2010.

Norn but not forgotten. BBC Radio Scotland, 20 December 2010.
The Book Café. BBC Radio Scotland, 22 April 2012.
Book of the Week. Readings from *Sightlines*: 'Aurora', 'Pathologies', 'The Woman in the Field', 'The Gannetry', 'On Rona'. BBC Radio 4, 23–27 April 2013.
Rumours of Guns. Drama by Kathleen Jamie and Andrew Grieg. BBC Radio 4, 1 December 2012.
Poetry Please. Discussion of tree poems, including Jamie's 'Alders'. BBC Radio 4, 9 December 2012.
Front Row. Jamie discusses *The Overhaul*. BBC Radio 4, 17 January 2013.
The Verb: Writing Mid-Life. Discussion with presenter Ian McMillan. BBC Radio 4, 1 March 2013.
The Echo Chamber. Discussion of middle-age writing, with Paul Farley. BBC Radio 4, 23 March 2013.
Poetica: 'Who Do You Think You Are? The Poetry of Kathleen Jamie'. ABC Radio National (USA), 14 July 2012, http://www.abc.net.au/radionational/programs/poetica/2012-07-14/4066098 (last accessed 25 May 2014).
Poetry Please. Features 'The Queen of Sheba'. BBC Radio 4, 15 June 2013.

INTERVIEWS (ALPHABETICAL)

Anon., 'Kathleen Jamie in interview', *Scottish Book Collector*, April–May 1992. Discusses *The Golden Peak*.
Anon., 'Interview with Kathleen Jamie', *Books from Scotland*, 13 March 2006, http://www.booksfromscotland.com/Authors/Kathleen-Jamie/Interview (last accessed 25 May 2014).
Blyth, Caroline, 'Autonomies and Regions: an Interview with Kathleen Jamie', *Oxford Poetry* 7:2 (1993), http://www.oxfordpoetry.co.uk/interviews.php?int=vii2_kathleenjamie (last accessed 25 May 2014).
'Book Festival Review', *The Scotsman*, 25 August 2010, p. 5. Kathleen Jamie is quoted in this piece.
Brown, Clare, and Don Paterson (eds), 'Kathleen Jamie', in *Don't Ask Me What I Mean: Poets in their Own Words* (London: Picador, 2004), pp. 125–8.
Connolly, Cressida, 'A writer's life: Kathleen Jamie', *The Telegraph*, 21 November 2004, http://www.telegraph.co.uk/culture/3632092/A-writers-life-Kathleen-Jamie.html (last accessed 25 May 2014).
Crawford, Robert, 'Hugh MacDiarmid: A Disgrace to the Community', in *P. N. Review*, Jan/Feb 1993. Transcript of BBC Radio Scotland broadcast on the centenary of MacDiarmid's birth, 11 Aug 1992, interviews several poets including Kathleen Jamie.
Crown, Sarah, 'Kathleen Jamie: a life in writing', *The Guardian*, 6 April 2012. http://www.theguardian.com/culture/2012/apr/06/kathleen-jamie-life-in-writing (last accessed 25 May 2014).
Dósa, Attila, 'Kathleen Jamie: More than Human', in *Beyond Identity: New Horizons in Modern Scottish Poetry* (Amsterdam: Rodopi, 2009), pp. 135–46.
Fraser, Lilias, 'Kathleen Jamie', in *Scottish Studies Review* 2:1 (Spring 2001), pp. 15–32.
Gilchrist, Jim, 'Behind the veil', *Scotland on Sunday*, 13 May 2002, http://www.scotsman.com/news/behind-the-veil-1-566846 (last accessed 25 May 2014).
Goring, Rosemary, 'Kathleen Jamie: The SRB Interview', *Scottish Review of Books* 8 (2012): 2, http://scottishreviewofbooks.org/index.php/back-issues/volume-8-2012/volume-seven-issue-four-mainmenu/473-kathleen-jamie-the-srb-interview (last accessed 25 May 2014).
Jones, Sarah, 'Anatomy of a natural poet', *Scotland on Sunday*, 16 May 2006, http://www.scotsman.com/news/anatomy-of-a-natural-poet-1-1411760 (last accessed 25 May 2014).

McKeon, Belinda, 'Kathleen Jamie, Poet', *The Irish Times*, 15 June 2005, http://www.
   belindamckeon.com/work/kathleen-jamie-poet (last accessed 25 May 2014).
Scott, Kirsty, 'In the nature of things: Kathleen Jamie', *The Guardian*, 18 June 2005.
   http://www.theguardian.com/books/2005/jun/18/featuresreviews.guardianreview15 (last accessed
   25 May 2014).
Ramaswamy, Chitra, 'Interview: Kathleen Jamie, author of *Sightlines*', *The Scotsman*, 9 March
   2012, http://www.scotsman.com/lifestyle/books/interview-kathleen-jamie-author-of-
   sightlines-1-2233424 (last accessed 25 May 2014).
Wilson, Rebecca E., 'Kathleen Jamie', in Gillean Somerville-Arjat and Rebecca E. Wilson (eds),
   Sleeping with Monsters: Conversations with Scottish and Irish Women Poets (Edinburgh: Polygon,
   1990), pp. 91–9.

AWARDS

1981 Eric Gregory Award
1982 Scottish Arts Council Book Award, *Black Spiders*
1988 Scottish Arts Council Book Award, *The Way We Live*
1995 T. S. Eliot Prize (shortlist), *The Queen of Sheba*
1995 Somerset Maugham Award, *The Queen of Sheba*
1995 Mail on Sunday/John Llewellyn Rhys Prize (shortlist), *The Queen of Sheba*
1996 Geoffrey Faber Memorial Prize, *The Queen of Sheba*
1996 Forward Poetry Prize (Best Single Poem), 'The Graduates'
1999 T. S. Eliot Prize (shortlist), *Jizzen*
2000 Geoffrey Faber Memorial Prize, *Jizzen*
2000 Forward Poetry Prize, Best Poetry Collection of the Year (shortlist), *Jizzen*
2001 Scottish Arts Council Creative Scotland Award
2003 Griffin Poetry Prize (Canada; shortlist), *Mr. and Mrs. Scotland Are Dead: Poems 1980–1994*
2004 T. S. Eliot Prize (shortlist), *The Tree House*
2004 Forward Poetry Prize, Best Poetry Collection of the Year, *The Tree House*
2005 Scottish Arts Council Book of the Year Award, *The Tree House*
2006 Scottish Arts Council Book of the Year Award (shortlist), *Findings*
2006 Ondaatje Prize (shortlist), *Findings*
2012 T. S. Eliot Prize (shortlist), *The Overhaul*
2012 Costa Prize Poetry Award, *The Overhaul*
2013 Dolman Travel Book Award (co-winner), *Sightlines*
2014 John Burroughs Medal, *Sightlines*
2014 Orion Book Award for Non-Fiction, *Sightlines*

REVIEWS OF KATHLEEN JAMIE

Akbar, Arifa, 'Nature poet wins £10,000 prize for scaling lyrical heights', *Independent*, 7 October
   2004. Report on *The Tree House* winning the Forward Prize.
Blyth, Caroline, 'Rumours of a Massacre', *Times Literary Supplement*, 10 December 1993.
Clanchy, Kate, Don Paterson, Kathleen Jamie et al., 'Forward, looking backwards', *The Guardian*,
   8 October 2011.
Clark, Polly, 'Polly Clark reviews: *The Tree House* by Kathleen Jamie', *Poetry Matters*, 2004,
   http://www.towerpoetry.org.uk/poetry-matters/poetry/poetry-archive/144-polly-clark-reviews-
   the-tree-house-by-kathleen-jamie (last accessed 25 May 2014).
Colton, Julian, 'Kathleen Jamie: *The Tree House*', *The Eildon Tree*, 2006.

Crawford, Robert, 'Pinning Down the Snowflake', *The Scotsman*, 10 September 1994. Review of *The Queen of Sheba*.

Dahouk, Angel, 'Kathleen Jamie : *The Overhaul*', *Times Literary Supplement,* 13 December 2013.

Deming, Alison Hawthorne, 'Kathleen Jamie: *Findings*', *Orion Magazine*, September/ October 2007.

Falla, Jonathan, 'Referendums and Refugees: a Return to Pakistan', *The Scotsman*, 19 May 2002. Review of *Among Muslims*.

Fraser, Lilias, 'Review of *Sightlines*', *Bottle Imp*, November 2012.

Greig, Andrew, 'A White Elephant in Anstruther', *The Scottish Review* 32 (November 1983), pp. 3–8.

Greig, Andrew, 'Taking the High Road', *The Scotsman Weekend*, 15 May 1993. Review of *The Autonomous Region*.

Johnston, Maria, 'Shadow-play with the Soul', *The Guardian*, 10 November 2012. Review of *The Overhaul*.

Kinnes, Sally, 'A Lone Voice', *Radio Times*, June 1990. Review of *A Matter of Weeks*.

Lezard, Nicholas, '*Sightlines* by Kathleen Jamie – review', *The Guardian*, 7 August 2012.

Linklater, John, 'Best of British Poetry with a Scots Accent', *The Herald*, 13 January 1994. Review article on New Generation Poets.

Longley, Michael, 'Perfect river: beautiful lines', *Irish Pages*, 2007, *Scottish Poetry Library* Cut 3.Dun.2007. Text of an introduction of poets Douglas Dunn and Kathleen Jamie at Symposium on Irish and Scottish poetry since 1890, Queen's University of Belfast, 23 November 2006.

Mangan, Gerald, 'Romantic risks', *Times Literary Supplement*, 16 August 2002. Review of *Mr and Mrs Scotland Are Dead*.

Marsack, Robyn, 'Is there really anything worth celebrating on National Poetry Day?' *The Scotsman*, 5 October 2002.

Marsack, Robyn, 'Poems That Last More Than Just a Day', *Scotland on Sunday*, November 1994. Review of *The Queen of Sheba*.

Marshall, Alan, 'Love, war – and a spot of DIY', *The Telegraph*, 3 August 2002. Review of *Mr. and Mrs. Scotland Are Dead*.

Phillips, Janet, 'Supple, undammable song', *Poetry Review* 2004/5. Review of *The Tree House*.

Pollard, Clare, 'The Scale of Things', *Poetry Review* 103:1 (Spring 2013). Review of *The Overhaul*.

Ramaswamy, Chitra, 'A Natural Selection', Edinburgh: *Scotsman,* 14 April 2012. Review of *Sightlines*.

Rush, Christopher, 'Elephants in Anstruther: in search of the Scottish identity', *The Scottish Review* 31 (Aug 1983), pp. 43–8. Review of *Black Spiders*.

Troupes, David, 'Review of *The Overhaul*', *EarthLines*, February 2013.

ARCHIVE

Literary papers: Accession 11599 (papers relating to the period 1988–98) and Accession 12107 (papers relating to the period 1978–93), National Library of Scotland.

ONLINE RESOURCES

Kathleen Jamie:
    http://www.kathleenjamie.com (last accessed 25 May 2014)
    Includes recording of Kathleen Jamie reading from 'Hvalsalen' in *Sightlines*.

University of Stirling:

   http://www.creativewriting.stir.ac.uk/staff/kathleen-jamie (last accessed 25 May 2014)

The Poetry Archive:

   http://www.poetryarchive.org/poetryarchive/singlePoet.do?poetId=190 (last accessed 25 May 2014)

   Includes audio recordings of Kathleen Jamie reading 'Mr and Mrs Scotland Are Dead', 'The Tay Moses', 'Crossing the Loch', 'Lochan', 'Pipistrelles', 'The Wishing Tree'.

Scottish Poetry Library:

   http://www.scottishpoetrylibrary.org.uk/poetry/poets/kathleen-jamie (last accessed 25 May 2014)

   Holds an extensive collection of reviews and articles on Jamie.

British Council:

   http://literature.britishcouncil.org/kathleen-jamie (last accessed 25 May 2014)

Picador:

   http://www.picador.com/authors/kathleen-jamie (last accessed 25 May 2014)

   Publisher of Kathleen Jamie's poetry.

Sort Of Books:

   http://www.sortof.co.uk/authors/kathleen-jamie (last accessed 25 May 2014)

   Publisher of Kathleen Jamie's prose works.

Graywolf Press:

   https://www.graywolfpress.org/author-list/kathleen-jamie (last accessed 25 May 2014)

   Publisher of Kathleen Jamie's writing in the USA.

SECONDARY CRITICISM

Boden, Helen, 'Kathleen Jamie's Semiotic of Scotlands', in Aileen Christianson and Alison Lumsden (eds), *Contemporary Scottish Women Writers* (Edinburgh: Edinburgh University Press, 2000), pp. 27–40.

Borthwick, David, '"The tilt from one parish / into another": estrangement, continuity and connection in the poetry of John Burnside, Kathleen Jamie and Robin Robertson', *Scottish Literary Review*, 2011, pp. 133–48.

Broom, Sarah, *Contemporary British and Irish Poetry: An Introduction* (Basingstoke: Palgrave, 2006).

Brown, Rhona, 'Twentieth-Century Poetry', in Glenda Norquay (ed.), *The Edinburgh Companion to Scottish Women's Writing* (Edinburgh: Edinburgh University Press, 2012), pp. 140–51.

Collins, Lucy, '"Toward a Brink": The Poetry of Kathleen Jamie and Environmental Crisis', in Anne Karhio, Sean Crosson and Charles I. Armstrong (eds), *Crisis and Contemporary Poetry* (Basingstoke: Palgrave Macmillan, 2011), pp. 150–66.

Corcoran, Neil, *The Cambridge Companion to Twentieth-Century English Poetry* (Cambridge: Cambridge University Press, 2007).

Dósa, Attila, 'Kathleen Jamie: More than Human', in *Beyond Identity: New Horizons in Modern Scottish Poetry* (Amsterdam: Rodopi, 2009), pp. 135–46.

Dowson, Jane, and Alice Entwistle, *A History of Twentieth-century British Women's Poetry* (Cambridge: Cambridge University Press, 2005).

Entwistle, Alice, 'Scotland's New House: Domesticity and Domicile in Contemporary Scottish Women's Poetry', in Berthold Schoene (ed.), *The Edinburgh Companion to Scottish Literature* (Edinburgh: Edinburgh University Press, 2007), pp. 114–23.

Friel, Raymond, 'Women Beware Gravity: Kathleen Jamie's Poetry', *Southfields* Vol. 1, 1995.

Gairn, Louisa, 'Clearing Space: Kathleen Jamie and Ecology', in Berthold Schoene (ed.), *The*

Edinburgh Companion to Contemporary Scottish Literature (Edinburgh: Edinburgh University Press, 2007), pp. 236–44.

Gairn, Louisa, *Ecology and Modern Scottish Literature* (Edinburgh: Edinburgh University Press, 2008).

Gifford, Douglas, and Dorothy McMillan (eds), *A History of Scottish Women's Writing* (Edinburgh: Edinburgh University Press, 1997).

Gish, Nancy, 'Complexities of Subjectivity: Scottish Poets and Multiplicity', in Romana Huk (ed.), *Assembling Alternatives: Reading Postmodern Poetries Transnationally* (Middletown, CT: Wesleyan University Press, 2003), pp. 259–74.

Hubbard, Tom, 'Contemporary Poetry in Scots', in Matthew McGuire and Colin Nicholson (eds), *The Edinburgh Companion to Contemporary Scottish Poetry* (Edinburgh: Edinburgh University Press, 2009), pp. 36–48.

Kossick, Kay, 'Roaring Girls, Bogie Wives, and the Queen of Sheba: Dissidence, Desire and Dreamwork in the Poetry of Kathleen Jamie', *Studies in Scottish Literature* 32, 1 (2001), pp. 195–212.

Lilley, Deborah, 'Kathleen Jamie: rethinking the externality and idealisation of nature', in *Green Letters: Studies in Ecocriticism* Vol 17:1 (2013), pp. 16–26.

Lucas, John, 'Souls, Ghosts, Angels, and "things not human": John Burnside, Alice Oswald and Kathleen Jamie', *PN Review*, 2007.

Mark, Alison, and Deryn Rees-Jones (eds), *Contemporary Women's Poetry: Reading/Writing/Practice* (Basingstoke: Macmillan, 2000).

McCulloch, Margery Palmer, 'Women and Poetry 1972–1999', *Irish Review* 28 (2001), pp. 58–74.

McCulloch, Margery Palmer, *Scottish Modernism and its Contexts 1918–1959: Literature, National Identity and Cultural Exchange* (Edinburgh: Edinburgh University Press, 2009).

McGuire, Matthew, and Colin Nicholson (eds), *The Edinburgh Companion to Contemporary Scottish Poetry* (Edinburgh: Edinburgh University Press, 2009).

McGuire, Matthew, 'Kathleen Jamie', in Matthew McGuire and Colin Nicholson (eds), *The Edinburgh Companion to Contemporary Scottish Poetry* (Edinburgh: Edinburgh University Press, 2009), pp. 141–53.

McMillan, Dorothy, 'Twentieth-Century Poetry II: the Last Twenty-Five Years', in Douglas Gifford and Dorothy McMillan (eds), *A History of Scottish Women's Writing* (Edinburgh: Edinburgh University Press, 1997).

Norquay, Glenda, Florence Boos, and Rhona Brown (eds), *The Edinburgh Companion to Scottish Women's Writing* (Edinburgh: Edinburgh University Press, 2012).

O'Brien, Sean, *The Deregulated Muse* (Newcastle upon Tyne: Bloodaxe, 1998).

Pollard, Natalie, *Speaking to You: Contemporary Poetry and Public Address* (Oxford: Oxford University Press, 2012).

Rees-Jones, Deryn, *Consorting with Angels: Essays on Modern Women Poets* (Tarset: Bloodaxe, 2005).

Riach, Alan, 'The Poetics of Devolution', in Matthew McGuire and Colin Nicholson (eds), *The Edinburgh Companion to Contemporary Scottish Poetry* (Edinburgh: Edinburgh University Press, 2009), pp. 8–20.

Sampson, Fiona, *Beyond the Lyric: A Map of Contemporary Poetry* (London: Chatto & Windus, 2012).

Schoene, Berthold, *The Edinburgh Companion to Contemporary Scottish Literature* (Edinburgh: Edinburgh University Press, 2007).

Severin, Laura, 'A Scottish Ecopoetics: Feminism and Environmentalism in the Works of Kathleen Jamie and Valerie Gillies', *Feminist Formations*, 2 (Aug. 2011), pp. 98–110.

Smith, Jos, 'An archipelagic literature: re-framing "The New Nature Writing"', in *Green Letters: Studies in Ecocriticism* Vol 17:1 (2013), pp. 5–15.

Volsik, Paul, 'Somewhere Between the Presbyterian and the Tao: Contemporary Scottish Poetry', *Etudes Anglaises* 60.3 (2007), pp. 346–60.

Watson, Roderick (ed.), *The Literature of Scotland: the Twentieth Century*, 2nd edn (Basingstoke: Palgrave Macmillan, 2007).

Whyte, Christopher, 'The 1990s', in *Modern Scottish Poetry* (Edinburgh: Edinburgh University Press, 2004), pp. 207–35.

Wilson, Fiona, 'Scottish Women's Poetry since the 1970s', in Matthew McGuire and Colin Nicholson (eds), *The Edinburgh Companion to Contemporary Scottish Poetry* (Edinburgh: Edinburgh University Press, 2009), pp. 23–35.

GENERAL ECOCRITICISM

ASLE (Association for the Study of Literature and Environment (UK and Ireland)): http://asle. org.uk/ (last accessed 25 May 2014).

Andrews, Malcolm, *Landscape and Western Art* (Oxford: Oxford University Press, 1999).

Arnold, David, and Ramachandra Guha (eds), *Nature, Culture and Imperialism* (Delhi: Oxford University Press, 1995).

Bate, Jonathan, *The Song of the Earth* (London: Picador, 2000).

Berry, Wendell, *Sense of Place and Sense of Planet: The Environmental Imagination of the Global* (New York: Oxford University Press, 2008).

British Library, 'Writing Britain: Wastelands to Wonderlands' (exhibition, 2012). In this video, a selection of British poets and novelists discuss the importance of landscape: www.youtube.com/ watch?v=yrCCF3IMN2k (last accessed 25 May 2014).

Buell, Lawrence, *The Environmental Imagination: Thoreau, Nature Writing and the Formation of American Culture* (Princeton: Princeton University Press, 1995).

Buell, Lawrence, *The Future of Environmental Criticism: Environmental Crisis and Literary Imagination* (London: Blackwell, 2004).

Cocker, Mark, 'Introduction', in J. A. Baker, *The Peregrine*, ed. John Fanshawe (London: HarperCollins, 2011), pp. 4–15.

Coupe, Laurence, *The Green Studies Reader: From Romanticism to Ecocriticism* (London: Routledge, 2000).

Cowley, Jason, 'Editor's letter: The New Nature Writing', *Granta 102* (2008), pp. 7–15, http:// www.granta.com/Archive/102/Editors-Letter (last accessed 25 May 2014).

Cronon, William (ed.), *Uncommon Ground: Rethinking the Human Place in Nature* (New York: W. W. Norton & Co, 1996).

Dee, Tim, 'Nature Writing', *Archipelago* 5 (Spring 2011), http://www. valuesofenvironmentalwriting.co.uk/Dee.pdf (last accessed 25 May 2014).

Gaard, Greta, and Patrick D. Murphy (eds), *Ecofeminist Literary Criticism* (Urbana, IL and Chicago: University of Illinois Press, 1994).

Garrard, Greg, *Ecocriticism* (London: Routledge, 2004).

Gifford, Terry, *Pastoral* (London: Routledge, 1999).

Gifford, Terry, *Green Voices: Understanding Contemporary Nature Poetry*, 2nd edn (Manchester: Manchester University Press, [1995] 2001).

Gifford, Terry, and Anna Stenning, 'Editorial: Twentieth-century nature writing in Britain and Ireland', in *Green Letters: Studies in Ecocriticism* Vol 17:1 (2013), pp. 1–4.

Glotfelty, Cheryl, and Harold Fromm (eds), *The Ecocriticism Reader: Landmarks in Literary Ecology* (Athens, GA: University of Georgia Press, 1996).

Harrison, Robert Pogue, *Forests: The Shadow of Civilization* (Chicago: University of Chicago Press, 1993).

Heise, Ursula K., *Sense of Place and Sense of Planet: The Environmental Imagination of the Global* (New York: Oxford University Press, 2008).

Hochman, Jhan, *Green Cultural Studies: Nature in Film, Novel and Theory* (Moscow, ID: University of Idaho Press, 1998).

Kerridge, Richard, 'Environmentalism and Ecocriticism', in Patricia Waugh (ed.), *Literary Theory and Criticism: An Oxford Guide* (Oxford: Oxford University Press, 2006).

Kinsella, John, 'On Nature Writing', 31 October 2012, www.picador.com/Blogs/2011/10/John-Kinsella-On-Nature-Writing (last accessed 25 May 2014).

Knickerbocker, Scott, *Ecopoetics: The Language of Nature, the Nature of Language* (Amherst, MA: University of Massachusetts, 2012).

LeMenager, Stephanie, Teresa Shewry, and Ken Hiltner, *Environmental Criticism for the Twenty-First Century*, Vol 1 (New York: Taylor and Francis, 2012).

Luke, Tim, *Ecocritique: Contesting the Politics of Nature, Economy and Culture* (Minneapolis: University of Minneapolis Press, 1997).

Lupton, Hugh, 'The Dreaming of Place', *Earthlines* 3, August 2012, pp. 24–7.

Mabey, Richard, 'Nature's Voyeurs', 15 March 2003, www.guardian.co.uk/books/2003/mar/15/featuresreviews.guardianreview1 (last accessed 25 May 2014).

Mabey, Richard, 'The Lie of the Land', 31 March 2007, www.guardian.co.uk/books/2007/mar/31/art.art (last accessed 25 May 2014).

MacFarlane, Robert, 'The Wild Places', *Granta*, 2008.

MacFarlane, Robert, 'Introduction', in Nan Shepherd, *The Living Mountain* (Edinburgh: Canongate, 2011).

McKusick, James, *Green Writing: Romanticism and Ecology* (New York: Palgrave Macmillan, 2000).

Manes, Christopher, 'Nature and Silence', in Cheryll Glotfelty and Harold Fromm (eds), *The Ecocriticism Reader: Landmarks in Literary Ecology* (Athens, GA: University of Georgia Press, 1996), pp. 15–29.

Morton, Timothy, *Ecology without Nature: Reconsidering Environmental Aesthetics* (Cambridge, MA: Harvard University Press, 2007).

Morton, Timothy, *The Ecological Thought* (Cambridge, MA: Harvard University Press, 2010).

Murphy, Patrick, *Literature, Nature and Other: Ecofeminist Critiques* (New York: State University of New York Press, 1995).

Oelschlaeger, Max, *The Idea of Wilderness: From Prehistory to the Age of Ecology* (New Haven, CT: Yale University Press, 1991).

Parham, John, *The Environmental Tradition in English Literature* (London: Ashgate, 2002).

Plumwood, Val, *Environmental Culture* (London: Routledge, 2001).

Rigby, Kate, 'Ecocriticism', in Julian Wolfreys (ed.), *Introducing Criticism at the Twenty-First Century* (Edinburgh: Edinburgh University Press, 2002), pp. 151–78.

Rozelle, Lee, *Ecosublime: Environmental Awe and Terror from New World to Oddworld* (Tuscaloosa, AL: University of Alabama Press, 2006).

Schama, Simon, *Landscape and Memory* (London: HarperCollins, 1995).

Slovic, Scott (ed.), *Nature and the Environment* (Ipswich, MA: Salem Press, 2013).

Soper, Kate, *What is Nature?* (Oxford: Blackwell, 2004).

Tonkin, Boyd, 'Call of the Wild: Britain's Nature Writers', 18 July 2008, http://www.rainforestportal.org/shared/reader/welcome.aspx?linkid=103277&keybold=global%20warming%20conflict (last accessed 25 May 2014).

Williams, Raymond, *The Country and the City* (London: Hogarth Press, 1993).

Index